THE RACIAL POLITICS OF DIVISION

The Racial Politics of Division

Interethnic Struggles for Legitimacy in Multicultural Miami

Monika Gosin

Cornell University Press

Ithaca and London

First published 2019 by Cornell University Press

Library of Congress Cataloging-in-Publication Data

Names: Gosin, Monika, author.
Title: The racial politics of division : interethnic struggles for legitimacy in multicultural Miami / Monika Gosin.
Description: Ithaca [New York] : Cornell University Press, 2019. |
    Includes bibliographical references and index.
Identifiers: LCCN 2018047433 (print) | LCCN 2018048413 (ebook) |
    ISBN 9781501738258 (pdf) | ISBN 9781501738265 (ret) |
    ISBN 9781501738234 | ISBN 9781501738234 (cloth ; alk. paper) |
    ISBN 9781501738241 (pbk. ; alk. paper)
Subjects: LCSH: Miami (Fla.)—Ethnic relations. | Miami (Fla.)—Race relations. | Minorities—Florida—Miami—Social conditions. | Ethnic conflict—Florida—Miami.
Classification: LCC F319.M6 (ebook) | LCC F319.M6 G67 2019 (print) |
    DDC 305.8009759/381—dc23
LC record available at https://lccn.loc.gov/2018047433

Contents

ACKNOWLEDGMENTS

This book would not have been completed without the support and generosity of so many people. I want to begin by expressing my profound thanks to the people I interviewed for this project, whose identities I have kept anonymous. I am humbled that they not only chose to entrust this stranger with their stories, but that they befriended and welcomed me in the process.

I began the research for this project while a graduate student at the University of California, San Diego (UCSD). It was an honor to be guided by the esteemed scholars on my committee, Charles Briggs, Raúl Fernández, Daniel Hallin, and Sara Johnson. I am eternally indebted to my chair, Ana Celia Zentella, who remains a trusted advisor. As an accomplished and well-respected scholar who maintains a strong connection to the community and demonstrates true and enduring affinity for her students, she is an example of the type of scholar I could only hope to become. I am grateful too that Raúl Fernández has continued to be a mentor. I cannot thank him enough for the many, many nuggets of savvy wisdom he has imparted along this journey and for his enthusiastic support and advocacy. My cohort members Faye Caronan Chen, Tere Ceseña Bontempo, Ashley Lucas, Theo Verinakis, and Thuy Vo Dang, along with Myrna García, Gina Opinaldo, and Cecilia Rivas, were a needed source of laughter and encouragement. I thank you for allowing me to feel, even today, that we are always in this together. I cannot forget the contributions of colleagues and friends such as José Fusté, who encouraged me to pursue my work by putting me in touch with contacts. Mama Kialueka in Miami and Cousin Michelle Archie in Los Angeles took me in whenever I needed a place to stay while conducting field research. Thank you for opening your homes to me.

I am grateful for the institutional support I have received in grants and fellowships at various stages of the research and writing for the book from: the UC-CUBA Academic Initiative; California Cultures in Comparative Perspective (UCSD); the UCSD Center for the Study of Race and Ethnicity; the Center for Citizenship, Race and Ethnicity Studies at the College of Saint Rose in Albany, New York; the Program in Latino/a Studies in the Global South at Duke University; and the College of William and Mary's Faculty Summer Research Grant program. I am truly appreciative for my postdoctoral experience in the Program in Latino/a Studies in the Global South at Duke, where I gained from the leadership of then-director Antonio Viego and assistant director Jenny Snead Williams, and from the intellectual guidance of my truly inspiring advisors William (Sandy) Darity and Holly Ackerman. I am thankful too for the Duke Center for the Study of Race, Ethnicity and Gender (REGSS), for granting a book manuscript workshop award that provided me the opportunity to benefit from the invaluable expertise of Marvin Dunn and Nancy R. Mirabal, to whom I am also very grateful.

The book was in its final stages and completed after I joined the faculty in the Department of Sociology at the College of William and Mary. I have been fortunate to have such supportive departmental colleagues, every single one of which has helped me in profound ways. I give Amy Quark special mention because she volunteered to help me navigate the book publishing process. She ended up reading the whole manuscript several times, helping to reorganize and evaluate final drafts. I could not be more thankful for her investment of such a significant amount of time and effort to mentor a junior colleague. I appreciate also the welcoming friendship of Jennifer Bickham Mendez and the great advice and leadership of chairs Kay Jenkins and

Graham Ousey. Several William and Mary students took interest in my research and worked as assistants: thank you Jennifer Fay, Benoit Mathieu, Jamesha Gibson, Olivia Leon Vitervo, and also Abbey Potter from the University of Virginia.

The careful eyes of Lennox Archer, Maria Teresa Ceseña Bontempo, Susan Silver, Philip Christman, Petra Rivera-Rideau, and Ali Neff helped me refine the writing at various stages. Joseph Jiménez served as a Spanish translator and blessed me with his firsthand knowledge of Cuban Miami and Miami culture more broadly. There simply are no words to express the gratitude I have for you all and the roles you took in this process.

I am elated that this book found a home at Cornell University Press. I thank Jim Lance for believing in the book when it first crossed his desk. As an editor he was a kind and calm presence, whose efforts allowed me to further develop the book to greater potential. I also want to thank the anonymous reviewers, whose close reading of the book, expertise, and insights helped me truly transform the work. While exploring the book publishing market, the manuscript was simultaneously reviewed by another press; I thank their readers as well, who contributed ideas that I ended up incorporating into the final work.

Writing a manuscript can sometimes be a lonely undertaking, so I cherish the social and emotional support I have received from my friends. Here I name just a few: Jennifer Dabu, Perlita Dicochea, Cherie Espinosa, May Fu, Esther Hernandez, Dalida Lim, Erin Malone, Jennifer Mata, Shannon Norwood, Angie Roberts-Dixon, and Estella Robinson. Though you have not been directly involved in this book and many of you are outside my current academic circles, you have sustained me and have inspired my work in ways you don't even know.

Space does not allow me to elaborate on the immeasurable contributions of all the people who have helped shape this book. But I reserve these final words for a note of thanks and dedication to my family. I draw upon the strength of my parents, who, having fought the good fight for so long, encourage me directly and through their example. I give thanks to them for inspiring me through their love to keep the faith, and I give thanks to the One who makes all things possible. My siblings Jamal and Lennox have provided years of comradery and laughter. Lennox, though you are the youngest, we can all agree you are the smartest! Thank you for reading and improving all my work. My friendship with Tere Ceseña Bontempo began when we were both pursuing our doctorates, but she has become truly a sister to me. I count your presence in my life a tremendous blessing.

The love, care, and patience of Scott Wisniewski is a treasure. We met just as this project was getting underway. Though we are in totally different professional worlds, you have stuck by me, absorbing all the specific challenges my kind of work can bring to a family and a partnership. Together we have built a loving family that now includes two beautiful little humans. The three of you interrupt and complicate all my plans—to bring me the utmost joy. You inspire me to hold fast to the only things that truly matter in the end.

THE RACIAL POLITICS OF DIVISION

INTRODUCTION

In the United States, race operates through a politics of division. This politics has traditionally served the purpose of maintaining white dominance—white elites needed to exclude nonwhites and "Others" from full membership in the nation to consolidate power and resources into the hands of the privileged few (Feagin 2010; C. Harris 1993; Lipsitz 2006; Roediger 2002). The need to account for and determine who is *not* white is crucial for these purposes, and thus race, and the black/white division in particular, became particularly rigid. However, racialized individuals find that they too are compelled to engage in this politics of division, which strips away various kinds of co-belonging. Marginalized groups are obliged to set their group apart from the "Others" to prove they belong in the United States, because improving one's position within the hierarchical racial structure shapes one's access to important legal, political, and economic resources and the extent to which one can live as a full citizen with a sense of human dignity and respect (Cacho 2012; De Genova 2005; Horsman 1981; Kim 2000). This is not to say that people cannot oppose and resist the exclusionary values of the nation—

they do. But power operates in such a way that marginalized groups must negotiate and contend with exclusionary politics; their very survival could depend on the strategies they use to gain favor with or avoid the ire of the ruling elite.

The divisive racial politics of U.S. inclusion is powerfully illustrated in an oft-cited *New York Times* story about two men who immigrated to Miami, Florida, from Cuba. The story is introduced with a striking summation: "Joel Ruiz is Black. Achmed Valdés is White. In America they discovered it matters."[1] The two men had been best friends since their childhood in Cuba. However, on reaching Miami in 1994, their friendship began to flounder for a reason neither had expected—race. Although racism indeed exists in Cuba, one can be black, white, or mixed and still be "Cuban."[2] In Miami, however, the identities of "Cuban" and "black" have often been taken to be mutually exclusive, and the men were cast as *either* black *or* white by the people they encountered in their everyday lives. Notwithstanding Cuba's own racial problems, the two friends had shared the same social groups and resided in the same Cuban neighborhood. In an extremely residentially segregated Miami, however, race would determine where they lived, with whom they socialized, and their prospects for mobility. These social forces so changed their relationship that, by the time of the 2001 story that profiled their friendship, it had dwindled into "mostly a friendship of nostalgia." The two men could not fully relate to each other's U.S. experiences.

Valdés began learning of his place in the unfamiliar U.S. racial landscape when, as part of the lessons his relatives taught him on how to be "American," he was cautioned to be wary of African Americans and avoid their neighborhoods. As a white Cuban and Latino, Valdés found that he could feel happy and at home in Miami, where, despite initial economic struggles, he is part of the majority group. He could benefit from the fact that the mostly white Cubans who came to the United States before him following the rise of communist leader Fidel Castro had amassed much power in the area. But erecting a barrier between himself and African American blackness, as his relatives proposed, would also separate Valdés from Cuban blackness. For Ruiz, meanwhile, white reactions to his black color had the greater consequence. A particularly frightening incident happened to Ruiz one night when police ordered him and his friends to exit their car at gunpoint. A white Cuban officer had seen him and his uncle at Versailles, Miami's famous Cuban restaurant. Possibly motivated by anger that they had been accompanied by white Cuban female companions, the officer made it clear that Ruiz was stopped because he was black.[3] As the story reads, the officer "said something in Spanish that forever changed Mr. Ruiz's perspective on race. 'I've been keeping an eye on you for a while,' Mr. Ruiz recalls the officer saying, 'since you were in the restaurant. I saw you leave and I saw so many blacks in the car, I figured I would check you out.'"[4] As an authority figure charged with literally policing boundaries, the officer illustrated an internalization of the structure wherein he must take it upon himself to maintain the system of racial oppression. After this encounter, among others, Ruiz soon learned that he could not walk around as freely as he had in Cuba; he has to be vigilantly aware of the particular ways his blackness is criminalized in the United States and conduct himself in a manner that quells racist fears.

Miami has a very complex social environment marked by a foundational history of strict racial divisions between whites and blacks. Since the late 1950s, racial meaning there has also been shaped by mass migrations from Latin America and the Caribbean; U.S.–Cuban Cold War politics, which brought a large and powerful Cuban population to the area; and the development of contentious relations between members of the Cuban and African American communities. Despite this complexity, Ruiz and Valdés found that navigating their new society meant interacting with forces that sought to reduce their multifaceted identities to a black/white binary. While Valdés was encouraged to claim a white identity and the privileges associated with it, as a black Cuban, Ruiz found that negotiating race and identity meant facing the denigration of blackness that is both systemic and consciously perpetuated by Anglos, as well as a racism transplanted by white Cubans, left unchecked in the "ethnic enclave." Anti-black racial notions brought from Cuba, intersecting with the dominant racial ideologies that circulate in the U.S. context, ultimately bolster the idea of white superiority and black inferiority. For these friends, the pressure to be "black" or "white," reinforced not only by the overarching white Anglo power base and white Cuban Americans but also by local African Americans among others, pulled them apart.

This book represents an effort to understand and counteract the forces that create divisions between the two friends, between African Americans and Cubans in Miami, and between racialized groups more broadly. Exploring dynamics of conflict as they operated in histories of race making in Miami, I analyze discourses exemplifying and driving divisions between the primary populations Ruiz and Valdés found they had to define themselves in relation to: African Americans and Cubans; generations of Cuban immigrants; and black and white Cubans.[5] I argue that divisive notions about what it means to be "white" or "black" shaped contests between these groups over the benefits attached to national belonging. Indeed, conflict between "minority" or "non-Anglo" groups is rooted in the sometimes unconscious and often strategic embrace of these divisive white nativist perspectives. As Aihwa Ong (2003) suggests, the white elite have remapped biological notions of race onto morality-based ideals of "worthy citizenship," the idea that the privileges of U.S. belonging must be earned by demonstrating one's worthiness as hard-working, self-reliant, law-abiding, and freedom-loving (see also Gans 1999; Gray 1995; Urciuoli 1996).[6] I discuss how this dominant framework of worthy citizenship encourages interethnic conflict as marginalized groups are obliged to prove their worthiness by setting their group apart from the Others. Racialized individuals are compelled to claim binary identities—white/black but also native/foreigner or good/bad immigrants—as they jockey for status within a system that perpetually questions their legitimacy or claims of belonging. In short, white supremacist narratives intended to maintain white elite positioning atop a racial hierarchy govern the conflicts between groups of color: they set the stakes, the rules of engagement, and, often, the outcome.[7] These power dynamics play out just as sharply in those American places, such as Miami, that are celebrated as emblematic of the country's growing diversity.

The racialized framework of worthy citizenship not only foments competitive relationships among minority groups but, in doing so, also elides the complex lived experiences of racialized groups that foster mutual understanding and stronger interethnic alliances. I argue that the day-to-day lived experiences of racialized individuals reveal the multidimensional conditions of meaning-making that are flattened by the mainstream racial ideologies that compose worthy citizenship. For instance, in the opening story of the two friends, Ruiz's identity as black *and* Cuban became a problem as he navigated life in Miami because he had to contend with how the intersection of the United States' and Cuba's exaltation of whiteness over blackness leaves him, in the minds of others, unable to be fully Cuban *or* American. He does not see his Cuban identity as threatened by his blackness, and he aspires to be American despite the nation's tradition of blocking African American access to full citizenship. His positioning operates as a potential bridge between African Americans and Cubans, between Afro-Cubans and other black Americans, and between white and black Cubans by illustrating how all these identities are mutually constituted. However, his experiences teach him that his multiplicity is seen as a threat to the dominant order, even in a city with so much ethnic/racial diversity. As Miriam Jiménez Román and Juan Flores (2010, 10) contend, Afro-Latino positionality complicates notions of blackness in the United States and destabilizes dominant assumptions that racial identities such as Latino, black, and "American" cannot coexist (see also Rivera-Rideau, Jones, and Paschel 2016, 11).[8] Thus, by foregrounding the ways Afro-Cubans such as Ruiz negotiate and illuminate the transnational circuits of meaning-making around race, I draw out the greater complexity of racialized identities in the United States that are oversimplified by binary racial notions. By examining the nuanced and even unexpected ways that identities taken to be a priori such as "black" and "white" are constructed, negotiated, rejected, and (re)claimed in the context of multiethnic tensions in Miami, I deconstruct the exclusionary discourses that circulated and emphasize the porousness of the boundaries drawn by divisive politics. All in all, the book aims to expose the racist fabric into which interethnic contentions are woven so that it may be unraveled and reworked as a resource for building coalitions. As such, the book has broad application for the study of issues related to "interminority" conflict in multicultural America. My work also seeks to make a contribution to several scholarly fields, including scholarship on race and immigration, African American studies, Latino studies, and Afro-Latino studies. My specific focus on Miami, moreover, provides critical contributions to understandings of Miami race relations, studies on its "native" African American communities, and scholarship on the Cuban diaspora and on Afro-Cuban immigrants in particular in the United States.[9]

Conflict in Context

Miami has long been hailed "the city of the future" (Didion 1987; Portes and Stepick 1994; Rieff 1987; Woltman and Newbold 2009). The area began decades ago to experience the demographic trends now sweeping across the country. Indeed, Miami is an early example of the "majority-minority" spaces now becoming common in many cities and states. Today, Miami is a "mirror reflecting the debates over immigration, race, and economic transformation facing cities all over America" (Shell-Weiss 2009, 8). Its geographical prox-imity and long-standing ties to the Caribbean and Latin America make it a "zone of contact" where immigrants and "natives" confront each other all the time and have to work things out with each other (Aranda, Hughes, and Sabogal 2014). As a result, it is one of the most international and diverse cities in the United States with a Latino population of over 60 percent (Pew Research Center 2013). Miami also has one of the most diverse black popu-lations in the United States owing to post-1960 immigration to the area from the Caribbean. About one-in-three blacks (34 percent) living in Miami are immigrants.[10] Yet, Miami became Latino and international only in the second half of the twentieth century, with the influx of Cuban and other immigrants (Shell-Weiss 2009). Despite this growing diversity, the city's deep-seated his-torical black/white racial tensions have endured, and Miami remains among one of the nation's most segregated cities (Aranda et al. 2014).[11] African Amer-icans continue to be disenfranchised, and now the negative experiences and socioeconomic positioning of Miami's newer immigrant blacks (such as Hai-tians and Afro-Cubans) illustrate how entrenched Miami's anti-black climate is (Aja 2016). All these factors make Miami a critical "case study underscor-ing the prevailing importance of racial difference in an increasingly multi-cultural society" (Shell-Weiss 2009, 10).

I begin my study in 1980, the beginning of the period referred to as "the browning of America" and a pivotal year in Miami history (González 2011). By 1980, Miami was already being celebrated for its rich cultural diversity (Didion 1987; Portes and Stepick 1994; Rieff 1987; Woltman and Newbold 2009). Yet, despite its claims to diversity and inclusion, in 1980 Miami was, as we will see, fraught with racial tensions. The city not only saw continued conflict between a white majority and a black minority but was also beset by the racial tensions "of the future" that emerged as black/white relations in-tersected with a growing population of new immigrants: Cubans. As the United States fought the Cold War in opposition to Fidel Castro, it encour-aged mass migration from Cuba through its foreign policy. Bolstered by hard work—and the unparalleled aid that the U.S. government provided to these political exiles for adjustment to life in the United States—the Miami Cu-ban contingent that came in the first two waves of immigration gained social, economic, and political power in Miami (Grenier and Pérez 2003). The preferential treatment of Cuban Americans, coupled with Cuban Americans' staunch support of the Republican Party, worsened relations with African

Americans still shut out of the political and economic establishment. Still, despite the gains made by the Cuban community, local Anglos made it clear their welcome was tenuous at best. Separating themselves from their new neighbors, white Anglos moved out of the area in droves, illustrating the fact that nativist anti-foreigner sentiments were also running high (García 1996; Grenier and Castro 1999; Shell-Weiss 2009). Meanwhile, the African American community was particularly hard-hit by economic oppression and police brutality during this period (Dunn 1997, 2016; Dunn and Stepick 1992). Tensions came to a head when African American citizens staged a large-scale revolt in a protest known as the McDuffie Riot, named after Arthur McDuffie, an unarmed black motorist killed by police who were then acquitted. The McDuffie Riot was followed almost immediately by a new, third wave of Cuban migration: the 1980 Mariel exodus. The Cubans arriving during Mariel were stigmatized as criminals in both Cuban and U.S. press; thus, this wave of Cuban immigration would affect all Miami's communities in ways previous waves had not. Moreover, while previous waves of Cuban migrants were overwhelmingly white, the Mariel exodus (and the subsequent fourth wave of Cuban migration, the 1994 Balsero crisis) would bring more black Cubans to the United States than ever before.[12] Such dynamic forces occurring in 1980 would compel both Miami's African American and Cuban American communities to reexamine the terms by which they would define their identities and fight for their rights.

I situate my analysis during the 1980 Mariel exodus and the subsequent Balsero crisis. These two most controversial waves of Cuban immigration intensified the friction between African American "native minorities" and the growing Cuban immigrant population. During the Mariel exodus, 125,000 Cuban refugees were brought to the United States by boatlift, and during the Balsero, or rafter, crisis, 35,000 Cuban refugees came to the United States, fleeing a period of economic and political instability in Cuba brought on by the fall of the Soviet Union (Masud-Piloto 1996). I focus on these waves to analyze the dynamics of conflict between African Americans and Cubans, the city's two largest minority groups at the time. I focus on these waves, too, because they provide a population, Afro-Cubans, whose presence intervenes in and complicates the strict divisions imagined between African Americans, Cubans, and other populations in Miami.[13] Accessing African American and Cuban voices through a study of African American and Spanish-language newspapers, the *Miami Times* and *El Nuevo Herald,* I examine how members of these groups documented the drama that unfolded during these events. Given Miami's fraught racial history, these immigration "crises" would come to be narrated in ways that would heighten the perception of threat for both communities. Specifically, African Americans struggled with the fear that the newcomers would diminish any gains they were able to make after the civil rights movement, and Cuban Americans grappled with threats to their status as model anti-communist heroes. Mariel Cuban migrants were constructed as "black" deviants by the public, the government, and the press, and with the coming of the *Balseros*, Cuban migrants, for the first time, were made into economic migrants seeking illegal entry into the United States (Masud-Piloto 1996; Pedraza 1996). By analyzing the antagonistic discourses in the newspapers, which pit the various actors in the Miami scenario against one another, I illustrate how binary frames of worthy citizenship exemplified, and at times drove, Miami conflict during the period following Mariel and Balsero. I also illuminate how blackness functioned symbolically to create boundaries between the various communities in Miami. Centering Afro-Cubans in the analysis of the newspaper texts, and through in-depth personal interviews with Afro-Cubans who currently live in Miami and Los Angeles, the book also disrupts the exclusionary constructions exemplified in the papers. As the book weaves the voices of black Cubans throughout the text, we also gain insight into the specific issues Afro-Cuban immigrants face as they negotiate race in the United States.

Theorizing Interethnic Conflict in Multicultural America

Beyond the Race–Immigration Divide

Understanding interethnic conflict and racial dynamics more broadly in multicultural America requires us to bring together—but also critically reframe—multiple disciplines and subfields. First of all, and most simply, my research challenges the tendency within scholarship on the United States' changing racial and ethnic relations to maintain a separation between studies emphasizing the black/white or white/nonwhite divide and scholarship on the assimilation processes of immigrants of color. As Zulema Valdez details in her preface to the 2017 edited volume *Beyond Black and White*, in the post–civil rights era, one primary area of research focuses largely on racial differences between African Americans and non-Latino whites to better understand the persistence of inequalities between these groups despite civil rights gains. The other main area of research focuses on the assimilation processes of immigrants of color, as they seek integration into (white) American society (Entman and Rojecki 2000; Portes and Zhou 1993; Zhou and Bankston 1998). The separateness of these two realms of study does not sufficiently capture the complexities of race relations in a society transformed by profound demographic change (Romero 2008; Sáenz and Manges Douglas 2015; Valdez 2017; Valdez and Golash-Boza 2017). With more and more cities, counties, and states becoming "majority-minority," contests over power and resources in these spaces take place not just between nonwhites and the Anglo population but also between groups of color (Kasinitz, Mollenkopf, and Waters 2002). Miami is a case in point given its status as one of the first "majority-minority" cities in the nation. Yet, the separation between studies on the African American/white divide and on immigrant assimilation has also been reproduced in the literature on race relations in Miami. Although previous research has identified Miami as a site for investigating interethnic relations, with some attention to African American–Cuban relations in particular (for example, Aranda et al. 2014; Grenier and Castro 1999; Grenier and Pérez 2003; Shell-Weiss 2009; Stepick, Grenier, Castro, and Dunn 2003), relations between these two groups have rarely been the main focus. In general, African American and Cuban communities are treated as bounded in the numerous studies on Miami's Cuban community, and just a handful of book-length studies (for example, Connolly 2014; Dunn 1997, 2013, 2016; Rose 2015) have focused on Miami's "native" African American communities. We can tap into the rich insights that can be gained about how race operates in the multicultural United States, the possibilities for cooperation, and also the dynamics of conflicts that may arise by examining the relations between non-white immigrants and "native minorities" in Miami.

Some scholars have suggested that we are now "beyond black and white," that the black/white binary dynamics are no longer relevant to understanding race. Latinos in particular are seen as challenging the traditional color line given the greater flexibility they have in determining their racial identities, or at least the ways they challenge traditional categories (Fernandez 2008; Frank, Akresh, and Lu 2010; Yancey, 2003). Eduardo Bonilla-Silva (2004;

2018) offers a more nuanced take, arguing that the United States is becoming more like Latin America, with a tri-racial hierarchy, with whites on top, honorary whites (such as some Asian groups, lighter-skinned Latinos, and most multiracials), and blacks on the bottom. Bean, Feliciano, Lee, and Van Hook (2009), in contrast, believe the color line is moving from black/white to black/nonblack. These scholars have importantly recognized the growing complexity in U.S. race relations in theories about how the U.S. color line has shifted. Yet they risk neglecting the fact that the black/white binary remains at the root of these distinctions—the power differential with whites on top and blacks on the bottom remains the same. Michael Omi (2001) captures this tension in theorizing a multiracial America. On the one hand, he acknowledges the limits of theorizing with a black/white paradigm, arguing that "We would profit from more historical and contemporary studies that look at the patterns of interaction between, and among, a multiplicity of groups." But, on the other hand, he warns against decentering the black experience, as it is fundamental to ideas of race in our society. Thus, the challenge is to "frame an appropriate language and analysis to help us understand the shifting dynamic of race that all groups are implicated in" (2001, 251). Like Omi, I believe that despite the limits of the black/white paradigm, the power of white supremacy and the social devaluation of blackness remain foundational to our understanding of contemporary race relations. What we need is to examine how black/white binary dynamics are rearticulated in the present and intersect with issues related to immigrant incorporation.

Toward that end, rather than focusing primarily on immigrants *or* native African Americans, my discursive analysis gets at the heart of what is at stake for both immigrants *and* native minorities (African Americans and generations of Cuban exiles) as they lay claim to an American identity. In the periods I explore when the black/white racial dynamics "of the past" began to intersect with the racial tensions "of the future," African Americans and local Anglos in Miami grappled with what the new population of immigrants meant for them. Native-born African Americans in particular had to contend with a U.S. racializing frame that positions "black" as opposite to "American" and positions "natives" against "foreigners." At the same time, new immigrants seeking their fortune in the United States were confronted with historical white/black racial dynamics along with anti-immigrant sentiments. I explore the complexity of intersecting and transnational racial ideologies that shape how new immigrants negotiated their identities in relation to U.S. constructions of a white dominance and black subjugation.

Interminority Relations and the Quest for "Worthy Citizenship"

Most studies of interethnic conflict have attributed it primarily to causes such as limited resources, demographic shifts, or negative racial attitudes (Bobo and Hutchings 1996; McClain et al. 2007; Oliver 2010; Oliver and Wong 2003). Conceptualizing interethnic conflict in relation to changing racial dynamics in a more multicultural United States, I refocus our attention on discourse and ideology as key factors explaining the emergence of interethnic conflict. Analyses of conflict between groups of color have much to gain from shifting the focus onto racial ideology and the extent to which it becomes a "commonsense" way to make sense of difference, not only for whites but also for marginalized groups (Bonilla-Silva 2018; Feagin 2010; Lewis 2004).

Scholars have offered powerful explanations of how white elite Americans have constructed racial frames, or ideas about racial superiority/inferiority, to justify their power. Racial frames are social technologies that allow white elites to confer or deny the privileges of citizenship in the nation—privileges such as civil rights, protection, and freedom—on the basis of race (Feagin 2010; Kim 2000; Picca and Feagin 2007). In its history, the United States officially reserved the privileges of citizenship for whites—while denying them to African Americans. For instance, in 1787, the Constitution declared that blacks (as former slaves) counted as only three-fifths of a person for purposes of political representation and electoral votes. The earliest law governing the granting of citizenship to immigrants, the 1790 Naturalization Law, also made race fundamental in determinations of national belonging by stating that only "free white persons of good character" could become citizens. Today, the language of inclusion/exclusion can sometimes be coded but still relies on the traditional designation of "blackness" to signal the Other, while "white" is set as the normative reference point for "citizen," or the one that belongs (Feagin 2010; Horsman 1981; Ong 2003).

As Aihwa Ong (2003) argues, in the contemporary era, racial frames based explicitly on ideas of biological race have been rearticulated in terms of the moral characteristics of "worthy citizenship." To earn the privileges of citizenship, members of racialized communities must illustrate they are "worthy" by conforming to "proper"—that is, Anglo, middle-class, moral—standards (2003; see also Gans 1999; Gray 1995; Urciuoli 1996). This focus on individual achievements and morality legitimates the terms of "worthy citizenship," whereby belonging is rooted in the idea of who is most deserving (Aranda, Chang, and Sabogal 2009; Ong 2003; Urciuoli 1996, 2003). Because the qualities that make people ideal citizen-subjects are taken for granted as having moral value, the acceptance of such ideals can reinforce the status quo, making it difficult to realize the power dynamics that enforce them. Thus, as Ong (2003) suggests, the normative values embodied in worthy citizenship are intended to compel subjects to police themselves. Policies, programs, codes, and practices of the government seek to instill in subjects the values of worthy citizenship, thwarting resistance to dominance at the level of the individual (Ong 2003, 6). As such, social technologies of government designed to create ideal citizen-subjects reproduce the white elite power structure. Although Ong does not explore the topic of interethnic conflict, the concept of worthy citizenship, with its focus on how marginalized groups are disciplined into adopting the social norms that then police them, proves a useful starting point for unpacking it.

I examine how the racialized ideologies of worthy citizenship shape—and indeed encourage—interminority conflict, as they come to be accepted and perpetuated by groups of color themselves. Scholars have recognized that nonwhites may also adopt white racial frames and position others as outsiders, but scholars' focus has primarily been on white efforts to maintain power and on how groups of color *resist* white racial frames (Feagin 2010; Kim 2000; Picca and Feagin 2007). I argue that in the face of instability, members of racialized communities may also invoke language that affirms dominant assimilative models in order to secure their footing. This is because, as Lisa Marie Cacho explains, "recuperating social value [or achieving representation or acknowledgment by the establishment] *requires* rejecting the Other" (2012, 17). Given the exclusionary basis of white racial frames, invoking worthy citizenship necessarily involves claiming one's worthiness over and above other groups. Hence, as racialized communities seek to reposition themselves more favorably in society, they may draw on the language and ideals of worthy citizenship as it is defined in the United States, engaging in what amounts to a zero-sum battle over the benefits of belonging. Racialized groups may employ moralistic and exclusionary language to construct themselves as superior to or more of an insider than other groups (Aranda, Chang, and Sabogal 2009; Cacho 2012; Kim 2000). This often means claiming a position within what I argue are the binary identities constructed by the dominant framework of worthy citizenship: black/white; native/foreigner; and good/bad immigrant. In sum, attempts by marginalized groups to secure status as true Americans can reinscribe white racializing frames. The reinscription of these frames is a testament to the tenacity of the racial structure of power in maintaining white dominance.

Today, despite demographic shifts, white racial power continues to reproduce itself by requiring the complicity of minority and immigrant groups in exchange for a tenuous claim on U.S. citizenship. Groups of color have long sought to and succeeded in resisting the status quo in multiple ways. Still, these efforts to resist white dominance and to claim rights from below are always constrained by the exclusionary framework of worthy citizenship perpetuated from above (Ong 2003). Connecting conflict between groups of color to the often invisible workings of white racial power is necessary to circumvent the temptation to blame these groups themselves as interethnic conflict arises. Moreover, in order to avoid "blame the victim" mentalities that hold marginalized groups responsible for their subjugated positioning, our focus on how minorities work to gain rights and enact resistance must also attend to the ways regulation from above operates to maintain dominance—even after marginalized groups have worked hard and "achieved" the qualities that are supposed to ensure worthiness (Ong 2003).[14] Groups of color do play a role in generating conflict among themselves, yet they do so in large part because they are constrained by an exclusionary framework for citizenship designed to reproduce white elite power through strategies of divide and conquer.[15]

Cuban Whiteness and the Transnational Circuits of Race Making

Exploring how African Americans, Cuban Americans, and black and white Cubans draw on racialized discourses as they jockey for the benefits of "worthy citizenship," I examine how "black/white" racial dynamics continue to manifest and operate in different forms in the current more racially/ethnically diverse U.S. context. To more fully grasp how the black/white binary gets rearticulated in this context, we must explore the historically specific ways in which transnational circuits of race making intervene. In the case of Miami, this means delving into how whiteness plays a role in claims to citizenship and power by Cuban Americans in Miami. Moreover, focusing on white Cuban relations with both African Americans and black Cubans in Miami entails taking on what is a sensitive subject among Cubans—antiblackness among white Cuban Americans. But in doing so, I contribute to a "critical Latino whiteness studies," which interrogates the currency of whiteness in the hemisphere (López 2010, 190; see also Aja 2016).

In the United States, Cubans have been able to benefit from "implicit racial privilege" in ways that many other Latino groups have not because they have been constructed in the media as anti-communist heroes and because of their upward mobility (Aja 2016; López 2010; Molina-Guzman 2008). Immigration scholars have taken interest in the Cuban exiles because of the ways the latter have challenged the traditional assimilation model, meeting success by reshaping rather than assimilating into their environment. As such, Miami Cubans have been offered as an example of the "triumph of pluralism" (Shell-Weiss 2009). Yet, a closer look at the Cuban American community also demonstrates how they "can also serve as local state-level actors and producers in situating their privileged space in a white hegemonic sphere" (Aja 2016, 7–8). This book acknowledges and foregrounds Cuban American privilege and hegemony in Miami. At the same time, as I examine and critique Cuban American claims to a white identity in the United States, I unpack the complexity of Cuban American whiteness, or "off-whiteness"—its hegemony and its precariousness (Aja 2016; López 2012).

As is the case for other immigrant groups, the racial understandings Cuban exiles held before coming to the United States intersect with what they learn about race as they navigate a new and different racial climate (Roth and Kim 2013). Indeed, to understand Miami's racial dynamics, we must engage with how race operates in Cuba, paying attention to histories of slavery and discrimination there and assessing the impact of Cuban racial ideologies, which simultaneously idealize racial unity and discourage anti-racist organizing. The historical disenfranchisement of blacks in Cuba during and after slavery allowed whites on the island to be wealthier and more powerful than blacks. When Castro disrupted the class system and sought to redistribute the wealth of white Cuban elites, white Cubans were the most likely to be opposed to his government and to flee to the United States (Benson 2012, 2013; Clealand 2013; De la Fuente 2001; Helg 1995). Upon arriving in the

United States, white exile Cubans who held anti-black attitudes encountered the U.S. configuration of anti-black racism. The white Anglo dominant ideologies in the United States affirmed the attitudes of exiled Cubans and encouraged them to dissociate from African Americans (Aja 2016; Bailey 2000, 2001; Hay 2009; Landale and Oropesa 2002; López 2012). Bringing into focus the ways Cuban attitudes brought from Cuba intersect with U.S.-based anti-black attitudes, we keep in mind that transnational histories of white settler and colonial domination intervene in relations between non-Anglo groups in the context of the United States.

Along with taking account of racial dynamics in Cuba, it is essential to bear in mind the larger context of the U.S.–Cuba political conflict to understand the complexity of Cuban American whiteness (Grosfoguel 2003). "All in all, U.S. state intervention encouraged 'whitening' the perception of [the Cuban American] difference in the imaginary of 'White' America" (Grosfoguel 2003, quoted in López 2012, 191). Though Cubans have been afforded a "special status," this status is limited. United States Cuban immigration policies have become more restrictive over time, and these restrictions illustrate the precariousness of Cuban American claims to a "favored minority" or "whitened" status. Moreover, as Latino studies scholars note, people who would be considered white in Latin America are remade into "Latinos" in the United States through processes of racialization. These processes often position Latinos as perpetual foreigners (Chavez 2013; Mora 2014; C. E. Rodríguez 2000; Santa Ana 2002). Thus, though white Cubans were white in Cuba, in the United States their claims to whiteness are always in relation to a white American elite power base—they are perceived as nonwhite in relation to Anglo whites (López 2012; Mirabal 2003).[16]

I illuminate how (white) Cubans, not viewed as "true whites" in the United States, work to "reclaim" whiteness by distancing themselves from blackness (López 2012, 191). I do not deny that white Cubans are agents in making claims to a white identity, for some, even in ways that are more overtly racist toward blacks. I realize that several scholars would push back from even the slightest suggestion that Cubans have anything in common with other minority groups. However, I believe it is important to both acknowledge white Cuban hegemony and analyze their contradictory positioning. Because of my focus on the particularities of power dynamics in the U.S. national context, in my discussions about the battle over worthy citizenship in Miami, I describe Cubans, regardless of color, as a *minority* group, taking into account the ways they have been racialized as distinct from the white numerical majority. This is not to say that they experience their marginality in the same way as other groups, quite the contrary. However, Aihwa Ong reminds us that it is important to discern the domains where preexisting racial, ethnic, gender, and cultural forms and the analytics of power shape "peoples' attitudes, behaviors, and aspirations in regard to belonging to a modern liberal society" (2003, 15). Following Ong's recommendation that we emphasize the role of the social technologies of government in creating ideal citizen-subjects, I reveal how white Cuban Americans, responding to threats to their status as "true" Americans, invoke "worthy citizenship" in ways that reinscribe black/white and other binaries. The complex positioning of Cubans, who are white and not quite white, a minority and not quite a minority, blacks *and* whites, refugees and not (traditional) refugees, allows us to trouble racial categories and definitions. Furthermore, examining Cuban American antiblackness and the contradictions inherent in Cuban American whiteness advances a critique of the enduring stigmatization of blackness in the hemisphere (Aja 2016; López 2010, 190).

African Americans and the "New" Immigration

As non-European immigrants renegotiate whiteness/blackness to claim worthy citizenship within the United States, these struggles necessarily overlap with the struggles of African Americans who perceive themselves to be "native minorities." Despite the gains of the civil rights movement, the continued disenfranchisement of African Americans highlights the enduring legacy of a U.S. system that positions African American "others" against white "citizens." Yet the experiences of African American communities are often absent in studies of immigration, and existing research has failed to explain how the influx of new immigrants and the United States' growing ethnic/racial diversity intersects with the continued systematic disempowerment of blacks in the United States. Thus, my focus on African American negotiations of the racial climate of the late twentieth- and twenty-first-century United States provides a necessary and important scholarly intervention. In the case of Miami, because interethnic conflict has in large part been related to local reactions to mass immigration from Cuba, I offer a new look at the Mariel exodus and Balsero crisis, highlighting the voices of African Americans, which are often left out of the numerous studies on these migration waves (for example, Aguirre 1984; Aguirre, Sáenz, and James 1997; Bach, Bach, and Triplett 1981–1982; Camayd-Freixas 1988; Greenhill 2002; Henken 2005; Hufker and Cavender 1990; Masud-Piloto 1996; Nackerud, Springer, Larrison, and Issac 1999; Wilsbank 1984).

As descendants of slaves brought to the U.S. South, African Americans have a very different relationship to the United States than do immigrants (regardless of color). Because of their position in the United States as both minorities and as "Americans," African Americans have often sought to align racially with the "Other" but have also desired to establish their rightful place in the U.S. nation (Brock and Castañeda Fuertes, 1998). The alliances blacks have made with other groups of color historically is encouraging and demonstrates that conflict is not the norm. Nevertheless, the findings of scholars investigating black opinions on immigration from as far back as when the Chinese arrived between 1850 and 1882 and when Mexicans arrived during World War II, to the more recent post-1965 migration of the twentieth century, reveal a strong contradiction: blacks generally support the rights of immigrants but tend to oppose immigration when it infringes on their job prospects (Diamond 1998; Fuchs 1990; Hellwig 1981, 1987; Jaynes 2000; Pastor and Marcelli 2004; Schulman 2004; Thornton and Yuko Mizuno 1999). The response to the Cuban influx in Miami in 1980 and in 1994 demonstrates a similar contradiction, complicated by the fact that Cubans, who were the "Other," were constructed simultaneously as "white" and viewed as a privileged group.

Capturing a moment in time before Miami's black population grew to be as diverse as it is today, I explore how African Americans responded to the Cuban influx, as well as to a new black immigrant presence owing to the influx of black immigrants from other areas of the Caribbean. I examine how Miami-based African Americans contended with what the new diversity would mean for their still disenfranchised community and look into their struggles over the politics of black identity. For African Americans living lives in which they feel disempowered and ignored, some may voice their concerns in ways that flatten out geopolitical complexities and reinscribe racial binaries and white racial frames. But by taking the time to listen to their concerns and illuminating their struggles for "worthy citizenship," I not only undermine the simple binaries that compose worthy citizenship; I take seriously the concerns of African American "native minorities" who feel caught up in a zero-sum game. My focus on African Americans in Miami ultimately underscores that given changing demographics, scholarship on African American experiences must continually be in conversation with scholarship on immigrant experiences.

Today, African Americans and Latinos together constitute the majority of residents in most of the nation's largest cities, and the residential integration of blacks and Latinos will continue to increase (Telles, Sawyer, and Rivera-Salgado 2011). These demographic shifts make it important to put more scholarly attention on the relationships between these groups, whether in relation to the issue of conflict or otherwise. Clearly, African Americans have a long tradition of building coalition with immigrant groups and with Latinos (Behnken 2016; Johnson 2013; Kun and Pulido 2013; Márquez 2014). Thus, while heeding the warnings of scholars who argue that constructions such as "the Black–Latino divide" have been overhyped in U.S. media (Sawyer 2006; Telles et al. 2011), I also acknowledge a need to recognize the divisions that do exist. In places such as *El Nuevo South*—North Carolina, Alabama, Georgia, and other southern regions—"although cooperation and conflict coexist in Hispanic newcomers' relations with whites and blacks, often in ambivalent and contradictory ways, black-Hispanic tensions frequently outweigh a sense of shared racial solidarity vis-à-vis whites" (Marrow 2011, 118; see also Gay 2006; McClain et al. 2007).[17] As such, my study contributes to the burgeoning literature about black/brown relations in "new" contexts, particularly the South.[18] Given the longer history of raced immigration to Miami, which preempts the large-scale immigration of Latinos into other metropolitan areas, Miami acts as a predictor of how complex racial dynamics between blacks and Latinos may continue to unfold in other areas of the country (Grenier and Stepick 2001).

Afro-Cuban Immigrants—Confounding Racial Divides

As I have argued, it is necessary to capture how the poles of "black" and white" continue to be entrenched in today's multiethnic society and create divisions between groups such as African Americans and nonblack Latinos as they struggle for worthy citizenship. Yet it is equally important to challenge such binary divisions and the consequences they create for marginalized groups. The way forward, I would suggest, is to attend to the complexity of what it means for people who straddle black and Latino identities to assimilate into the national framework of the United States. Drawing from and contributing to Afro-Latino studies, I focus on Afro-Cuban immigrants to reveal possibilities for challenging the logic of worthy citizenship and of anti-blackness through alternative forms of identification and interethnic cooperation.

Latino studies scholarship, which centers the implicit heterogeneity of Latinos, has been instrumental in complicating U.S. racial politics and resisting the strict divisions of the U.S. black/white binary (Dominguez 1997; C. E. Rodriguez 2000). But despite the resistive potential found in embracing the ambiguities inherent in the category "Latino," Latino studies scholarship often neglects the issue of blackness and the specificity of black Latino experiences (Jiménez Román and Flores 2010; Rivera-Rideau et al. 2016; Torres-Saillant 2002, 2003, 2010). Afro-Latinos in the United States must contend with the black/white opposition in ways their nonblack counterparts do not. Furthermore, the exaltation of racial ambiguity lends itself to the affirmation of Latin American myths of racial democracy, which deny existing racism with the assertion that because of race mixture (and other multiplicities), specific Latin American countries have moved beyond race (Duany 2005; Jiménez Román and Flores 2010).

The scholarship on Miami race relations reflects this inattention to the black Latino experience. Afro-Cubans have been virtually absent from analyses of contemporary Cuban immigrant experiences (Aja 2016; Gosin 2010; Mirabal 2003), and until Alan Aja's (2016) important contribution, *Miami's Forgotten Cubans*, post-1959 Afro-Cuban immigrants have been excluded from most book-length analyses of both Cuban Miami and Miami race relations. Afro-Cubans remain a quite small proportion of Miami's population, which partially explains their absence from these studies. Yet their numbers in the United States grew substantially during the Mariel and Balsero immigration waves. Although previous studies focused on Mariel have considered the issue of race, with the observation that being categorized as black played a major role in the *Marielito* stigma as well as their rejection by some "white" Cubans (Aguirre 1984; Bach et al. 1981–1982; Camayd-Freixas 1988; Hufker and Cavender 1990; Masud-Piloto 1996; Wilsbank 1984), the issue of blackness has not been the main focus of these studies.[19]

The growing scholarship on Afro-*latinidades* works to resolve these tensions within the Latino studies and Miami immigration literatures. It highlights the ways political identities and categories such as "Latino" "are always historically and discursively constructed" (Beltrán 2010, 9) but also forces a re-looking at the poles of black and white as they operate in the lives of people who are phenotypically black (Jiménez Román and Flores 2010; Oboler and Dzidzienyo 2005; Rivera-Rideau et al. 2016; Torres-Saillant 2002, 2003, 2010). For the literature on Miami, this means, rather than taking the Mariel stigma for granted, as is done in most studies, we must explore how the stigma came into being through a language around blackness, making connections between what it means to be African American in the United States and what it means to be "black" for Afro-Cuban immigrants. More broadly, building on Afro-Latino scholarship allows me to explore how Afro-Cubans disrupt an anti-black racial politics of division. The Afro-Cuban experience illustrates the complexity, simultaneity, and porousness of identities taken to be discrete, pointing to alternative ways to claim belonging.

In my study, the Afro-Cuban presence among the Marielitos and Balseros brought into question a dominant narrative in African American newspapers that positioned African American "natives" against (white) Cuban "foreigners."[20] Their presence troubled the boundaries between "black" and "white" and between "African American" and "Cuban" as well as the very definitions of these identities. Their presence also challenged white Cuban Americans who sought to dissociate from African Americans in order to (re) claim their white identities, because white Cubans were forced to acknowledge their own "blackness" and the fact that the Cuban welcome in the United States was not as stable as they hoped. Furthermore, as revealed in interviews, Afro-Cubans recount stories illustrating instances in which they deliberately challenge divisive racial notions in face-to-face interactions. They challenge Cuban exile anti-blackness, the impulse among some African Americans to define black membership around a U.S. identity and the English language, and the idea that black and Latino identities are distinct. As they juxtapose the ways in which Cuban notions of "whiteness" and "blackness" are remade in the United States, the Afro-Cubans in this study enact a strategic use of racial discourses of a different sort, reclaiming problematic Cuban racial democracy discourses to combat negative racial experiences in the United States. Through their negotiations of the U.S. racial order, they challenge the limitations of racial categories and anti-blackness, as well as other oversimplifications necessary in the politics of division as manifested in the U.S. racial hierarchy. Making this challenge is important because such oversimplifications support a political order that many people in all groups find unlivable.

Charting the complex relations between African Americans and Cubans, generations of Cuban immigrants, and black and white Cubans during periods of radical transformation in Miami, I seek to illustrate how interethnic conflict must be understood as part of the broader effort of ethnic groups to make claim to the nation and construct their identities. In the chapters to come, I criticize the negative attitudes some African Americans harbor against Latinos as well as the anti-black racism that can be seen among some Latinos. But a main goal of the book is to bring to light how conflict between groups of color is connected to, even compelled by, the historically white dominant social order. Using Miami as an exemplary case, I explore a history of strict black/white divisions that provides the foundation of race making there. Connecting the current more "multicultural" racial context to these histories of white domination, I seek to more fully challenge the racial status quo and white power base that continues to limit resources of marginalized peoples, frames them as unfit for the nation, and creates a standpoint of precariousness that gives rise to the need among these groups to struggle for U.S. belonging. In this way, rather than blaming racialized groups for the conflict that exists, I affirm the desire among marginalized groups to more fully establish themselves or contest their exclusion from a "true" American identity. I also work toward rooting out and exposing the fallacy of subscribing to the white power base's exclusionary ideals of "the nation" as a tool for asserting power, unity, and identity. I reinforce the fact that the boundaries around racial/ethnic identities are in fact porous. But this is not the simplistic call to "get rid of racial categories," nor is it about challenging what people call themselves. Rather, I contend that looking at why these boundaries get made in the first place, and the power dynamics involved, is necessary to get to the book's ultimate goal—to direct us to the idea that the *people* being identified are not so separate; our oppressions are mutually constituted, and our fates are bound up together.

Research Strategy: Examining Text and Talk

To more effectively understand processes of racialization as they lay out divisions between groups and shape interethnic conflict, there is a need "to look at the cultural representations and discursive practices that shape racial meanings" (Omi 2000, 260). Race is constructed through discourses of text and talk, that is, through discourses circulating in the mass media and in face-to-face interaction (Van Dijk 1993; West-Durán 2004; Wetherell and Potter 1992). I explore dominant discourses on conflict between African Americans and Cubans in Miami, as well as how these groups draw on such discourses in different ways as they seek the benefits of "worthy citizenship." This dual focus requires analyzing discourse at different sites of production and paying attention to the production of dominant discourses about national belonging and how minority individuals and communities interpret, understand, and utilize these discourses to their own ends. As such, the research in this book draws both on textual analysis of newspapers as critical sites of the production and contestation of dominant discourse and on in-depth interviews that provide a lens into the interpretations and strategies of individuals as they reflect on how such discourses affect their daily lives.

Discourse and the Media

During the Mariel exodus and the Balsero crisis, the media functioned as an important multifaceted site of discourse production about race, immigration, and interethnic conflict. To be clear, the media and media processes are not the subject or main concern of the research per se, but rather the media are used as a tool or site for capturing discursive practices and understanding the framing of the concerns of the communities investigated. Media scholars Robert Entman and Andrew Rojecki define discourse as "how people understand, think, and talk about something, be it an issue or a category of people" (2000, 6). Following Marx, Gramsci, and the Frankfort School, Rojecki argues "that our tendency to take things as a given and not be self-reflective on them privileges a set of power relations, a rationalization of privileged class interest" (2000, 17). Such apathy can be exploited by privileged groups who may manipulate discourse to support their constructions of consensus through language and texts (Hall 1997; Van Dijk 1987, 1993). What is important is that "the media do not exist in isolation. They reflect and validate the existing social order and disparage those who are perceived as a threat" (Hufker and Cavender 1990, 333).

Accordingly, in regards to marginalized groups, the mainstream media have often painted a broad, negative, and decontextualized picture of these groups, further contributing to their marginalization. Toward the goal of avoiding such decontextualization, this book engages with mainstream as well as nonmainstream discourses by investigating African American and Spanish-language press. Ethnic news media were created in part to challenge the dominant elite voices prominent in mainstream media and to provide alternative readings of society. Newspapers are indeed mediated, reflecting the priorities of editors and journalists. Yet they (ethnic newspapers especially) are also always in conversation with their perceived public. This conversation can be indirect or more direct, as such newspapers act as an interactive space for their readers to voice their opinions and concerns (Jacobs 2000; Rhodes 1995; A. Rodriguez 1999). In this book, I access the voices of Miami's African American community through an examination of the *Miami Times*. As "the South's largest Black weekly circulation, serving Miami-Dade County since 1923," the *Miami Times*, based in Liberty City (one of Miami's historically African American neighborhoods), was and continues to be the most widely circulated black community newspaper in Miami.[21] In 1980, the paper reached 23,049 people on a weekly basis (National Research Bureau 1980). Established in 1929 during the heyday of the black press, it performs for Miami what Ronald Jacobs describes as the black press's role: it provides a forum for debate and to promote self-improvement, monitors the mainstream press by providing alternative readings of news, and increases black visibility in mainstream society (2000). Between 1900 and 1950, the black press in the United States was at its strongest and provided a valuable space for discussions of integration and issues of civil rights. Black newspapers were important venues for black organizations and leaders to mobilize the community (Jacobs, 2000). Similarly, the *Miami Times* reported on civil rights concerns (such as unfair hiring practices and so on), local events and politics, black firsts, and sports. The paper also contained a large section on local black church happenings, a poetry section, death announcements, classifieds, and a section where community members could offer thank you notes to other community members and supporters. Although the newspaper likely did not reflect the views of all blacks at the time, this official voice provides insight into leading African American opinions about current events.

The Spanish-language paper I examine, *El Nuevo Herald*, has a more complicated history with the Cuban American community. The Miami

Cuban community created a strong local news media with hundreds of newspapers, tabloids, and magazines dedicated to the defeat of Castro (García 1996).[22] Along with these smaller papers or *periodiquitos* more focused on the politics of Cuba, in 1980 Miami had two other prominent Spanish-language newspapers, *Diario las Americas* and *El Miami Herald* (later renamed *El Nuevo Herald*). *Diario las Americas*, a Nicaraguan-owned newspaper, catered to the right-wing, exile community (A. Rodriguez, 1999). Seeking to engage a Spanish-language paper with a primary focus on local concerns and capturing more diverse Cuban American political viewpoints, including more moderate views, I examined *El Nuevo Herald*. *El Nuevo Herald* was created by the Knight-Ridder Company in 1979 in response to Cuban American criticism of the company's English-language *Miami Herald*, which is Miami's flagship newspaper. By the late 1970s, the Cuban American community had become fed up with the *Miami Herald*, which they believed was insensitive to Cuban issues, painted Cubans and other Latinos as criminals, and was too soft on communism and Castro (Portes and Stepick 1994; Soruco 1996). Because *El Nuevo Herald* was created to attract the readership potential of the growing Cuban population and was created in response to dissatisfaction with the *Miami Herald*, it needed to strike a balance between Anglo-American or mainstream ideals and the concerns of the Cuban American community in order to sell papers. In 1987 *El Miami Herald* became independent of the *Miami Herald*, with a separate staff and editor, and changed its name to *El Nuevo Herald*. A Cuban American, Roberto Suarez, became the paper's editor, and the journalists were almost exclusively Cuban (Portes and Stepick 1994; Soruco 1996). Although the paper was still owned by the Knight-Ridder Corporation, the move to independence from the English-language paper allowed a more prominent Cuban voice and identity of the paper. Under the editorship of Suarez, *El Nuevo Herald* grew to a daily circulation of more than a hundred thousand by 1990 (Soruco 1996) and has continued to be the most widely read Spanish-language paper in Miami.

I analyze *El Nuevo Herald*'s coverage of Mariel because during the time it reflected several voices; in the same paper we are able to see coverage that reflects both mainstream depictions of the Marielitos as well as Cuban American reactions to those depictions. Controlled by the same editorial board that produced the mainstream paper, it reflected an often expressly negative view of Mariel, exhibiting the press's role in enforcing a racialized normativity by directly presenting the same overarching views promoted in the mainstream paper in editorials and news stories (often direct translations of the English version) (Portes and Stepick 1994). Yet the paper also engaged strategies that signaled the Spanish-language paper's attempts to align more closely with the exile community. For instance, it presented more explicitly Cuban voices in op-eds, letters to the editor, and other material more unique to *El Nuevo Herald*. Besides containing different op-eds and letters than the mainstream paper, *El Nuevo Herald* also differed from the *Miami Herald* in the placement of stories (giving stories about Mariel more prominence on the front page) and the amount of stories on Mariel (*El Nuevo Herald* published more). By paying close attention to these areas in which *El Miami Herald* and the *Miami Herald* differed, I tease out Cuban American engagement with the discourses being produced about the Mariel refugees in the English-language paper. By the time of the Balsero crisis, *El Nuevo Herald* had become independent and therefore more accepted within the Cuban American community. Thus, my analysis of the paper during the Balsero crisis captures a more solidified Cuban American voice.

Afro-Cuban Voices

To further expand the discussion about the complexities of racializing frames and expose their limitations, my study also includes a focus on unofficialized discourses of talk through in-depth interviews with a sample of Afro-Cubans from Miami and Los Angeles.[23] I interviewed Afro-Cubans living in the United States to gain a deeper understanding of their individual voices, examine how they negotiate their racial positioning, and connect their views to the structural and ideological issues affecting the construction of race. The interviewees include thirty individuals, fifteen in each city, gathered through snowball sampling and consisting of eleven women and nineteen men from nineteen to sixty-five years of age. The majority of interviewees came to the United States during the 1980s and 1990s (three arrived in the first decade of the 2000s) as adults or late teens. A little more than half of the interviews were conducted in Spanish and then translated.

The qualitative methodology captures nuances within subjective interpersonal interactions, which are difficult to capture in quantitative studies. I explore several questions: How do these Afro-Cubans believe Anglos, African

Americans, and other Latinos position them in the U.S. racial hierarchy? How do they determine their own place in society and in relation to the predominant racial structure and to other racialized groups? How do their present experiences relate to the findings from the newspapers? Having a small sample allowed an in-depth look into individual life experiences. I do not attempt to generalize the findings to a larger population but to identify patterns and concerns that can be expanded on in future studies. Ultimately, by centering Afro-Cubans through interviews, I seek to engage in a scholarly conversation about the complicated negotiations faced by transnational black immigrants and illuminate how through their multiplicity, post-1980 Afro-Cuban immigrants challenge assimilative models and impulses.

Notes on Terminology

There are several terms that are used repeatedly in the book that require explanation. One is "minority." According to a politics of division, white Euro-Americans have been pitted against "nonwhites" (Valdez 2017), and thus I use the term "minority" to describe populations (such as African Americans, Latinos, Asians, and Native Americans) that traditionally have been racialized as distinct from the white numerical majority. This polarity has remained consistent over time (Dominguez 1997; Feagin 2010; Urciuoli 2003). Thus, in the United States, the term "minority" has meant more than proportionally smaller numbers of people; it has signaled a group of people who have been denied full access to institutional power. Currently, there are moves away from using the term "minority" in part because the demographic trend is toward no one group being the majority or the minority. Although I continue to use the term, I also use terms such as "groups of color," "racialized groups," or "Others" as I work toward finding descriptive alternatives to a term that has a long tradition of usage in scholarship on race and ethnicity but needs to be rethought given demographic trends.

"*Latino communities*" or "*Black communities.*" I distinguish between "Latino" and "black" (African American) communities in the tradition of scholarship that seeks to identify trends and patterns. However, I acknowledge and highlight in this book that in reality, there is much heterogeneity within these populations; there is no one "Latino" or "black" community. Furthermore, as Afro-Latinos exemplify, these communities are not discreet.

Black.

The term "black" is used in two ways. It is used as a descriptor of African heritage or of black color (which could be applied to Cubans or other newer immigrants of African descent), and it is also used interchangeably with "African American." The term "African American" broadly refers to the descendants of slaves brought to the continental United States, but this category can include Afro-Caribbeans who share this quasi-"native" status in that they immigrated to the United States early in Florida's history (such as the mid-nineteenth century). These earlier black immigrants integrated themselves in a unified "black" African American community, often adopting an "African American" political and social identity (Rose 2015; Shell-Weiss 2009). What is important to know is that regardless of early origins, members of this group consider themselves to be "native" to the United States, in contrast to more recent immigrants (black or non-black) who arrived after the 1960s. Although using only "African American" to refer to "native" blacks could be simpler, I include the use of "black," because it was used most often in the *Miami Times* newspaper to describe the group that today is more commonly called "African Americans" in formal language. "black" is also a commonly used self-descriptor by African Americans.

Afro-Cuban. The term "Afro-Cuban" is used in this book because it is the term commonly used in U.S.-based scholarship to describe black people from Cuba. However, it is not used in Cuba; there Cubans who describe themselves as "black" (referring to phenotype) use the term "black" or "negro."

Chapter Outline

Chapter 1 develops Miami as a distinct location in the United States and expands on the concept of "worthy citizenship." The chapter provides more depth on Miami's history, demographics, and racial dynamics to provide background for understanding interethnic tensions during the 1980 Mariel boat lift and 1994 Balsero crisis. I argue that three dominant race-making frames are involved in the creation of worthy citizenship: the black/white frame, the good/bad immigrant frame, and the native/foreigner dichotomy. These binary frames, traditionally utilized by whites to divide themselves from groups of color, become useful for racialized groups when they are faced with political, economic, and social instability in the United States and are compelled to prove their worthiness by aligning with the dominant order. As such, these frames shape the contentious interethnic relations explored in the book.

Chapter 2 analyzes the coverage of the 1980 Mariel boatlift in *El Miami Herald*. This chapter illustrates how the black/white binary of worthy citizenship was perpetuated in the framing of the Marielitos as either potential "worthy citizens" or "black criminals." As exiles fleeing the Fidel Castro regime, Cuban Americans had presumably secured their welcome in the United States by proving their worthiness through an upward mobility that distinguished them from the nation's (black) underclasses. Yet, the newcomers from the 1980 Mariel boatlift, or Marielitos, were younger and poorer than Cubans who came during previous waves, a higher percentage of them were black, and they were criminalized in the Cuban and mainstream U.S. press (García 1996). Their criminalization created a dilemma for established Cuban exiles: they desired to both support the newcomers as their compatriots and escape the stigma that threatened the community's "Golden Exile" image. I argue that a language around blackness helped produce the Mariel stigma, as voices in the *Herald* invoked the good/bad immigrant binary through white dominant tropes about laziness, dependency, and criminality to distinguish "worthy" (white) from "unworthy" (black or nonwhite) citizens. Highlighting an intra-Latino struggle between black and white Cubans shaped by the racial context of Cuba, the chapter juxtaposes the newspaper discourse with Afro-Cuban testimonials as they discuss how public opinion about blackness affected their acceptance during Mariel. By examining how racist attitudes from Cuba intersect with a U.S. brand of anti-black sentiments in the context of the U.S. anti-communist imperatives, the chapter illustrates how and why anti-black discourses may be adopted by various racially marginalized groups to set themselves apart from "unworthy citizens."

Chapter 3 analyzes African American responses to the Mariel boatlift in the *Miami Times*. The Mariel boatlift came on the heels of what became known as the McDuffie Riot, an African American uprising against the latest notorious incident of police brutality. As the local government turned its attention to the influx of 125,000 Cuban newcomers, some African Americans feared Miami's white dominant infrastructure would continue to ignore their persistent concerns. Furthermore, the *Times* drew on the native/foreigner binary to endorse the idea that black Americans and white Americans were the "real Americans" who were "losing out" due to mass migration and that Cuban refugees (constructed as white) were receiving preferential treatment over another controversial group of migrants coming seeking U.S. refuge at the same time—"unambiguously" black Haitian refugees. The seeming disdain for Cuban immigration is, upon closer examination, directly related to African American desires to more fully challenge the persistence of anti-blackness in the United States. But the binary frames used to characterize "white" Cubans and "black" Haitians flattened out the greater complexity of a climate in which immigration and refugee policies were actually consistent with a reversal of civil rights movement gains. The chapter illustrates that the larger presence of black Cubans among the new refugees forced a reexamination of African American modes of solidarity that decide group membership and black identity according to a bipolar black/white racial paradigm. This critique becomes all the more important as African Americans are challenged by the nation's growing ethnic/racial diversity with how to fight anti-blackness while also incorporating other populations such as Latinos into their struggles for greater equality.

Chapter 4 examines the polarizing effect of the 1994 Balsero crisis on Miami's African American and Cuban American communities and the different interpretations of the crisis that were disseminated in both *El Nuevo Herald* and the *Miami Times* newspapers. My findings demonstrate the extent to which, for racialized native-born and immigrant communities alike, citizenship is implicitly understood as conditional and earned through suffering, an assumption that establishes the grounds for interethnic conflict. I contend that through its civil rights and immigration policy, the United States has created a hierarchy of suffering that makes human rights a zero-sum game. Accordingly, the newspaper coverage reveals that the varying interpretations of the Balsero crisis centered on the differential treatment of Haitian "boat people" and the Balseros. The Cuban and Haitian asylum seekers could be co-opted to make each community's suffering visible and to highlight the desirability of being included in the U.S. nation. The arrival of over 35,000 Cubans on makeshift rafts had led to the historic move of the Clinton administration to further close the open-door welcome on Cuban immigration, and the *Herald* conveyed Cuban exiles' anger over what they perceived as U.S. betrayal. The theme of Balsero suffering, captured in images depicting the desperation of rafters at sea, became a primary theme in the paper and was offered as proof that they deserved asylum.

Meanwhile, the *Miami Times* continued a critique of the differential treatment of Haitians and Cubans, reflecting African American discontent that all suffering is not equally recognized. The *Times* made the case that after more than a century as suffering "Americans," blacks were still deemed unworthy citizens by white elites. Taken together, the messages in both newspapers illustrate that in the quest for U.S. belonging, interethnic conflict emerges as racially marginalized groups are coerced to compete with one another over who has suffered most. Nonetheless, discussions of the struggles of Afro-Cubans in both papers, though limited, point in the direction of alternative ways of understanding the Balsero crisis. They highlight the racial origins and consequences of U.S. immigration policy and generate new potential for collaborative rather than competitive relations between Cubans and African Americans and other racialized groups.

In negotiation with the mainstream discourses I trace in earlier chapters (around black/white binaries, good/bad immigrants, and natives/foreigners), blackness, Cubanness, and Americanness are reimagined by Afro-Cuban informants in ways that are more nuanced and complex. Chapter 5 focuses on the narratives of post-1980 Afro-Cuban immigrants living in Miami and Los Angeles to foreground the often-neglected perspectives of contemporary Afro-Cuban migrants and to gain greater insight into how people situated on the borders and "in between" confront dominant racial frames. The stories they tell about their daily racial encounters shine a light on the spaces where they found a welcome and on the overlaps where coalitions between groups such as African Americans and Latinos are possible. But their stories also detail experiences of rejection by members of groups within which they might be expected to have affinity. In some of their encounters with Cubans and African Americans in Miami, and with African Americans and Mexican Americans in Los Angeles, they have been expected to choose one identity or the other or have been rejected because of their blackness. However, the interviewees strategically undermine the fixed notions of race and ethnicity that are embraced even by some nonwhites. Furthermore, they draw upon problematic "racial democracy" discourses from Cuba to contest such negative racial experiences. Although this chapter points to the resistive potential in the fluidity in Afro-Cuban identity, lauding this potential does not mean accepting an overly simplified U.S.-based "multicultural rhetoric" or the idea that "race does not matter" (which also comes through in Latin American racial democracy discourses). Rather, this chapter underlines that

Afro-Cuban negotiations illustrate just how much race continues to shape the social lives of those seeking U.S. belonging and highlights the continued strength of racial notions that denigrate blackness.

My conclusion draws together the broader implications of my arguments about how and why the binary frames of worthy citizenship come to be internalized and utilized as a strategy for marginalized groups to make claims to the nation and about how all those caught up in the Miami scenario—African Americans, (white) Cubans, and Afro-Cubans—actually help us disrupt these binaries. Their negotiations of race illuminate the greater transnational and geopolitical contexts that are mediated in U.S.-based race making. The conclusion also situates the historical analyses of previous chapters to the current Miami context and outlines the national implications of this book's study. The Obama presidency brought the greater political congruence between younger Cubans, Afro-Cubans, and African Americans to the fore, but Obama's opening of relations between the United States and Cuba and the Cuban vote during the 2016 election for Donald Trump have also reminded us of the continued hardline stance of older Cuban exiles. This chapter ponders what the new climate in Miami means for the future of race relations there. The lessons learned from the cases explored in the book allow us to anticipate and better understand contemporary struggles that arise between African Americans, Latinos, and other racialized groups across the nation and give us the background we need to contemplate solutions. Thus, the conclusion also discusses African American and Latino conflict in light of more recent examples and in light of anti-immigrant rallies used as a stage by powerful white politicians to play African Americans against immigrants. Ultimately, the conclusion reminds us that as whites become the numerical minority, challenging the pull to embrace white dominant exclusionary ideologies, as well as dismantling structural inequities, will be crucial for the forging of effective alliances between currently marginalized groups.

Chapter 1

RACE MAKING

Miami and the Nation

In 1990, Miami was set to play host to Nelson Mandela, who had been freed from prison after a twenty-seven-year sentence for his role in opposing South Africa's racial apartheid system. Arguably "the most powerful symbol of the battle for racial freedom at the time," Mandela had embarked on a worldwide speaking tour (Sawyer 2006, 165). He drew staggering crowds and high levels of adulation in cities like New York, and enthusiasm was also high in Miami, Florida, especially among African Americans. African American Miamians, who were continuing the fight for racial justice in their own city, anticipated his arrival keenly as he symbolized for them the worldwide pan-African unity needed to fight against the black/white apartheid that had characterized the culture not only of South Africa but also of the United States.

Yet many Cuban Americans in Miami had the exact opposite reaction to Mandela's visit. Before his scheduled appearance, Mandela gave a television interview with ABC network's Ted Koppel, in which he described a "complex web of friendships across national borders" and thanked them for their financial and military support of him and his cause (Sawyer 2006, 165).[1] Among these controversial friends was Cuba's leader Fidel Castro—the very leader Miami's Cuban exiles had come to the area to escape. As migrants invited to the United States because their presence bolstered the country's fight against communism and Castro, Cuban Americans primarily saw the United States as the land of opportunity to which they owed their thanks. To them, the black American struggle predated them, and local race relations were not their immediate concern. Cubans were incensed with Mandela's embrace of Castro, whom they saw as a tyrant guilty of a host of human rights offenses. Viewing themselves as exiles fleeing political persecution, their main political fight was against the leader whom they fled, a cause that they fought for with great vigor. Members of Miami's Cuban population, many of whom were powerful political and economic players in Miami's economy, acted quickly to mobilize against Mandela's appearance. As a result, in contrast to the warm welcome Mandela received elsewhere, in which he was given keys to the city and other honors, the mayors of Miami and Miami Beach, both of Cuban descent, refused to meet with Mandela or bestow any honors (Grenier and Pérez 2003; Sawyer 2006). Mandela still made his scheduled appearance, but the red carpet treatment was rescinded, and his presence was met by three hundred or so Cuban protesters (Sawyer 2006).

Miami's African Americans were appalled by the Cuban-led snub. To them, that Cuban Americans could disparage such a broadly recognized heroic figure, who had fought so hard and even suffered for racial justice, provided one more example of how Cuban Americans, since the beginning of their large-scale migration to the area after 1959, were not only uninterested in African American concerns but actively hostile to the African American struggle. African Americans accused Cuban Americans of racism, and when city officials supported the Mandela snub, African Americans nationwide launched a boycott of Miami tourism. Among other efforts, large black national organizations canceled events they had planned in the city. The boycott lasted three years and resulted in $60 million in losses for the city (Grenier and Castro 1999; Grenier and Pérez 2003). It finally came to an end after the Miami Beach Commission negotiated with African Americans, establishing a scholarship fund for black students at Florida International University and agreeing to the development of a black-owned hotel on Miami Beach. City officials also made retroactive statements honoring Mandela (Grenier and Pérez 2003). Although these moves ended the boycott, the day-to-day tensions between African Americans and Cubans, Miami's two largest ethnic/racial populations, continued to simmer.

Many scholars cite the Mandela incident as one of the most high-profile examples of the deep and persistent divisions between Miami African Americans and Cubans (Sawyer 2006; Shell-Weiss 2009). However, as Claire Jean Kim (2000) cautions, we should be careful, in narrating conflicts between non-Anglo minority groups, to avoid presenting whites as normative, uninvolved bystanders. For example, in the case of the Mandela incident, the white Anglo political and business establishment ultimately had the final say on whose case and whose ideas received the powerful "signal boost" of mainstream news coverage. Both groups had to appeal to white elite gatekeepers to achieve their aims. Cubans as powerful political constituents had to convince city officials to snub Mandela in spite of the warm welcome he received in almost every other place he went. African American boycotts of Miami businesses were the only thing that ultimately moved (white) elites toward appeasing African Americans.[2] The tension arose, too, from decades of governmental preference for Cubans over African Americans demonstrated via foreign policy, local business practices, and the granting of aid. From the initial U.S. decision to open immigration to Cubans in the early 1960s in service of the Cold War, while ignoring the concerns of long-resident African Americans, to the social service agencies that did more to incorporate Cuban newcomers than to help African Americans, white elites played a formative role in interethnic conflict. The Mandela controversy and other black/Cuban tensions were not just about the "natural" misunderstandings between a native minority group and foreign-born migrants but were cultivated by the U.S. history of anti-black racial practices and foreign policy moves that ultimately serve the white power base.

This chapter highlights the central role of white Anglo elites and of white supremacist ideologies in supporting a politics of African American/Cuban division. I will detail the histories that led to the Mandela conflict and beyond: strict black/white segregation practices in Miami, the specific historical forces that brought Cubans to Miami, and the clashes that would arise between whites, Cubans, and African Americans. In doing so, I argue that African Americans and Cubans were positioned by the white power base within a "racial order" that would create unavoidable tensions among these groups (Kim 2000). The chapter captures how racist forces and ideologies of worthy citizenship imposed a strict separation between the categories of

"African American" and "Cuban," and between "black" and "white," despite the actual heterogeneity of people placed in these categories in Miami. Developing the notion of "worthy citizenship," the chapter next discusses how non-Anglo groups may take on such ideologies in their own quest for national belonging. All in all, using the case of Miami Florida, the chapter reminds us of how histories of white colonial and settler domination in the United States and binary racializing frames that justify such domination are connected to interethnic conflict writ large.

Jim Crow and the Establishing of Black Miami

If you browse Florida tourism websites today, Miami is described as an "international hub of cultural diversity and world-class offerings."[3] A unique tropical paradise of sorts with its beaches frequented by "the beautiful people," Miami remains a popular tourist destination. But before the 1960s, blacks were not allowed as guests in the hotels that lined Miami's beaches. African Americans worked as the hotel maids and as cooks and servers in the restaurants. In order to enter these areas reserved for the enjoyment of white tourists, African Americans had to carry identification, and after work they were expected to make their ways back to their homes in the "negro areas" (Connolly 2014; Grenier and Pérez 2003). Since its incorporation in 1896, the region was typically southern not only in its population of mostly blacks and whites but also in its racial politics. Indeed as N. D. B. Connolly asserts, South Florida's exotic labels have served "to conceal the brutality and racism so often required to create and preserve one of the nation's most celebrated tourist destinations" (2014, 5). African Americans endured segregationist policies that denied them such simple pleasures as Miami's beaches and, far worse, subjected them to white brutality in the form or lynchings and police violence.

Like most other southern cities, Miami early on established a political, economic, and social structure that excluded nonwhites and defined white in opposition to black. In its earliest colonial history, Florida was controlled by the Spanish, who brought both free and enslaved blacks with them. From the 1700s to the early 1800s, the area was fought over by the Spanish, French, and the British, all of whom utilized black slave labor in their efforts to settle the region. As the land shifted between European colonial hands, Florida would also be a place where escaped slaves would flee to and often join in alliances with native Seminole Indians. In 1821, the United States gained control of Florida in an effort led by Andrew Jackson, "to rid Florida of foreign domination" (Dunn 2016, 28). After the United States mounted a brutal campaign of clearing the land of Seminoles, Florida was then settled by poor whites mainly from Georgia and South Carolina and of Scots-Irish descent, who brought already entrenched Southern ideals of anti-black brutality with them. They would be joined by wealthy whites from the North seeking to develop the Florida "wilderness" after it became a state in 1845. Whether the settlers were poor whites from the South or rich whites from the North, they saw themselves in opposition to blacks, who served as enslaved laborers. The Haitian revolt of African slaves in 1791, as well as rebellions in the United States, such as that of Nat Turner in Virginia in 1831, were recent in the memories of the white population and caused them to be even more fearful of revolt by black slaves in Florida. Thus, whites in Florida enacted, in historian Marvin Dunn's analysis, some of the most extreme measures to keep "recalcitrant" blacks in line (2016, 41).

The framework of defining white in opposition to black continued to be openly visible into the twentieth century. During the first third of the twentieth century, it was not uncommon for major newspapers in Miami such as the *Miami Herald* and the *Miami Metropolis* to refer to blacks as "coons" or similar epithets. Though black labor had originally brought progress to Miami's economy, blacks were systematically excluded from Miami politics and were segregated into a section of the city known then as "Colored Town" (since renamed Overtown) (Dunn 1997; Dunn and Stepick 1992). Miami had an active Ku Klux Klan (KKK) presence. The KKK was highly visible: it would hold parades during the 1920s, for instance, and terrorized blacks in various ways, including kidnapping black clergymen who preached racial equality to teach them to not disrupt the social order (Dunn 1997).[4] Later, during World War II, as a part of the war safety efforts, Miami heavily enforced Negro curfews so that blacks could generally be accounted for at all times. These curfews did not have to be enforced by police or officials; any white citizen could enforce them (Connolly 2014).

Although segregationist policies established a strong black/white division, the black population in Miami has always been heterogeneous in terms of their origins. The earliest blacks in the Miami area were migrants from the Bahamas seeking work after the collapse of the Bahamian economy in the

1880s. In Miami, they primarily worked as farm laborers (Dunn 1997).[5] They were joined by African Americans, descended from slaves from other southern states such as Georgia and South Carolina. The Great Freeze, which struck the southeastern United States in 1894–1895, prompted white planters to move to the Miami area for warmer climates. This agricultural catastrophe also spurred African American blacks to come to the Miami area as they sought field work (Dunn 1997). Despite the actual heterogeneity of the early black population, the binary black/white opposition lumped all blacks together. For example, in the 1930s, real estate appraisers would give neighborhoods ratings to assess residential market values for white buyers. Though areas such as Coconut Grove were settled primarily by Bahamians and Colored Town had a good percentage of West Indians along with native-born African Americans, white property appraisers simply labeled these neighborhoods "100 percent negro." With the "negro" designation would come a "D" rating, the lowest on the scale. In contrast, appraisers would distinguish whites by being either native or foreign born and have variations of grades (all higher than the D rating) depending on where they lived (Connolly 2014, 95).

Despite the racist conditions under which they had to live, blacks carved out spaces for themselves and a sense of connectedness to their Miami home. Ironically, segregation encouraged black-owned businesses because blacks, locked out of the white world, needed their own institutions. They created a black Miami which had a vibrant culture and commercial life (Dunn 1997, 144). As the center of black Miami, Overtown became a thriving business and cultural center between the 1900s and 1950s (Dunn 1997; Dunn and Stepick 1992). Overtown's streets reflected the Caribbean and native-born black mix that could be seen in the street festivals selling Bahamian foods alongside African American cuisine. Night spots would play host to famous black entertainers and be frequented by both black and white guests. Miami's black communities put on parades and hosted sporting events and other diversions. Blacks in Miami built businesses, churches, organizations, schools, and a history. In essence, they established cultural practices that tied them to the Miami area and gave them a sense of ownership and identification with the places in which they lived (Connolly 2014; Rose 2015). This was especially true of the African Americans who were the descendants of slaves brought to the continental United States and had centuries-long historical connections to the southern United States.

Still, blacks in Miami were not satisfied to simply leave the racial status quo unchallenged. African Americans in Miami, with their long ties to the southern region, felt connected to the various black challenges to the white power base that were taking place throughout the south. Indeed, Miami's blacks were active in this fight and had important civil rights fights that even predate those in other areas (Dunn 1997; Rose 2015; Shell-Weiss 2009). By the 1960s, African Americans were beginning to see the signs that their own efforts were bringing about profound changes. Perhaps blacks would gain the right to be treated with human dignity, to evade white brutality—to take a casual stroll on the beach.

Contending Forces: The Birth of Cuban Miami and Shifting Power Relations

As African Americans were mounting their fight for civil rights in Miami, Fidel Castro was establishing the Cuban Revolution in nearby Cuba. The Cuban Revolution, along with U.S. responses to it, would spur the large-scale migration of Cubans to the Miami area and forever change the face of Miami. As Raymond Mohl points out, the Cuban Revolution and the civil rights movement were "two powerful forces for change [that] not only coincided, but they collided with one another" (1990, 39).

After functioning as allies during World War II, relations between the Soviet Union and the United States began to worsen. The United States decided to take a stance of resisting Soviet expansion in the world and entered into an arms race with Russia as both nations sought to bolster its weaponry in case of the need to defend against one another. Meanwhile the United States always had interest in Cuba. From the early 1800s to the mid-1900s, Cuba was dependent on the United States for trade. The United States occupied Cuba between 1898 (after Cuba's war of independence from Spain) and 1902. Later, while supporting the Batista regime in the mid-twentieth century, it held some political control over Cuba (Boswell and Curtis 1984; Soderlund 2003). In 1959, Fidel Castro overthrew the U.S.-backed rule of Batista and made Cuba the first communist state in the Western Hemisphere. It quickly aligned itself with the Soviet Union and against U.S. imperialist efforts. The United States responded under President Eisenhower with the breaking of all diplomatic ties, establishing the difficult relations that would continue into the twenty-first century (Boswell and Curtis 1984).

Via land reforms, the nationalization of businesses, and other policy changes, Castro stripped rich Cubans of much of their economic and political power (Boswell and Curtis 1984; García 1996). Thus, the first wave of Cuban refugees included landed elites, some of whom had supported the previous Batista regime and whose lives and livelihoods were threatened within the new regime (Pedraza-Bailey 1985). Lisandro Pérez estimates that between 1959 and 1962, a total of 200,000 families with children under eighteen years old arrived from Cuba (2001, 93). The second wave of Cuban immigration began in the fall of 1965 and lasted until 1973: approximately 5,000 people were retrieved by boat lift, and 260,000 were brought to the United States by plane (Grenier and Stepick 1992). This wave consisted mainly of the relatives of those who had arrived in the previous wave. A higher percentage of the second wave represented the "petit bourgeoisie," or small business owners (Pedraza-Bailey 1985). Those who arrived during the first two waves are commonly thought of as the groups who established the (white) Miami exile community (Grenier and Pérez 2003).[6] During the second wave, the United States instituted the Cuban Adjustment Act (1966), which stated that all newly arrived Cubans could become naturalized citizens (Pedraza 1996). President Lyndon B. Johnson promised the Cuban people that the United States would serve as a haven for them, beginning a unique relationship between the Cuban people and the United States. Significantly, the United States played a crucial role both in Cuba's own politics before the rise of Fidel Castro and in creating the conditions encouraging Cubans fleeing the Castro regime to come to the United States.

Though many of the Cubans who first arrived were from the upper classes of Cuba, in the United States they took on jobs dramatically different from what they did before. People who had been teachers, lawyers, and doctors became cab drivers, janitors, and maintenance workers. Women who were not accustomed to being employed entered wage work in the tourism industry and manufacturing (García 1996; Shell-Weiss 2009, 176). The exiles settled southwest of the central business district in the area that became "Little Havana" and in other areas such as Hialeah, then a working-class white city (Aranda et al. 2014; García 1996). They hoped their stay in the United States would be short and that they would be able to help facilitate the overthrow of Castro and go right back (García 1996). However, the exiles also established roots in the United States and thrived in Miami.

The Cuban influx could not be ignored as it was "the single largest mass immigration to the United States in more than half a century, and the largest in Miami's history" (Shell-Weiss 2009, 172). As the Cubans came in, the local government was under the imperative to find ways to incorporate them. Helping the Cubans was seen as an immediate need to help foreign policy and national security during the height of the Cold War (Shell-Weiss 2009). So arriving Cubans were welcomed with open arms at a time when long-resident African Americans fought to be recognized at all (Mohl 1990). This welcome, along with U.S. support of their anti-communism, meant Cuban exiles saw the United States as an ideal place of refuge, to which they came in large numbers. The U.S. government underscored its welcome of the Cubans with unparalleled aid to these political exiles for adjustment to life in the United States (Grenier and Stepick 1992; Stepick et al. 2003). Some of the types of aid they received included automatic legal status with a fast track to citizenship, occupational training, scholarships for higher education, low-interest loans, English-language classes, and hundreds of millions of dollars in aid to establish businesses (Aranda et al. 2014; García 1996; L. A. Pérez 2003).

As white political elites in Miami embraced the cause of Cuban exiles, they gave even less attention to the African American social justice efforts. This laid the groundwork for interethnic conflict. For example, on April 29, 1959, the newly established Greater Miami chapter of the Congress of Racial Equality, a pivotal African-American civil rights group, staged a sit-in at two segregated restaurants on Flagler Street. Normally sit-ins like these would be the top story in the newspapers in the Miami press and even gain national attention. However, the sit-in efforts received little press in contrast to the continued influx of Cuban refugees. White employers added to the tension by championing the hiring of immigrants over African Americans. The extensive federal, state, and city efforts to find work for Cuban immigrants stood in contrast to rising rates of unemployment among African Americans and Puerto Ricans (Shell-Weiss 2009, 178). A new racial division seemed to be emerging in Miami—whites and Cubans (as honorary whites) against African American blacks.

But if Cubans seemed to be favored by whites, this favoritism was complicated—it was not pure good will on the part of whites toward

Cubans. Industrialists and policymakers, driven by the desire to lower labor costs, maximize tourism profits, and reach untapped markets, saw Cubans as an exploitable and perhaps temporary labor force that would not get embroiled in battles for equality or better labor conditions. Hence whites could use "one vulnerable population [Cubans] to exploit several others." The groups were placed in direct competition, and whites "ultimately stood to gain from eroding cross-ethnic alliances" (Shell-Weiss 2009, 181).

When Cubans first began to arrive, African Americans viewed them as possible allies. But the seeming political favoritism of Anglo elites, along with the subsequent economic and political gains that emerged for Cubans as they settled into the city, led to an increasing sense of rivalry between African Americans and the exiles. The feeling of blacks losing ground came from the idea not only of white favoritism and Cuban power but also of being displaced because of sheer numbers. Indeed, the onset of mass Cuban immigration in the 1960s would radically alter Miami demographics. There was a thirty-fold increase in Cubans in the area from the time right before the Cuban Revolution, when there were 20,000 Cubans in Miami, to the early 1980s, when the numbers had risen to 600,000 (Boswell and Curtis 1984, 71). In 1960, African Americans greatly outnumbered Cubans, but by 1980 there were more than twice as many Latinos as non-Latino blacks (see Figure 1).

Not only did Cubans come to outnumber African Americans, but generous governmental support for Cuban exiles helped them achieve economic,

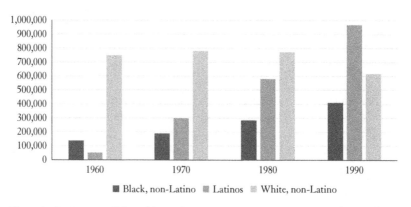

Figure 1. Comparison of Miami Metropolitan Area Population by Race/Ethnicity: 1960–1990. Source: Metro-Dade Planning Department (1990).

political, and cultural gains that African Americans had long struggled for unsuccessfully. The traditional trajectory of immigrant assimilation in the United States is understood this way: immigrants arrive and, in successive generations, lose their ethnic distinctiveness, becoming more like the mainstream culture (Gordon 1964; Park 1950). As Alex Stepick and his colleagues (2003) point out, though, Miami Cubans have begun to exercise assimilative power, meaning that, in Miami, acculturation went in reverse (146). Reverse acculturation occurs "when established residents self-consciously adopt some traits of the newcomer culture, [for instance], learning Spanish" (31). In just a few decades, Cubans would transform Miami into a place where Spanish was widely spoken, and Cuban-owned businesses, such as restaurants, supermarkets, and salons, proliferated. Cuban culture flavored every corner of the city with the welcoming smells of Cuban cuisine and *café Cubano*. The Miami Cuban contingent would also grow to be enormously powerful socially, economically, and politically, unlike migrants to other places (Grenier and Pérez 2003). Cubans began to consolidate power and influence in such a way that they in fact seemed to displace white Anglos as the ones in power in the city (Mohl 1990). The mainstream media celebrated their entrepreneurship as popular magazines such as *Life, Fortune,* and *Newsweek* offered them as proof of the storied direct link between hard work and the ability for all to achieve the American Dream, with little attention to the fact that U.S. aid helped launch their success (García 1996, 110).

The U.S. intervention in Cuba and Cuban immigration policy also encouraged a heightened sense of patriotism among Cuban Americans, and political differences would play a major role in African American–Cuban conflict. Over time, Miami Cubans established a tradition of vocal political involvement and advocacy for the concerns of Cuban Americans regarding U.S.–Cuba relations and immigration policy. Cuban American patriotism, based on fervent opposition to Castro and staunch support of the Republican Party, has been defined as "exile politics," a primary unifying element for the Miami exile community (Stepick et al. 2003). In fact, as Alejandro Portes and Alex Stepick note, the Golden Exiles, as the earliest arrivals fleeing the Castro regime were called, created a "moral community" that dictated that Cuban exiles *must* take on this political point of view (1993, 139). The staunch conservatism of the Cuban exile community and support of the Republican Party contrasted greatly with the political point of view of the Miami African American community, which has traditionally aligned itself with the Democratic Party. The strong political stance of the Cuban community and the clear affinity with the Republican Party meant Cubans would vote against measures supported by African Americans. Their political power has been a force to be reckoned with. When it became clear that the Cuban community could significantly influence the result of not just Floridian but also presidential elections, politicians became attuned to the community and their needs to advance their own political goals. Despite the ulterior motives of many Anglo politicians in currying Cuban favor, it is not surprising that some Cubans felt embraced by the United States and responded with patriotic allegiance. However, the United States' prioritizing of the Cold War fight over local social justice concerns positioned "patriotic" Cuban Americans against "complaining" African Americans. As Melanie Shell-Weiss emphasizes, growing conflict between minority populations was caused neither by ethnic diversity nor by local dynamics alone; "federal intervention played a direct and prominent role" (2009, 182).

While U.S. Cold War priorities created conditions that made opposition between African Americans and Cuban Americans inevitable, it cannot be denied that some Cubans also held anti-black attitudes, were directly dismissive of African Americans, and looked down upon them (Aja 2016; López 2012). As will be discussed in more detail in Chapter 2, Cuba has a history of colonization, slavery, and racism similar to that of the United States, and whites there also sought to maintain power through the denigration of blacks. Although Cubans who came to the United States in the first two waves were overwhelmingly white, Cubans are not racially homogenous, and a large percentage of Cubans on the island are black. The Cubans who came to the United States in the first waves were most likely to have directly benefited from black labor in Cuba. These Cubans likely brought anti-black attitudes with them to the United States (López 2010, 2012). Indeed, the view that Cubans are racists, and that some privileged Cubans abuse their power, plays a major role in African American resentment toward Miami Cubans (Mohl 1990). Miami's Spanish-language press was often inattentive to the issues of the African American community, perpetuated a denial of Cuban racism, identified African Americans with crime, and supported the comparison of Cubans as hard-working, self-reliant, and family-oriented in contrast to blacks, who were perceived as being dependent on welfare and so on (Aja 2016; Grenier and Pérez 2003). Hence, as Cubans began to gain power in

Miami, they came to be viewed by African Americans as a new (white) oppressor (Grenier and Stepick 2001, 156).

In his history of ethnic relations in Miami, Raymond Mohl (1990) provides as an example a *Miami Times* quote by a black columnist discussing the 1989 Miami riot (which occurred the year before the Mandela visit), a response to an incident of police brutality against a black resident. The unrest was in part blamed on Cubans. The columnist wrote, "The reality of Miami today and in the foreseeable future, is that the Cubans are the new masters in Miami. They should not be surprised when those who feel they have nothing to lose rise up against the new rulers" (Mohl 1990, 54). In his statements, the columnist exhibits the more overtly antagonistic views of members of the black community while seeking to bring attention to the often more subtle ways Cubans demonstrated racism toward blacks. But the emerging view that Cubans were somehow to blame for many of the problems African Americans faced offended many Cuban Americans. They saw African American problems as centuries old related to slavery, racism, and segregation and advanced the opinion that the newly arrived Cubans were being used as scapegoats (Mohl 1990, 55). As scholar Antonio López argues, Cuban exiles cannot be taken off the hook and should be held responsible for seeking to benefit from a white identity at African Americans' expense (López 2012, 191). I agree with this wholeheartedly. At the same time (as López would likely agree), when analyzing Cuban–African American conflict, placing all the focus on Cuban exile attitudes would blind us to a very important part of the story—the ways the already entrenched black/white binary helped facilitate such attitudes and shaped the repercussions of these attitudes in the U.S. context.

Though demographics and power were shifting dramatically over time with the new Cuban migration, the historical "racialized institutional structures" put in place by the white Anglo power base lived on and were actively defended (Aranda et al. 2014). Though whites nationally were celebrating Cubans as the new "Horatio Algiers" (García 1996), the rapid change to Miami was alarming to many whites locally. With the large-scale migration from Cuba, in just a little over ten years Miami became one of the country's largest immigrant cities (Shell-Weiss 2009, 7). By 1970, Miami had become a "city of immigrants," with 40 percent of its residents foreign born (in comparison to only 12 percent in 1960), and was now "majority-minority" as together

Latinos and African Americans outnumbered whites (Shell-Weiss 2009, 206–207). Although the old black/white divisions remained strong and foundational to race relations in the area, nativity, along with race and class, would polarize people (Shell-Weiss 2009). The area experienced substantial "white flight"; between 1970 and 1980, there were 30,000 fewer whites in Dade County (Boswell and Curtis 1984, 68; Shell-Weiss 2009). Whites also showed their contempt for Cuban immigrants in other ways, such as refusing to rent to Cuban apartment seekers, with apartment owners posting signs reading "No Cubans Allowed" (García, 1996, 29). In 1980, after the Cuban community was well established, local political leaders made an even clearer statement that they did not like the changes that were happening when they passed an anti-bilingual county referendum, which set off the English-only movements of the United States (Stepick et al. 2003, 99). The proposal sought to repeal the Bilingual-Bicultural Ordinance originally passed in 1973 and to prohibit the use of Metro Commission funds for programs that used any language other than English (García 1996).[7] The proposal affirmed the white dominant assimilationist view that all newcomers should speak English. By 1980 Miami had become the "Cuban capital of the United States." Anglos saw the transformations in the city as proof that Cubans refused to assimilate and were in fact unassimilable (García 1996, 89). Thus, just as Cubans began to consolidate economic, political, and social power in Miami, their threat to the white Anglo power base also began to expose their vulnerability as not-quite-white foreigners.

Racial Order and Worthy Citizenship in the Miami Scenario

As this chapter has illustrated thus far, racist forces in Miami imposed a strict separation between people placed within the categories of "African American" and "Cuban," and between "black" and "white," creating distinct categories despite their actual heterogeneity. A close look at Miami's history demonstrates that despite the diversification of the population over time due to immigration, racialized structures remained intact as whites actively worked to maintain power. Coming from a country with its own black/white divisions, the largest migrant group, Cuban exiles, reinforced rather than disrupted the racial status quo. Yet, although they did not disrupt the black/

white division, they did underscore a new division that was beginning to
matter more and more in the U.S. nation as newer immigrants arriving from
non-European countries retained their ethnic distinctiveness rather than following the traditional assimilation narrative. The white Anglo power base
found this problematic because they felt the newcomers would ultimately be
a threat to what they had defined as American culture. In this context, divisions between Cubans and African American ensued, a division the white
Anglo establishment encouraged through foreign policy moves, through
local business and hiring practices, and through the perpetuation of discourses deeming one group worthier of their access to the American Dream
than the other group. As such, this chapter has argued that the conflict that
emerged between African Americans and Cubans was not simply the natural
result of two different groups living together but directly related to the ways
African Americans and Cubans were actively positioned by the white power
base within what Claire Jean Kim (2000) calls a "racial order"—a system of
dominance.

important name + term

In Kim's notion of racial order, the positioning of groups within a racial
hierarchy serves the purpose of maintaining white power by disciplining
groups of color. Racial categories, she says, are reproduced relationally to
other groups in a distinct (but dynamic and continuous) order, in a field
structured by at least two axes: superior/inferior and insider/foreigner. Blacks
and whites are major anchors, with whites on top and blacks at the bottom;
incoming immigrants are positioned in relation to these anchors. Immigrants "are racially 'triangulated' both as inferior to whites and superior to
blacks (in between black and white) and as permanently foreign and inassimilable (apart from black and white)" (Kim 2000, 16). Kim illustrates this
in her important analysis of African American and Korean conflict in New
York City during the Red Apple boycott of 1990. African American and Haitian activists boycotted Korean grocery stores after a physical altercation between a Korean female grocer and a Haitian female customer. The exact details of the altercation are confusing and disputed. Nevertheless, members of
the black and Haitian communities felt discriminated against and targeted in
the incident. After the incident, blacks were constructed in the press as irratio-
nal actors targeting "model minority" Koreans. Kim argues against such constructions, asserting that the tensions among these groups arose from both
groups' positioning: Asians in her study were positioned above blacks because

also lies on
inassimilable
non ns plane

5

• Cuban

• white anglo C

• black am

of their economic and educational success in the United States. Because the black population as a whole is stereotyped as being like the poorest of these groups, the successes of the black middle class that are similar to those of immigrants are often erased. Nevertheless, Kim argues that the popular focus on immigrant success absolves the nation from its responsibility in African American disenfranchisement and allows the United States to blame poorer African Americans for their own "failures." In effect, legitimate problems are erased by the focus on the successes of model immigrants.[8] Still, immigrants aren't clear winners here, as they are often simultaneously positioned as unassimilable outsiders when they retain aspects of their ethnic distinctiveness (such as the languages they spoke in their country of origin). Because these ethnic qualities are seen as incongruent with being "American," these immigrants never get to be fully "American." Regardless of whether immigrant groups are positioned as unassimilable outsiders or as superior to blacks, whites remain neutral or normative in this racial order. The ability for whites to remain neutral in instances of interethnic conflict is related to what Kim terms "racial power," the fact that the racial status quo tends to reproduce itself in ways that maintain white dominance atop the social hierarchy (2000, 2).

In the Miami scenario, African Americans and Cuban Americans were placed within the racial order by the white establishment in ways that maintained crucial racializing binary frames that have been essential for maintaining white dominance. It is these racializing binary frames that I argue compose worthy citizenship. Within the notion of worthy citizenship, groups are deemed more deserving of citizenship or national belonging by the extent to which they can prove that they conform to "proper" Anglo, middle-class, moral standards. I identify three main overarching racializing frames that groups working to position themselves more favorably within the nation may draw upon: (1) the black/white frame, the seemingly antiquated primary frame that still exists today and that most overtly reinscribes biological race; (2) the good/bad immigrant frame in which immigrant groups can make claim to the nation on the basis of their "proper" morality; and (3) the native/foreigner dichotomy, in which groups claim to be more entitled to citizenship on the grounds that their group has a longer history of time or investment in being included in the United States. These frames are adapted from the racial ideologies that have justified the positioning of whites above other groups within a racial hierarchy. These frames, which govern interethnic conflict, can be distinct at times but are more often overlapping and interconnected in their work of maintaining dominance.

Black/White Frame

In Miami as in the rest of the nation, the idea that black equals "noncitizen" and white equals "citizen" was promoted. African American writers and scholars have long theorized about the dominant racializing frame that positions black as opposite to American—reaffirming the supremacy of whiteness by eschewing blackness (for example, Ellison 1952; Morrison 1992, 1994).[9] Scholars of whiteness studies point out how blackness was used as the pole against which whiteness was defined, as lower-class whites and Irish immigrants were able to elevate themselves by distinguishing their status as free laborers against black slaves (Ignatiev 1995; Roediger 1991). Despite the various forms of nonbelonging constructed in the United States (slaves, unwanted native inhabitants, expendable immigrant labor from various countries, and inhabitants of conquered lands), the polarity of white and nonwhite has remained consistent (Feagin 2010; Urciuoli 1996, 2003). In the Miami scenario, we see the strength of the black/white frame in the ways Miami enforced the idea of white superiority with measures that not only kept whites and blacks separate but reinforced the idea of black criminality and inferiority. Laws and practices that kept blacks "in their place" and brutalized their very bodies enforced the idea that blacks did not deserve human dignity and that their lives were expendable.

As can be seen in Miami's history, the poles of white and black remain salient even for immigrants who do not perfectly fit in as black or white. They must negotiate their own identities in relation to a "dominant whiteness and a subjugated blackness" (De Genova 2005, 8). New immigrants soon learn that it is better to be anything other than black and that they must define themselves not only vis-à-vis whiteness as the normative U.S. identity but also in relation to U.S. blackness (Noguera 2003; see also Horsman 1981; Ong 2003). In the Miami scenario, Anglos played a role in teaching Cuban Americans to look down on African Americans in their positioning of Cuban Americans above blacks in the racial hierarchy as it prioritized its Cold War efforts while resisting civil rights advances (López 2012). Locally, Cubans received unprecedented aid while African Americans were still struggling

whites created distinction b/w
black and Cuban work ethic

(Grenier and Stepick 1992; Stepick et al. 2003). Moreover, discursively, white employers propelled age-old stereotypes about black laziness and incorrigibility while praising "hard working" Cubans. As such characterizations were stated by white employers and repeated over and over in the press, Cubans would learn just what those in power in the United States valued and would be provided a language they could use to maintain their own positioning within their new home. It became clear that African Americans were not well regarded and it would not be advantageous to be associated with then.

Yet the black/white frame does not only discipline blacks, keeping them at the lowest rung in the social order; it also serves to discipline other groups, such as the Cubans in Miami, teaching them to "stay in their place." Guinier and Torres call this disciplining tactic the "racial bribe"—"a strategy that invites specific racial or ethnic groups to advance within the existing black-white racial hierarchy by becoming 'white'" (2002, 225). Other scholars contribute similar concepts of "conditional" or "honorary" whiteness (Bonilla-Silva 2004; Mirabal 2003). These groups are in fact never fully included but are given enough concessions (such as legal rights, the prominent promotion of minority leaders, and so forth) to feel as though they are. Whiteness is painted as achievable, but their own ideas or ideals, if too different from the mainstream, must be excluded. In Miami, the "racial bribe" came in the form of the model designation given to Cuban exiles. The conception of a "model minority" is defined in opposition to African Americans and predicated on immigrant groups demonstrating the ability to compare favorably against African Americans in terms of social mobility, crime statistics, health, and so on (Okihiro 1994). Furthermore, immigrants, such as Cuban exiles in this case, become model citizens or "model minorities" when they are viewed as contributing more than they take and are not a burden to society (R. G. Lee 1999).

As Asian American studies scholars have long theorized, the "model minority" stereotype reinforces the polarization between white and black at the same time that it reveals the actual subjugated positioning of those deemed "models." Historically, Asians have been used to discipline black workers (blacks can always be replaced as laborers by Asians if they get out of hand) (Okihiro 1994). Today such disciplining continues, and immigrants get the message they must assimilate away from blackness toward whiteness to become model citizens. Such reasoning encourages immigrant groups to disparage blacks and blackness. At the same time, model minorities hold a tenu-

racial bribe become white in power only and who provide

ous claim to their near whiteness because their "alien-ness" makes them more exploitable. If they do not conform they can be expelled, whether literally by deportation or figuratively by exclusion from structures of power. As a result of U.S. failures to keep the promises of citizenship, they incur greater surveillance, exploitation at work, and other exclusions.

Good/Bad Immigrant Frame

The nation's ability to expel "foreign others" creates an instability that gives many immigrants all the more reason to work to prove they conform to the terms of worthy citizenship. In the Miami history recounted thus far and as we will see in closer detail in coming chapters, Cuban Americans confronted with historical white/black racial dynamics along with anti-immigrant sentiments felt this instability and sought to maintain a good place in the United States by adopting the "good/(bad) immigrant" idealization. The idea of the "good immigrant" (Saito 2001) is related to the model minority idea but is about not just how outsiders impose an identity onto "model" groups but how these groups also self-impose these ideals. The "bad" part of the dichotomy comes into play because determining what makes one a "good" immigrant also sets out what it is to be a "bad" immigrant.[10] Leland Saito illustrates this in his investigation into how long-term residents (white, Latino, native-born Japanese, and Chinese Americans) in Los Angeles adjusted to new immigrants from China arriving in the late 1980s and early 1990s. Nisei (second-generation Japanese) shared concerns similar to those of other long-term residents, but, as Asians, they also shared experiences with the incoming Chinese immigrants. The good immigrant depiction was a way for Nisei to affirm their own acceptance in U.S. society and to maintain a sense of power as the "arbiters of what was 'correct' in their community" (Saito 2001, 341). According to Saito, the image of the good immigrant reflects "the process through which long-term residents of the city, rapidly becoming a numeric minority, attempted to cling to political and social control of the city and influence over the new immigrants' pattern of adaptation by invoking a mythical image of how 'good immigrants' were supposed to act" (332). Nisei expected newcomers to blend in and adapt to the United States and its ways by being passive and subservient.[11] Nisei did not view this position or requirement as "racist" but rather viewed it as the natural way to become U.S. Americans. Saito argues, as I do with respect to the politics of race in Miami, that Nisei did not recognize how their ideas stemmed from the racism of the United States, which is based on Eurocentric ideals of propriety that position whites as the norm.

In Miami, we see a similar deployment of the good immigrant ideal. The United States demonstrated it valued Cuban Americans because they helped propel the treasured narrative about the nation being a place where all who work hard can achieve the American Dream, as well as the inherent value of the American Dream in contrast to communism. Through their labor and entrepreneurship, Cubans also brought wealth to white Miami elites. Hard work is certainly a factor in the Cuban success story and is not to be discounted. But the "Golden" label also resulted from their being constructed as a "model minority" without accounting for the generous U.S. immigration, education, housing, and economic policies that helped the exiles immensely (Pedraza-Bailey 1985). Cuban Americans took pride in their economic prosperity and propagated it to contest communism and to bolster their good standing in the United States. Arguably, taking pride in one's achievements and seeking to undermine a regime one sees as oppressive is not a problem in and of itself. However, as we will see in more detail in coming chapters, narratives of worthy citizenship and especially the good/bad immigrant narrative were used in ways that maintained and reinforced divisions between not only Cubans and their new African Americans neighbors but also between black and white Cubans and generations of Cuban immigrants.

Native/Foreigner Frame (New Nativism)

The tensions around whiteness, blackness, and power in Miami both reinscribe and complicate the traditional white/black narrative in south Florida. Analyzing the Miami scenario allows for an examination of how black/white binary dynamics are rearticulated in the present and intersect with issues related to immigrant incorporation. Such an examination requires an analysis of the complex ways anti-immigrant nativists position non-European immigrant newcomers within the existing racial hierarchy.

As Asian American scholars and Claire Jean Kim in her notion of racial order have pointed out, even when immigrants achieve a "model" status, they are not securely positioned above blacks. Rather, they can also be positioned as permanently foreign and unassimilable (apart from black and white). As such, the division of natives versus foreigners gains primacy when whites take on a nativist stance. The definition of nativism used by most analysts is "negative sentiment of various kinds towards foreigners"—"[an] 'antiforeign' feeling" (Bosniak 1997, 281). Perceiving immigrant groups that have already arrived or aspiring immigrants as a threat, nativists may exhibit animosity, bias, or an exclusionary impulse (Bosniak 1997). This impulse is central to the native/foreigner frame, which draws on Kim's (2000) notion of the insider/foreigner axis within the racial order, wherein immigrant groups are positioned as permanently unassimilable foreigners in contrast to native insiders.[12] In the United States, this powerful narrative continually gains new political life as white elites deploy it in the interest of "protecting" the country. In Miami, as Cubans continued to come into the area and transformed it, Anglos conveyed the message that Cubans were a foreign element threatening to take over "their" city.

White nativist constructions of immigrants as outsiders may be adopted by African Americans, as I discuss in the Miami context; other nonwhite groups, such as second-generation immigrants; or even recent newcomers who make claim to the nation.[13] In Miami, whites did not clearly place blacks along with themselves as apart from the Cubans. Yet, local Anglos began to disparage Cubans in the local media, demonstrated they did not want to live with them by moving away from the area, and characterized them as foreign invaders. In doing so, they provided a discourse blacks also drew upon as they sought to establish themselves more securely in the nation. As we will see in more detail in coming chapters, some African Americans took on a nativist stance that argued, in particular, that a longer history of oppression and suffering makes them worthier of inclusion. African Americans argued that Cubans were in a sense receiving "handouts" because they were the beneficiaries of African American efforts to create more equal conditions for all during the civil rights movement (García 1996, 40). As we will see in Chapter 3, another major strategy African Americans used for underscoring their greater claim to the United States was putting primacy on their command of the English language, which they spoke exclusively, and, like many of their Anglo neighbors, disparaging the fact that Cubans held onto the Spanish language. African Americans are not to be simply excused when they promote such ideals and disparage immigrants. Yet we must also remember that when black people play this game, they did not make its rules; they are attempting to win, or at least stop losing, a game written primarily to exclude and exploit them.[14] As we can see in the Miami scenario and in the nation more broadly, the theme of morality and who is most deserving undergirds the native/foreigner frame, encouraging a nativist stance against new immigrants. These nativist sentiments can also be held by nonwhite groups making claims to an American identity by asserting worthy citizenship.

Conclusion

Miami has a racial history that is distinctive from other areas of the country but not entirely unique. Like most other southern states and arguably the nation as a whole, the city was founded by white settlers whose powerful positioning relied on the subjugation of blacks. During the civil rights era and thereafter, the city became increasingly diverse, preempting the patterns of increased migration and diversity that would be seen across the country. What is most unique about Miami is that one of those immigrant groups, Cubans, managed to become immensely powerful unlike post-1965 immigrants to other cities. The fact that they were invited to the United States as refugees and were provided unprecedented aid not offered to other migrants allowed them to gain a "model status" and strengthened their desire to become patriotically aligned with the United States and against the ruler of the nation they left. Moreover, coming from a country where they were considered white and where blacks are also denigrated, they brought with them already entrenched ideas about the superiority of whiteness and the inferiority of blackness. These distinctive qualities intensified divisions that would ensue between African Americans, still fighting for their place within the U.S. nation, and the Cuban newcomers. Yet, the dynamics of interethnic conflict, particularly between a minority group that sees itself as "native" to the United States, such as African Americans, and Spanish-speaking newcomers, are quite similar in other U.S. cities where groups also adopt binary racializing frames of reference to position one group above another. Because of the constant bombardment of the white racial frame, people of color can internalize and operate from the dominant frame "using the language, stereotyping, imaging, or emotions of that white racial frame" (Feagin 2010,

190). The tenuous hold on an American identity felt by groups of color at times gives rise to the need for them to fight to (re)gain their standing. I utilize the concept of "worthy citizenship" to describe not only the desires of groups of color to become "true" Americans but also the ways excluding others in the process seems necessary for such inclusion. As such, despite the diminished presence of white people in Miami over time, and in many of the nation's cities currently, white Anglo elites and white supremacist ideologies continue to play a central role in supporting a politics of interethnic division.

The Miami situation provides an illustration of why and how this all plays out. By pointing out the uses of binary racializing frames by African Americans and generations of Cuban immigrants in Miami, I seek to illuminate their concerns about jobs, family, social standing, and, ultimately, their quest for human dignity. I contend that underneath antagonistic attitudes between "minority" groups lays a critique of the continued disenfranchisement of people of color. When we read between the lines, we discover a challenge to the discourses that claim Americanness is exclusive to whites and illuminate the need for a broader picture of the way racism is working today, particularly how it works in communities where Anglos are the minority and the enemy is an "other" racialized group. By exposing the fallacy of worthy citizenship, the analysis contributes to the reformulation of ideas about what qualifies as "belonging" or being accepted as part of the nation.

In the coming chapters, we will gain a closer look at how marginalized groups may draw upon the racial binaries of worthy citizenship in attempt to place *themselves* in positions of power. But we also see how these same groups, as well as newcomers that would come on the scene, such as two new waves of Cuban immigrants as well as Haitian refugees, illuminate the fallacy of racial binaries and exclusionary politics. In Chapter 2, I begin with a look at Cuban American reactions to the 1980 Mariel exodus, a migration wave from Cuba that would dramatically challenge the divisions that had been set up between African Americans and Cubans. The exodus would also illustrate how racial identities taken to be distinct are actually much more complex. The Mariel Cubans would differ from previous Cuban waves because a much higher percentage of them were black. The Mariel Cubans were also different from previous waves in that rather than being regarded as anti-communist heroes, they were more immediately stigmatized in the U.S. press and public. This new Cuban stigma derived both from Castro's depiction of the Mariel refugees as criminals and from their blackness. In the face of this new stigma, Cuban Americans grappled with threats to their status as model anti-communist heroes. As exile Cubans attempted to regain their status, they deployed U.S.-based ideals of worthy citizenship, intersecting with a Cuban white/black racial dynamic, in an attempt to distinguish "good immigrant" Marielitos from the "bad" ones. Although Cuban Americans were less overt in pitting themselves against African Americans, their reaffirmation of the black/white narrative through strategies of dissociation from blackness promoted (or perpetuated) ideologies that would undergird tensions between African Americans and Cubans, black and white Cubans, and Cuban immigrant cohorts. Yet the Afro-Cubans who were arriving in the Mariel wave presented a challenge to the use of "race" by Cuban Americans to make claims to the nation. By including Afro-Cuban voices, Chapter 2 will allow a look into how Afro-Latino positionality complicated notions of blackness for Cuban Americans and destabilized the idea that multiple racial identities cannot coexist (Jiménez Román and Flores 2010, 10; Rivera-Rideau et al. 2016, 11). Moreover, the chapter's focus on Afro-Cuban immigrants provides a view into how Afro-Cubans interpret the effects of the antagonistic racial discourses that were circulating in their daily lives.

Chapter 2

Marielitos, the Criminalization of Blackness, and Constructions of Worthy Citizenship

[handwritten margin notes: "white elites", "blk under-crim", "imm come in and see this bx is replicate it"]

The black/white frame that has historically portrayed "black" as the opposite of "American" remains in full effect. This opposition continues to function as the mechanism by which immigrants are placed or may place themselves within the nation (De Genova 2005; Ellison 1952; Kim 2000; R. G. Lee 1999; Morrison 1992, 1994; Noguera 2003; Roediger 1991; Urciuoli 1996, 2003). Newer immigrants receive the message that to properly assimilate as Americans they must progress "upward" toward a white middle-class ideal rather than "downward" toward the black underclass (Portes and Rumbaut 2001; Portes and Zhou 1993). Notions that the "underclass" and "criminality" are associated with blacks are taken for granted, and such notions are publicly utilized by white elites to defend the current social order (Katz 2013). As Lisa Cacho (2012) notes, crime is so associated with blackness that black bodies make crime legible; the same actions committed by whites may not be recognized as crimes. Thus, rather than taking into account that in urban settings high rates of crime among African Americans are correlated with high rates of poverty and concentrated disadvantage (McNulty and Bellair

2003), it is assumed that black criminality is innate (Cacho 2012). Given that "the law is presumed to be both ethical and irreproachable," immigrants encountering narratives that equate black people with criminality are then encouraged to differentiate themselves from them (Cacho 2012, 4). This project of dissociation from the "black Other," often perceived to be necessary to ensure one's place as a worthy citizen of the nation, feeds interethnic conflict.

As we saw in Chapter 1, white elites have throughout Miami's history used foreign policy, businesses practices, and even the allocation of aid to oppose African American and Cuban Americans to each other. Rhetoric that positioned Cubans as "more deserving" and harder working underscored these practices. Such rhetoric promoted the idea that the poverty conditions and unemployment African Americans were experiencing due to a depressed economy and discriminatory practices was their own fault. Such rhetoric could then be utilized by Cuban Americans, happy with their model "whitened" status, to capture their distinctiveness and bolster their standing within the U.S. nation (Aja 2016; López 2010). In this chapter, I use the 1980 Mariel wave of immigration as a lens to understand the relentless stigma that remains attached to blackness and examine how taken-for-granted narratives equating "black" with "unworthy citizen" set up divisions between racialized groups. During Mariel, such narratives set up divisions between black and white Cubans and generations of Cuban exiles and promoted frames of reference that also set African Americans and white Cuban Americans at odds. The Mariel exodus mattered, in short, because it challenged the Cuban "model immigrant" story. The Marielitos were younger and poorer than those who had arrived in previous waves, and a much larger percentage of them were black (García 1996). The reception of the newcomers from this third wave of large-scale Cuban migration contrasted sharply with how previous waves had been received. U.S. policy had changed, and Cubans began to be treated more like economic immigrants than as political refugees (Aguirre et al. 1997).[1] Furthermore, rather than being lauded as anti-communist heroes, they were regarded as criminal suspects. Scholars have analyzed and roundly criticized this criminalization (Aguirre 1984; Bach et al. 1981–1982; Camayd-Freixas 1988; Hufker and Cavender 1990; Masud-Piloto 1996; Wilsbank 1984). But although there is passing mention of the fact that the characterization of the Marielitos as blacks added another layer to the Mariel stigma, few studies make blackness the main focus. I assert that the criminalization of the Marielitos cannot be completely understood without full attention to the ways the Mariel refugees came to be "blackened." Through an examination of public discourse within the Spanish-language *El Miami Herald* newspaper, I deconstruct the taken-for-granted stigma attached to blackness and plot out how a language around blackness helped to produce the Mariel stigma. More specifically, in the chapter I illustrate how narratives that equate blackness with "unworthy citizen" became useful in the service of making claim to the nation as some Cuban Americans sought to preserve their whitened status by distinguishing "worthy" (white) Cuban citizens from "criminal" (black) Marielitos.

The chapter also deconstructs these binaries and their utilization to construct distinctions between categories such as "African American," "Cuban," "Afro-Cuban," and "white Cuban," by putting a spotlight on Afro-Cubans, who had gained greater visibility during Mariel. The Afro-Cuban presence among the newcomers brought into focus the transnational circuits of race making that intervened in Miami racial conflict. I provide context on how race operates in Cuba and on how Afro-Cubans are positioned within Cuban society, to help illustrate how anti-black attitudes from Cuba intersect with and reinforce U.S. anti-black attitudes in the context of the United States. Juxtaposing the newspaper discourse with interviews I conducted with black Cubans who arrived during Mariel, the chapter highlights Afro-Cuban voices as they comment on their experiences of marginalization. Concluding with an analysis of a *Herald* exposé focusing on an Afro-Cuban family, the chapter captures how specific national contexts influence how anti-black stigma is deployed and experienced and offers further challenge to such stigma, its role in conflict between groups of color, and its continued effect on black peoples.

Tarnishing the Golden Image: The Crisis of Mariel

On April 1, 1980, six Cubans seeking asylum used a bus to crash through the gate of the Peruvian embassy in Havana, Cuba. One Cuban guard was left dead after the ensuing gun battle, but the embassy refused to surrender the gate crashers to the Cuban government. The Cuban government responded by announcing that it would remove the guards from outside the embassy and allow anyone seeking to leave Cuba to go to the embassy. Within seventy-two hours, a staggering ten thousand people gathered there (Masud-Piloto 1996; Portes and Stepick 1994). Though the situation at the embassy became chaotic and dangerous, the people who gathered there were intent in their protest. Angered at this sign of the public's defiance, Fidel Castro announced on April 20 that anyone who wanted to leave for the United States could do so through the port of Mariel. This action would serve two purposes—to rid Cuba of political dissenters and to allow the Cuban government to thumb its nose at the U.S. government and its anti-Castro sanctions and other policies. The move would also use the U.S. open-door Cuban immigration policy against it by overwhelming the nation, particularly south Florida, with thousands of migrants (Greenhill 2002; Skop 2001). The Mariel boatlift, one of the most controversial waves of Cuban immigration, had begun. Cuban Americans seeking relatives secured boats to bring the Mariel refugees to the United States. Most often, they ended up transporting complete strangers. A total of 6,000 refugees arrived in the first week, and in May, about 3,000 refugees arrived every single day. By the time the exodus ended in October, more than 125,000 Cubans were brought to the United States by boat lift (Masud-Piloto 1996).

When the refugees from Mariel began to come to the United States, the government's official stance was to welcome them as it had since 1959, when Fidel Castro first came to power. The United States had maintained an open-door policy toward Cuban exiles, who, fleeing communism, came to be viewed as model immigrants. But as massive numbers of Cubans continued to arrive from Mariel, the Carter administration became less welcoming. The local and federal governments were caught off guard by the high numbers and had no effective means of incorporating them. The Mariel migrants were much less likely than previous exiles to have family in the United States who could take them in. As a result, large numbers were held in tent cities and on military bases (Masud-Piloto 1996). According to one source, 55 percent were sent to camps in Florida, Pennsylvania, Wisconsin, and Arkansas to be screened and processed (G. A. Fernández 2002, 41). Besides the issue of the high numbers and the difficulty of incorporating the new arrivals, the boat lift was also controversial because it had not been instigated by the United States as had the first two waves but had been instigated by Castro. Moreover, as a strategy for making demands on the U.S. government, Castro released people some considered undesirable (criminals, homosexuals, and the mentally ill) into the population of those leaving. Notwithstanding the prob-

lematic characterization of these subsets of the Cuban population as "unde-
sirables," they were but a small proportion of the people leaving Cuba. Yet
the Castro government played up the characterization of the Marielitos as
deviants in the media (Pedraza-Bailey 1985).

Although the United States had previously refuted Castro's disparagement
of those seeking U.S. asylum, in the case of Mariel the U.S. public and popular press magnified the criminal image put forward by Castro (Aguirre
1984; Bach et al. 1981–1982; Camayd-Freixas 1988; Hufker and Cavender
1990; Masud-Piloto 1996; Wilsbank 1984). Indeed, the popular U.S. press
legitimated Castro's depiction of the Marielitos in reports that fanned domestic fears of crime and deviance (Pedraza-Bailey 1985). The U.S. nightly
news and the popular press helped solidify the idea that the Marielitos were
a burden to society by repeatedly reporting on the large numbers arriving,
the unfavorable results of public opinion polls, Mariel criminality, and other
negative consequences of the exodus (Hamm 1995; Masud-Piloto 1996). The
crime wave of the time had in fact started before the Marielitos came to
the United States and was a result of drug trafficking. Furthermore, most
crime that involved the Marielitos was found to be against other Marielitos
(Hamm 1995). Nevertheless, the Miami Police Department adopted the word
"Marielito" as an epithet to identify the city's worst threat: "'Marielito' became
a synonym for thief, drug dealer, rapist, and murderer, and was analogous to
racist terms such as 'nigger,' 'spic,' and 'kike'" (Hamm 1995, 76).[2] Such depictions made the Miami public fearful; an ABC News survey reported that
by mid-May 1980, most Miamians disapproved of accepting the Marielitos;
57 percent of adult respondents said they should not be allowed to live in the
United States, 68 percent thought President Carter should not have let them
enter, and 62 percent said Castro had made the United States look foolish
when he sent the "social misfits" (Aguirre et al. 1997, 494). The image of the
Marielito as criminal has been forever captured in U.S. popular culture as
well—in the character of the American film icon Tony Montana of *Scarface*
(1983). The depictions of the new immigrants as posing a cultural and literal
criminal threat fed into the growing anti-immigrant sentiment across the
country. Indeed, the Mariel boatlift "marked the beginning of a major shift
in how Americans regarded immigration" (Gonzalez 2011, 113). Demographic change had ushered in a nativist backlash, with public and media
discourse reflecting increasing concerns over national identity, border security, and economic resources (Chavez 2001; Gonzalez 2011; Santa Ana 2002).[3]

Thus, a major reaction to the sheer numbers coming in during Mariel was that the United States was taking in too many of the world's poor and needy at the expense of native citizens.

The newcomers' deviant image was compounded as stereotypes about blackness or black people intersected with media depictions of the Marielitos as criminals (Skop 2001). The majority of Cubans who had come in the previous waves were white, but anywhere from 10 to 40 percent of the Marielitos were black (García 1996, 60).[4] Thus, the Mariel wave was significant in that it brought more blacks from Cuba to the United States than ever before. As Nancy Raquel Mirabal points out, the migrations of Afro-Cubans "reconfigured a language of race, sexuality, culture, and gender that was not always understood or employed in community making among Cuban exiles" (2005, 203). For Cuban Americans, the change in public opinion was a "rude awakening" (Portes and Stepick 1994, 31). With the public backlash, Mariel immigrants disrupted the image of Cubans as model citizens, at the same time that they disrupted the idea that Cubans were white (García 1996, 60). For Cuban Americans observing the backlash against their incoming compatriots, the Marielito deviant image meant that the public image of Cubans as a whole was under threat.

Cuban Whiteness in Cuba and the United States

The popular characterization of the Marielitos as black, in spite of the fact that the majority were white by most definitions operating in a U.S. context, is reminiscent of the United States' one-drop rule, whereby one drop of black blood (or a few immigrants with black skin) has a polluting effect.[5] Cuban American efforts to counteract the polluting effects of the Mariel stigma would then become an effort of dissociation from the criminality of blackness. As Toni Morrison and others have observed, immigrants from various countries are often socialized to understand that to be a good American they must dissociate from African Americans or blackness (Morrison 1992, 1994; and see Marrow 2011; Smith 2006). But for Cuban exiles, their racial socialization in Cuba in a black/white frame fit quite easily into the similar frame in the U.S. imaginary. The United States and the island of Cuba share a history of colonization, slavery, and imperialism (Clealand 2013; Guridy 2010; Helg 1995; Sawyer 2006;). Cuba was originally peopled by the Ciboney, Arawaks, and Tainos, who were colonized and enslaved by Spanish settlers following Columbus's arrival there in the early 1500s (Pérez 1995). To supplement Indian slavery, Spain began importing African slave labor in 1505. The slave trade grew as Cuba became an important sugar colony. With the growing number of enslaved and free blacks in Cuba, many whites feared the possible "Africanization" of Cuba as the population fluctuated between a white and black majority during Cuba's early history (Ferrer 1998, 1999). Prohibitions of marriage between blacks and whites existed at various times during slavery, although they were not strictly enforced.[6] Still, some whites sought to maintain "una limpieza de sangre" (purity of white blood). These racist ideals exalting white over black and the historical disenfranchisement of blacks in Cuba during and after slavery worked to maintain wealth and power in the hand of whites on the island.

Yet, early on, anti-racist discourses celebrating ideals of pluralism and equality of the races infused Cuban ideas of their nation (Ferrer 1998, 1999). During Cuba's fight for independence from Spain over a period spanning 1868–1898, Cuban patriot Jose Martí rallied for racial unity with the now famous quote, "A Cuban is more than white, more than mulatto, more than black" (quoted in Greenbaum 2002, 11). With such racial democracy discourses, white patriots sought to rally African slaves and free blacks to help them fight for a free Cuba. Some black generals rose to great prominence, one of the most revered being Antonio Maceo, praised for his military heroism (Benson 2016). In short, blacks played a prominent role in the Cuban nation-building project. Given this history, the ideal of Cuban racial unity continues to pervade Cuban society so much that today, Cubans of all colors overwhelmingly place their national identity above their racial identity (Clealand 2013, 2017). However, despite the seeming progressiveness of ideologies championing racial unity, these same ideologies have been used by powerful whites to discourage blacks from organizing around race when they have had grievances or perceived they were being racially targeted and discriminated against. Blacks seeking to remedy legitimate issues surrounding their treatment would be met with cries that, by bringing up race, they undermined national identity (Benson 2012, 2013; Clealand 2013, 2017; De la Fuente 2001; Helg 1995). Racial democracy discourses have also been used by white Cubans in the United States to deny the existence of racism among Cubans (Aja 2016).

Cuba's racial history set up conditions wherein whites would be wealthier and more powerful than blacks, and thus, by the time Castro came to power, whites were the people most affected by Castro's efforts to redistribute wealth. Accordingly, the majority of people who first contested his government by seeking political exile in the United States were white. Blacks stood to gain most from the Castro government because they were the poorest of Cuba. However, this does not mean that all blacks automatically supported Castro. Rather, any who might have wanted to leave for the United States had fewer resources to do so. But by 1980, Cubans of all colors had lived under the Castro regime for twenty years, enough time to assess whether the promises of the revolution would be upheld. Although the Castro government did allow many gains for blacks, such as higher economic standards of living than before and gains in health standards, education levels, and literacy levels, there were also many problems, such as political and economic instability. Moreover, the suppression of individual freedoms, intolerance for dissent, and human rights abuses wore down individuals' support of the revolution (Boswell and Curtis 1984). Thus, when Castro opened the opportunity to leave Cuba after the incident at the Peruvian embassy, Cubans of all colors took their chances.

But the whites who had come to the United States in the 1959–1973 migrations had already established a "white" Cuban Miami (Aja 2016; López 2012). It is likely some of the earliest arrivals had directly benefited from black disenfranchisement when they were in Cuba and already had preconceived notions about the "place" for blacks—in servitude to whites (López 2010, 2012). Cubans have also been able to benefit from "implicit racial privilege" in the United States because the larger context of the U.S.–Cuba political conflict had promoted a broader discourse celebrating the Cuban exiles and the U.S. role in saving them from the perils of communism (Molina-Guzman 2008). Cuban Americans then felt embraced by the U.S. nation. But by 1980, local white Anglos were increasingly concerned that the Miami Cuban population was becoming "uncomfortably large" (Portes and Stepick 1994, 27), and they clearly differentiated Cubans from "native" whites. Anglos worried their control of the city culture and resources was slipping away. As the government worked to incorporate the new Mariel arrivals, whites expressed in the local press their anger that the government had "abandoned" them and their efforts to "save Miami from the Cubans" (Portes and Stepick 1994, 30). Moreover, with the nationwide media reporting on the criminality of the Mariel refugees, local Anglos worried Cubans were beginning to be bad for (tourism) business (Portes and Stepick 1994). As further example of the Anglo backlash and their efforts to reassert their own dominance, politicians rallied people to vote for an anti-bilingualism initiative that would overturn a 1973 Bilingual-Bicultural Ordinance and would prohibit Metro funds from being used for programs that used languages other than English (García 1996). The campaign for the measure went on during the Mariel exodus and passed in November, just months after the boat lift had come to an end (Castro 1992). Thus, the Anglo backlash against the Mariel wave of Cubans illustrated the precarity of Cuban whiteness in the U.S. context. As Antonio López points out, because white Cubans are not viewed as "true whites" in the United States, they have had to work to "reclaim" whiteness (López 2012, 191). Since all Cubans were now affected by the stigma attached to perceived "blackness" as a result of anti-Mariel prejudice, the reclamation of whiteness felt especially urgent, as its loss felt especially painful—a reminder of Cubans' provisional status within America. Thus, the difference between "white" and "black" Cubans would have to mean something different in the United States than it had meant even in Cuba. As we will see, even when the word "black" was not directly used, distancing themselves from (the criminality of) blackness became a primary tool for reclaiming their whiteness (and therefore moral notions of worthiness) to make claim to the U.S. nation.

El Miami Herald and Mariel

As the drama of Mariel unfolded, *El Miami Herald* was poised to capture every detail. As the paper was run by the same editorial board as the mainstream newspaper, the *Miami Herald,* and news stories were often direct translations of those in the English-language paper, stories in *El Miami Herald* reflected both the mainly negative views of the incoming Cubans expressed in the mainstream paper and Cuban American reactions to those views, which could be found in op-eds, letters to the editor, and other material unique to the Spanish-language paper. Although editorial choices influence the extent to which conflicting views are presented in newspapers, an analysis of the contradictions illustrated in the article types (editorials, news, op-eds, letters to the editor) reveals the complexity of the struggle the Cuban

American community had with the dominant discourses circulating about their incoming compatriots. Cuban American voices as reflected in the paper would sometimes affirm but also counter the mainstream negative portrayals of the incoming Cubans.

While previous studies of *El Miami Herald* coverage of Mariel discuss the depiction of Marielitos in polarized terms (as negative or positive) or highlight only the negative portrayals (see, for example, Camayd-Freixas 1988), my study captures more ambivalence. The three most prominent themes in the close to four hundred articles collected from *El Miami Herald* for the six-month period from the start of Mariel on April 4, 1980, to two weeks after the end of the exodus on September 16 illustrate what the paper depicted as the primary concerns of the exile community in reference to their compatriots. The first impulse captured in theme 1, Marielitos as compatriots (34 percent), was to embrace the newcomers, framing them as "good immigrants," worthy of citizenship and thus of help and acceptance. As time went on, however, the coverage reflected theme 2, criminality, or the local fixation on the Marielitos as criminal or deviant (48 percent). This theme conformed to a black/white frame, which more clearly invokes race and positions outsiders as "black." The national media attention to reports about Mariel deviance, and the fact that the process of incorporating Marielitos into U.S. society was much more difficult than that of previous waves, made it tough for exiles to continue to project the Golden Exile image they wished to preserve, that is, the idea that Cubans were (inherently) law-abiding, patriotic, and hard-working model immigrants. Hence, theme 3, Marielitos as "immigrants needing reform" and thus not yet worthy citizens (18 percent), often sought to defend the Marielitos but emphasized finding ways to explain and help correct the Marielitos' "deviant" behaviors. The three major themes that arose in the Mariel coverage and how the themes classify the newcomers as either inside or outside of the Cuban American community (and therefore outside or inside the configuration of "American") makes evident the overlaps between dominant racializing frames such as native/foreigner (whereby groups perceive themselves as having more claim to a U.S. identity because they have been established in the United States for a longer period), the black/white frame, and the good immigrant frame. It is apparent that the articles most reflective of the public Cuban voice—the letters to the editor—demonstrate great ambivalence among the Cuban American community in regard to the Marielitos. They contained the largest percentage

(40 percent) of the articles demonstrating theme 1 and the largest percentage (46 percent) of the articles with theme 3. When theme 2 was broached, it was overwhelmingly within news articles; thus, they reflected the mainstream paper's voice (82 percent).

Theme 1. *"¡Que Vengan los Asilados!": Marielitos as "Good Immigrant" Compatriots*

Early news stories provoked sympathy for the newcomers by appealing to the notions of family and family unification and by bringing the readers' attention to the tremendous hardships they faced in Cuba under Fidel Castro's tyranny (for example, "Families of Cubans That Survived Torture Are Arriving").[7] A report in April on the crowds that had congregated at the Mariel military base before they could be brought to the United States reads, "At least 1,000 future Cuban-Americans are waiting at the Mariel military base to be transferred to the United States."[8] With the descriptor "future Cuban-Americans" the piece shows the expectation that these people, women, children, and the elderly among them, would indeed make their way to the United States and become incorporated, as previous waves had, into the (Cuban) American family. A powerful line of discourse also invokes U.S. patriotism and the rhetoric of the American Dream to highlight the right of the new exiles to come and join the greater American family. One of the first news reports on the Mariel exodus emphasizes the right of the newcomers to be in the United States and calls on the nation's historical commitment to accept the world's "poor, tired, and needy." The article encourages support for the newcomers by quoting the plaque at the Statue of Liberty and Lyndon B. Johnson's original promise to the Cubans. Johnson, as quoted in the article stated : "I declare this afternoon to the people of Cuba that those who seek refuge here in America will find it. The dedication of America to our traditions as an asylum for the oppressed is going to be upheld." The article argued that "By signing a new immigration law in the United States and speaking these words at the feet of the Statue of Liberty, President Lyndon B. Johnson opened the doors of this country for hundreds of thousands of Cuban refugees."[9]

The quote refers to the speech made by President Johnson (October 3, 1965) when he signed into law the Immigration and Nationality Act, which did away with the national origins quota system and officially declared Cuban asylum seekers as good immigrants, giving first priority to family reunification, then asylum for political prisoners.[10] The article is optimistic about the newcomers' ability to be incorporated in the United States and responds to the public outcry against the Mariel exodus, which also lamented the growth of the established Cuban community. Using the words of an American president and the Statue of Liberty, the article reminds the general public that all Cubans were indeed "good immigrants" who had as much right to be in the United States as Anglo immigrants of the nineteenth and early twentieth centuries, whose claim to the United States is unquestioned. Hence, in the article, the "good immigrant" frame comes through as it supports the Golden Exiles' efforts to maintain their own position in the white-dominated hierarchy.

But as time went on, it became increasingly clear that the transition for the Marielitos would not be easy. With their relentless depiction of the newcomers as deviants, the English-language *Herald*, reflecting the views of many Miami Anglos, began to turn some older Cuban exiles against the Mariel refugees. But it also fostered what Alejandro Portes and Alex Stepick call "reactive ethnicity"; in the face of outside disparagement of their group, Cubans began to view themselves as stigmatized minorities and mobilized together to preserve their self-image (Portes and Stepick 1994, 30). An op-ed by Cuban American Roberto Fabricio (who would later become an editor of the independent *El Nuevo Herald*) titled "¡Que Vengan los Asilados!", or, "Let the Asylees Come!" celebrates the newcomers but acknowledges the reality that the Marielitos might not be fully accepted in U.S. society or by their fellow Cubans: "What I believe is that we cannot give ourselves the luxury of turning our backs on them. It would be cruel and treacherous. And this is a city built around hopes and dreams."[11] In his statements, the editorialist makes a plea to his fellow Cuban exiles, who on the premise of the American Dream were actually able to build a successful enclave. This success, he contends, demonstrates that the American Dream can be realized, but it is the job of the previous exiles to extend access to the newcomers.

Because maintaining the idea of unity was so crucial to the exile identity and their strength in the Miami economic, cultural, and political economy, the rejection of newcomers by previous exiles was viewed as a problem. In an op-ed later in the year acknowledging a growing rejection, Fabricio underscores the need for Cuban Americans' support. The op-ed reads, "Many Cuban families that generally would have been able to serve as foster parents have not responded because there has been so much said or written about whether or not these children could have been imprisoned, that they have stopped considering the reasons why these children were in Castro's prisons."[12] The op-ed decries the power of the media to scare off support for the Marielitos, which had become apparent by July.

The attitudes of some Cuban Americans who prided themselves on leaving Cuba when Fidel Castro came to power are chided in several articles that acknowledge a distinction being made between the old guard, or *antiguos*, and the recently arrived, or *recién llegados*. In this news report, a Cuban American interviewed for the story says,

> Many prior refugees also feel that the new refugees are different from those who came from Cuba previously. Some believe that those who have recently arrived do not want to make the same sacrifices that they made for free passage to the United States. . . . The previous exiles take on an attitude of superiority because they abandoned the island much earlier than those who just arrived.[13]

This article goes on to present the idea that "we Cubans should stick together"—asserting that people from Cuba, regardless of when they arrive, should view one another as brothers and sisters. An op-ed written by a Cuban American journalist from Miami continues this theme of Cuban unity as he comments on the new division:

> And one of the most deplorable aspects of this crisis is that, as a part of it, the Cuban colony has divided against itself. Because, effectively, for many of the "old refugees," the ones who came through Mariel are plagued. . . . . The only realistic attitude is to help the decent people that have come through Mariel, who are the majority, and to help them integrate economically and socially into our community in order to strengthen it.[14]

These articles hold to the tradition of Cuban American support of any newcomers from Cuba. Yet they also recognize the growing split that was occurring between the *antiguos* and the *recién llegados*, a split that threatened to contribute to the disempowerment of the Cuban American community as a whole.

Crucial to Cubans' identity in the United States is their being officially defined as good immigrants through favorable immigration policy because of their anti-communism. Congruent with the exiles' acceptance of this designation, embracing the idea that they were "worthy citizens" meant that Cuban exiles needed to explain why the Mariel refugees had a more difficult incorporation into U.S. society than previous Cuban immigration waves. To not undermine their own claims to the nation, placing blame on Castro seemed the most acceptable way to explain why waves of refugees from the same country could be so different. Thus, the Castro regime was most often invoked to explain the difference between the established Cubans and the newcomers. For example, in the op-ed "The Youth of Mariel," the author, an ex-political prisoner turned journalist, defends the Marielitos by discussing the psychological effects of living in Cuba under Castro: "In a society whose values are officially imposed by the State and violently rejected by the nation, social and individual stability cannot exist. Men who have aged chronologically continue to be social infants."[15] The op-ed is intended to defend the new arrivals, but the author's words could just as readily be used as evidence against the Marielitos. While his words offer an indictment of the state of the Cuban government in contrast to the United States, he infantilizes the Mariels, describing them as in a state of underdevelopment. The author goes on to assert that the new Cubans suffer from a personality disorder and that in today's Cuba the youth do not want to work or study and do not have discipline. On the one hand, the problems with the Marielitos are attributed to Castro and his regime, but on the other hand, the author implies that these deficiencies have become ingrained in the Marielitos themselves and does not offer reasons why the reader should believe that in the United States they would overcome this upbringing. The focus on Castro erases other complicating factors, such as the role of race, discrimination, and the U.S. contradictory stance toward immigrant groups based on imperialist goals. The anti-Castro stance also served to preserve faith in the bootstrap ideals about upward mobility in the United States that "worthy" Cuban exiles were able to achieve.

Interviewees who arrived during Mariel commented that this view of Marielitos as somehow degraded by the Castro regime also shaped how they were treated by established exiles. In my interview with Antonio, he affirmed the idea that the Cuban government creates a situation where people do not have the ability for self-determination and must do what they are told. But he also criticized his fellow Cuban American compatriots who made him feel unwelcome when he arrived. In answer to the question of whether he felt accepted by various groups in the United States, he responded, "the only people to discriminate against me have been Cubans, my fellow countrymen, who came before us in the sixties and seventies. Those people truly discriminated against me. I have always said it and am not afraid to say it." Asked for an example of such discrimination, he talked about how "Marielito" was used as a pejorative term. He noted that other Cuban Americans treated him as if he was not the right kind of Cuban, and he asserted that because he can trace generations of family members to his hometown of Matanzas, "I am as Cuban as him [who criticizes me] or might be *more* Cuban than him."[16] Antonio points out the irony that many of the Cuban Americans he met may have no direct familial ties to Cuba or memories of specific places, but nevertheless they position themselves as arbiters of the good immigrant narrative and as having the authority to determine who qualifies as a "real Cuban."

By arguing that the newcomers had been corrupted by Castro, defenders of the Marielitos implied that the newcomers were in a sense "real Cubans." Hence, arguments in the newspaper suggested that the Marielitos suffered from guilt by association and were wrongly accused of being deviants. That the Cubans who had endured his regime for twenty years could be so corrupted from their "true" form, that is, law-abiding and respectable, was viewed as testament of the failures of the Castro government. As such, defenses in the paper did not question the deviant label per se but rather emphasized and demonstrated how the newcomers actually did fit the ideal of the worthy citizen who would contribute to U.S. society. Letters to the editor written in their defense had titles such as "The New Exile Has Initiative," by an ex-political prisoner;[17] "Condemn Attacks on Those Who Have Recently Arrived," by a recent arrival;[18] and "The Refugees Are Not Scum," by a writer with a Spanish surname who was affiliated with the Christian Community Service Agency in Miami.[19] A news article (part of a series of news reports on the adaptation of Marielitos) titled "'Scum' Is a Defamation of the New Exile" attempts to repudiate negative labels attributed to the Marielitos by citing a Brookings Institute study by Robert Bach, which found that only 1 percent of the new arrivals had criminal histories.[20] A related news story reporting on the same Brookings study attempts to paint the new arrivals in a positive light by emphasizing the contributions they could make to Miami as a workforce.[21] The study disputes the claim that Marielitos are lazy and do not work and likens them to the already-established Cuban community, which had been portrayed as having a good work ethic. Mounting a defense against the stereotypes levied against the Marielitos, such articles utilize the idea of worthiness to put forth the idea that "they (we) belong here." The articles include the newcomers in the Cuban American family and demonstrate that in the face of rising anti-immigrant and anti-Cuban sentiment reflecting dominant societal views, the exile community would fight for their (own) honor. Because of the moral elements of dominant notions of worthy citizenship, doing so required exiles to "prove" they were worthy through strategies of disassociation from the racialized "Other."[22]

Theme 2. *"¡Esos No Son Compatriotas Nuestros!"*: *Contending with Criminality*

The explicit linking of race to worthiness becomes apparent when looking at the criminality theme in *El Miami Herald*. In stories regarding Mariel criminality, the black/white frame that positions blacks and blackness outside the "worthy citizen" ideal was invoked to explain and dissociate from Mariel difference. Blackness was a primary trope used in news articles to construct the group from Mariel as undesirable and criminal, playing into already-existing Cuban stereotypes about blacks (from Cuba) and U.S. stereotypes about African Americans. The newspaper articles, as well as narratives recounted here drawn from interviews with black Cubans living in the United States, also point out that despite the idealization of Cuban unity so important in constructing the notions of the "good immigrant" as "worthy citizen," this idea of membership in the Cuban family was not extended to black Cubans.

The practices of dissociation from "the black Other" seen here fits in with the growing racial explanation of social and economic problems in Florida and in the nation. At the time of Mariel, media discourses about blackness and black bodies were used by conservatives to achieve particular political objectives: blackness became an important tool of the new right to define worthy citizenship and "Americanness" (Gray 1995). Concern over "the black (African American) problem" was a hot media topic in the nation as a whole.

By the late 1970s, economic recession, deindustrialization, rising unemployment, and the growing disparity between the top 20 percent and bottom 20 percent of the population had adversely affected African Americans (Gray 1995). At the same time, by 1980 the African American middle class had grown significantly. Neoconservative groups pointed to the black middle class as proof that capitalism and bourgeois individualism worked and that poor African Americans were therefore to blame for their own problems. Threatened by the gains of the civil rights era, affirmative action, and programs designed to fight poverty, neoconservative groups sought to protect the privileges associated with whiteness by exposing the social problems affecting the United States and defining them in racial terms (Steinberg 1995). The black underclass was discussed as the "unworthy poor" who suffered because they had the "wrong" moral and family values and took advantage of the welfare system (Gray 1995; Katz 2013). The media incited fears about black welfare cheats, the pathological black family, and drugs and violence in the black community, all with a specific focus on black males, who were constructed as a socially irresponsible menace (Gray 1995). These U.S.-based discourses heightened any anti-black notions Cuban exiles brought from the home country and were drawn upon by some exiles to dissociate from their "criminal" compatriots.

El Miami Herald captured and reflected the mainstream focus on Mariel criminality as the criminality theme became predominant in the newspaper. This coverage was primarily in the form of news stories, in the sections reflecting the voice of the English-language *Miami Herald*. Not all the stories focusing on criminality were fervent portraits of the Marielitos as deviants. Several criticized the U.S. government for being slow to help the Cubans resettle in the United States. In addition, stories reporting on criminal acts were often meant to invoke sympathy for the refugees or give voice to advocates: for instance, allowing the Hispanic American League against Discrimination to make the point that the public should realize criminals were but a small percentage of the refugees.[23] Still, the language of the headlines of even these stories served to alert the community to the criminality and other forms of deviance among the Marielitos. There was a dramatic increase in the percentage of stories covering Mariel criminality between the beginning of the exodus in April and June, from 6 percent in April and 12 percent in May to a peak of 41 percent in June. From July to September, the criminality theme remained a popular topic: between 29 and 39 percent of stories

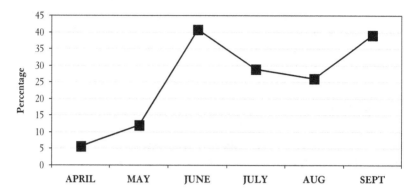

Figure 2. Percentage of Total *El Miami Herald* Articles (*n* = 394) Containing the Criminality Theme per Month.

focus on it. In the coverage, titles abounded singling out refugees and associating them with crime, such as "Dade Jail Is Packed with Refugees" and "Refugees Kill a Man in a Bar."[24] Such titles and reports helped frame the arrival of the Mariel Cubans as a crisis and the group as violent criminals. In June, there was a spike in coverage, then a downward trend; however, the reporting on criminality never again dipped to the lows reflected in the beginning months of the exodus. In September, there was another spike in criminality coverage (though not as dramatic as the rise in June) (see Figure 2). This rise is due to coverage of incidences of plane hijackings by Marielitos attempting to return to Cuba.

The sudden increase in articles addressing criminality in June is a result of reports on the June 1 Fort Chaffee rebellion. Fort Chaffee in Arkansas was the largest of the settlement camps and held Marielitos who were the hardest to process, many of them black (G. A. Fernández 2002; Hoeffel 1980, 47). Although the then governor Bill Clinton at first welcomed the Marielitos, Arkansas locals became increasingly hostile to their arrival. In mid-May 1980, Ku Klux Klan leader David Duke led a KKK protest against them. Fort Chaffee had an atmosphere of a "little Cuba" when the Marielitos first settled in. But the camp routine grew monotonous, and efforts to resettle the people there dragged on with no results. Marielitos inside the camp and their supporters outside the camp demonstrated their frustrations with sit-ins and hunger strikes, culminating in the Fort Chaffee riot (G. A. Fernández 2002).

On June 1, 1980, two thousand Fort Chaffee Cubans armed with clubs rioted, and four buildings were burned. More than two hundred Marielitos escaped. The Mariel protestors were met with armed resistance from police outside the camp. Citizens of the city became vigilantes: approximately three to four hundred people armed themselves and gathered near the city limits. According to early reports, fifteen troopers and four refugees were injured, and, as later reports revealed, five Cubans were shot. Clinton responded by declaring a state of emergency and increasing security. Ninety "leaders" of the crisis were detained in an effort to quell the fears of the public. Changes were made in camp leadership, and more concentrated efforts were undertaken to speed the processing of the remaining Marielitos (G. A. Fernández 2002). Although governmental inefficiency created the conditions that spurred the discontent of Fort Chaffee's inhabitants, it was the image of the Marielitos that was most damaged. Because of the notoriety of the Fort Chaffee camp, Marielitos came to be defined by the goings-on there, even though less than 2 percent of the eighteen thousand people held there were involved in the protests (García 1996).

Following the Fort Chaffee uprising, by July the idea that Marielitos were criminals was firmly established. In a news report reflecting a non-Cuban point of view, the Miami police attribute the rise in rape and transport of arms in the city to the Marielitos.[25] In fact, the article reports that police had begun the practice of distinguishing the arrests of refugees with an "R" to keep track of how many crimes were committed by refugees. The Marielitos are also described as dangerous, young, single males who may rape women. According to the article, these men do not comport themselves in the "proper" fashion: "The refugees, generally young and single, represent a cultural impact for the previous residents as well. The men walk around shirtless. They like to talk on the street corners while drinking beer. . . . They speak only Spanish, and they have their radios turned all the way up." The article does attempt to include an unbiased explanation of the Mariel behaviors, attributing them to Cuba's customs, where drinking in public is acceptable, and to the fact that the prohibitive signs in the neighborhood were all written in English. It also includes the testimony of a recent arrival who does not fit the stereotype and who says, "All of my family members work. We don't wander around the streets like vagabonds."[26] The story also acknowledges that the rise in crime in Miami Beach had begun even before the Marielitos arrived. Yet these disclaimers do little to diminish the impact of the title, "Rise in Crime in Miami Beach Is Attributed to the Refugees," or that of most of the rest of the story.

By September, the rupture between the established Cuban community and the newcomers was more clearly distinguished, as exiles reacted or responded to such negative depictions of the Marielitos.[27] A September 1 letter to the editor, "Castro Benefits from the Mariel Exodus," calls for the established Cubans to completely disassociate from the Marielitos because of their criminality. The self-identified Cuban author maintains that the Marielitos were sent to the United States by Cuba for the purpose of infiltrating the United States with communists. Furthermore, he says, "And there are the acts that embarrass the Cubans so much: burned encampments and violence provoked by those elements, miserable and despicable rape of children. These delinquents who have come to damage the constructive image of the Cuban, *esos no son compatriotas nuestros* (these are not our compatriots)."[28] The letter draws attention away from the fact that the Mariel exodus also included many more people who, just like the previous waves of Cubans, came to the United States with the intention not of committing crimes or of spreading communism but of working to achieve the American Dream.

The split between the old and new Cubans is similarly illustrated in a story discussing how Little Havana had changed for the worse with the arrival of the Marielitos. The story describes how the Antonio Maceo Park in Little Havana, which used to be where older Cuban Americans went to play dominos, was now a place where criminals congregated and drugs abounded. The story cites a 51.3 percent increase in police calls for service in Little Havana in August. It makes the point that the evidence is circumstantial, because the statistics document only the increase in calls for service without any indication of exactly who had committed the crimes. Yet simply by discussing the increase in calls for service, and indicating the areas from which the calls originated, the article makes a case for attributing the rise in crime to the Marielitos despite the lack of clear evidence. Because this rise in crime took place in the well-known Cuban community of Little Havana, a contrast is made between the established "law-abiding" Cubans and "law-breaking" Marielitos.[29]

On the whole, the stories on the criminality of the Marielitos do not directly implicate blackness (in a biological sense). Only one story, about the response of Arkansas residents to the Cubans who had been brought there, is explicit in describing a Mariel as both black and criminal:

> The residents of Jenny Lind [Arkansas] insist that the fugitive crowd "wields
> knives and clubs" and were hitting cars and shouting hysterically. "It seemed
> like a pack of wild animals," said . . . (a resident) on Wednesday. . . . [A] truck
> driver . . . threw back his cowboy hat and told a visitor that, during the es-
> cape on Monday, a black Cuban ran up to his truck and grabbed the driver's
> side window.[30]

Here, a Cuban is gratuitously described as "black" by one of the Anglo residents, who seems to use the word to intensify the negative image of the man.
Although the bulk of the article actually highlights the hysteria among the
Jenny Lind residents, the imagery invoked in this passage is of savage fugi-
tives, at least one of whom was black, wildly attacking the (white) innocent
residents of Arkansas. Words historically associated with blacks, particularly
black males (wild, animal), and qualifying the descriptor "Cuban" with
"black," make blackness central in the idea of threat. Given the historical association in the United States of "threat" with "black male," this depiction
resonates with the characterization of Marielitos as a whole as black.

Although the Marielitos were not often described explicitly as black, *El
Miami Herald* characterized them with many surrogates for blackness. For
instance, the use of the word "ghetto" functioned in this way, making a concrete association between the Marielitos and African Americans. An editorial, "No Plan Exists for Integrating the New Cuban Exiles," discusses the
profound impact of the refugee crisis, given the other various problems plaguing Miami at the time. The new arrivals are described as young people who
grew up in a repressive regime and repeats the refrain that they had learned to
work as little as possible and to rely on the underground market. The language and imagery of lazy youths waiting for a handout or too willing to turn
to crime, juxtaposed with the editorial's discussion of the recent and notorious
African American riot in response to the police killing of an unarmed black
man, Arthur McDuffie, compounds the implied idea of black threat.[31] Furthermore, the word "ghetto" is employed in the editorial to contrast the Mariel
immigrants with the Golden Exile entrepreneurs as polar opposites:

> This isn't the working class that moved in 15 years ago and converted a de-
> clining community into a bustling commercial district. These men are the
> building blocks from which a true Cuban *ghetto* can emerge, with all of the
> problems that that word implies.

The editorial claims we know the problems that the word "ghetto" suggests without actually filling in that blank for us—but the association with poor African Americans is what is implied.[32] The articles using the word "ghetto" also make a strong statement about the peculiarity of Cubans being characterized as deviant and living in conditions similar to those of African American ghettos, preserving the good image of the Cuban American community.

The emphasis on the word "ghetto" in the news story "Tent City: Cuban 'Ghetto' in Miami" provides an example, with the implication that the word is most appropriately associated with African Americans or blacks. The story, about the deplorable living conditions in the tent cities housing the refugees, asserts that the camps are the first Cuban ghetto: "The camp is an open wound; in less than four weeks it has been transformed into the first Cuban *ghetto* in Miami. If the conditions do not improve, they could provoke the first Cuban riot in Miami." The fact that so many of the Marielitos were black, especially those whose transition in the United States was more difficult, also appears to be a factor in the use of "ghetto" because of the association of the word with African Americans. We see the direct linking of the Marielitos and African Americans in a report on a fight that occurred between refugees in the camps and the police. The article quotes a threat made by a Cuban who was upset about how they had been treated by the police: "'The American blacks set the zone on fire, causing $200,000,000 in damage,' yelled a refugee. 'We have more guts than they do and we're going to set this place on fire.'"[33] With reference to rioting African Americans, U.S. blacks are depicted as instigators of the problem—as models of deviant behavior. Hence, although the news article calls attention to the deplorable living conditions in the tents and by implication the failures of the local and federal government, the ultimate message demonstrates a concern that the real problem and threat to the local community and the Cuban image was the Marielitos themselves.

By framing the Marielitos as deviant/black with the use of the word "ghetto," the coverage in *El Miami Herald* illustrates John Fiske's argument that predominant social orders contain possibly dangerous bodies in "their place"—in spaces such as ghettos that are usually ignored. He states, "The ghetto is not surveilled, because it is that which the eye of power does not wish to see, the regime of truth [it] does not wish to know" (2000, 60). On the one hand, poverty, degradation, and crime are viewed as naturally occurring in the ghetto and thus naturally associated with certain bodies. The plight of the people in the ghetto and the government's contribution to their condition, then, can be ignored. On the other hand, when the problems of the ghetto begin to have an impact on those outside of it, they become issues of intense scrutiny and concern for which a solution must be found.

Depictions of the Marielitos as unworthy citizens who do not know how to live in freedom, who are lazy and less inclined to work hard, who are the black rioting "inmates" at Fort Chaffee, and whose deviant natures affect the environment around them by creating ghettos define them as outside the white middle-class norm and distinguish them from the law-abiding exiles. The characterization of a large proportion of Marielitos as criminal further racialized and blackened the Marielitos and justified that they be put under the same type of surveillance experienced by other black (and brown) bodies in the United States.

My interviews with Afro-Cubans suggest that the black/white frame in turn shaped how established Cuban exiles treated black Cubans as they worked to dissociate from the stigma attached to the Marielitos. Interviewees confirmed the idea that a disconnect exists between white and black Cubans and pre-1980 and post-1980 refugees, based on real or perceived differences in politics, class, and race. Digna, a fifty-two-year-old woman living in Miami who arrived during Mariel, explained, "In Hialeah, many were welcoming family members and such, but we did not have family. There were many signs of racism. People here were welcoming Mariel people into their homes, with the conditions that they were not black. You know, [the unwelcoming people] were Cubans just like us." For Digna, the message was explicit: blacks were not wanted. Another Mariel entrant, Luis, found that he too would not have the opportunity to benefit from being sponsored. He recounts the experience of many single black males such as himself. He was shipped straight to Fort Indiantown Gap in Pennsylvania, one of the several holding centers for Mariel arrivals. He was later transferred to Fort Chaffee, Arkansas. "From there, I was one of the last to leave, so I didn't have no sponsor or nothing like that, so there was about a few hundred of us left." His journey then took him to halfway houses in Seattle, Washington, and then finally to Los Angeles in 1991. Far from the storied tale of Cuban ease of incorporation, Luis did not get settled in to begin "living the American Dream" until a decade after he arrived. His story and stories like it are living testament to what Cuban refugee centers during Mariel found to be a major obstacle; representatives from the Cuban Refugee Resettlement Center stated that they had the most difficulty resettling single, black, adult Cuban males (Boswell and Curtis 1984). One of very few stories in *El Miami Herald* about Mariel to talk about black Cubans even makes notes of the more difficult situation for blacks, asserting that being male, single, and black or *mulato* makes it difficult for the Marielitos to find sponsors in the United States.[34] This acknowledgment that being black made it harder to benefit from the U.S. framing of all Cubans as worthy of U.S. citizenship highlights the strength of the stigma attached to blackness. Indeed, it was difficult for black Marielitos to get sponsors among the established Cuban community, but they met rejection from the U.S. general population as well. The media framing, which equated criminality with blackness, played a strong role in promoting the idea that the Marielitos, purported economic immigrants rather than immigrants fleeing a dictator to whom they were morally opposed, were indeed (potential) criminals and thus bad immigrants.

Theme 3. *"Aquí versus Allá": Teaching the Marielitos to Be Worthy Citizens*

> They can't think that those who arrived here 20 years ago are better or worse; we are all human beings and we all possess virtues and, unfortunately, defects, but there is something that does differentiate the recently arrived, and that is that they need to learn how to live in freedom. . . . It is now time to close the lines—we need to unify all the people of good faith from both sides so the Cuban community can grow in this land; those who have spent more time [in the U.S.] could serve as tutors for the new refugees in their new lives.[35]

In light of the "evidence" that reports of the criminality and deviance of the Marielitos constituted, preserving the image of Cubans as the Golden Exiles meant finding ways to either dissociate from the Marielitos or explain and help correct the Marielitos' "deviant" behaviors. Portes and Stepick (1993) and Yohel Camayd-Freixas (1988) argue that the English-language *Miami Herald* purposively sought to turn its readers against the newcomers in its editorials and news reports. Articles in the Spanish-language *El Miami Herald* with the theme "Marielitos as immigrants needing reform" advanced the mainstream newspaper's stance while at the same time they communicated Cuban American anxiety over the Mariel stigma. Beginning as early as May, approximately 10 percent of each month's articles sent a message to the newcomers that they were not acting like "good immigrants" and thus "worthy citizens"; that is, they were not among those who adhered to laws, who were hard working, and who educated themselves, and thus they needed to change their ways to more fully fit the "Golden Exile" image. They needed to distinguish between how to comport themselves *aquí* in the United States, versus *allá* (in Cuba). Some of the stories also communicated that those who committed unlawful acts deserved to be punished. As Herman Gray points out, discourses about the "rehabilitation" of the (black) underclass involve "the idea that the inculcation of appropriate moral values, self-discipline, and a work ethic can effectively break the vicious cycle of dependency that cripples the poor and disadvantaged" (1995, 24). In *El Miami Herald*, the opinions about Mariel Cubans as immigrants needing reform were delivered mostly in the form of editorials and op-eds or letters to the editor. These were written primarily by news staff or members of the public who identified as Cuban or who had a Spanish surname. The articles reflect the variations of opinion in the Cuban community toward the newcomers by demonstrating a desire to help the Marielitos in the spirit of Cuban unity, but they also included veiled criticism.

Some letters and op-eds detailed the skills the newcomers would need to learn to "live in freedom," including how to adhere to U.S. laws and to value hard work and education. One letter to the editor paints the United States as the undisputed savior of the Cuban people and argues that each individual Cuban is a representative of the Cuban people and needs to behave in ways that demonstrate gratefulness to the United States. The letter outlines several lessons about the gratitude, language, and behavior that the author, a Cuban American, believes newcomers needed to learn upon arriving on the beaches of freedom:

> I believe it is necessary to offer counseling to the thousands of compatriots who are now arriving to these free beaches. . . . Above all, we all owe gratitude and recognition to the people and government of the United States for everything they have done in our favor. . . . Secondly, understanding life and the customs of the United States is a necessity. . . . Obviously, it must be said that there is no chance at improving the conditions of one's life if one does not learn the [English] language. In the third place, the behavior. . . . Here,

people do not fear the police. . . . Here, order, in addition to being the result of general education, has a higher purpose—to maintain a standard of living for all of us.[36]

The letter declares that newcomers should become accustomed to the way the United States works as soon as they can and learn English so that they can make a contribution (rather than be a liability) to the nation. The letter advances the idea of the "good immigrant," which is really about affirming the exile community's own acceptance in U.S. society and maintaining their sense of power. With the title "Behavior in the United States," the advice seems to be a response to the increasing reports on the criminal or deviant actions of some Marielitos. The letter also asserts white Cuban privilege in its reference to how policing works to protect them, not accounting for the differential police surveillance experienced by black subjects.

The extensive coverage of the June 1 Mariel uprising at Fort Chaffee also prompted members of the Cuban community to write letters to the editor of *El Miami Herald*. Most letters in reference to the uprisings criticize the Marielitos rather than the mistakes made by the United States in the resettlement of the refugees. "Refugees: You Are in a Law-Abiding Nation," written a day after the uprising, exemplifies the widespread concern about the Marielitos' lack of adherence to laws and the negative repercussions for the exiled community: "These hoodlums, in addition to harming the image of the Cuban exile—who in their vast majority are orderly and respectful of the laws—are hurting the refugees themselves. I believe that they should know that the United States is a Nation of Laws, which are very different from Castro's evil installation in Cuba, and that these laws should be obeyed."[37] The author goes so far as to insist that those who do not follow the laws should be sent back to Cuba. He expresses a fear of guilt by association and seeks to defend the image of the established Cuban community. This letter and others like it present a simplistic view that ignores things such as the fact that the U.S. political stance toward Cuba was changing and that its new stance toward the newcomers contributed to the problems faced by Marielitos in the United States. The United States' handling of the group is diminished in the reports, and difficulties faced by the exiles are blamed on their character and their unwillingness to obey laws, in a classic example of blaming the victim.

The negative role of the United States was not completely ignored in the coverage and was in fact highlighted in several articles, but, following the reporting in the *Miami Herald*, the stories focused on the U.S. role were more concerned with the economic effect of the government's indecision on the local community rather than the effects on the Marielitos themselves. For example, an editorial critical of President Carter's indecision regarding U.S. policy toward the new arrivals was also not supportive of the Marielitos. Its main point is a scathing critique of the new entrants and their lack of a work ethic:

> These new Cuban refugees will have to learn the American system in one form or another. They will have to quickly learn that freedom doesn't mean that you can have all the things you want at any time you want them. They will have to learn that the prosperous Cuban community in Miami earned their relative wealth through hard work, long hours of study, and diligent attention to learning the rules of the North American game.[38]

The editorial castigates the newcomers by praising the *antiguos* and makes the claim that the established Cuban community in Miami became affluent because they learned how to be worthy citizens. The newcomers are portrayed as having unrealistic expectations and desiring freedom and goods without sacrifice, and the hardships the group may have endured in Cuba, while traveling to the United States, and being processed in the United States are erased. This editorial and other items criticizing the Marielitos starkly distinguish the new arrivals, who are considered potential bad immigrants if they are not reformed, from *los antiguos*. Furthermore, in contrast to earlier articles that portray the Mariel refugees as good immigrants who are mostly compatriots in pursuit of similar goals, the articles framing the Marielitos as needing reform firmly place *los antiguos* in the role of the "native" group that has the authority to dictate what the "foreign" group should do to become good immigrants and to earn their place as worthy citizens of the nation.

Mariel Voices in El Miami Herald: *A Case Study of an Afro-Cuban Family*

In all the reports on the Marielitos, what are often lost are the voices of the Mariel refugees themselves. There were special interest stories and times when Marielitos were quoted in news stories, but for the most part they are a faceless group, pawns of either Castro or the U.S. government, a problem to be solved. Significantly, however, two months after the beginning of the Mariel exodus, *El Miami Herald* began a series of articles that follow the experiences of a recently arrived family, La Familia Casanova, to document their "immigrant story." It is also significant that the family chosen for the exposé is black. There is no direct reference to the family's race in the stories— their race is indicated in the accompanying pictures. As mentioned previously, there is little attention in the paper given to the fact that many of the Marielitos were black.[39] This may be related to the fact that in the U.S. context, the idea of the "black Cuban" was relatively new, because blacks were such a small percentage of those who came during previous waves. Cubans were most often discussed in U.S. public discourse as a homogenous group unified by their anti-Castro, anti-communist stance. Thus, non-Cubans involved in choosing stories to run may have been oblivious to differences among Cubans based on socioeconomic status, race, or gender. For Cuban writers in the newspaper, racial democracy discourse inspired by Cuban patriot Jose Martí, which has infused Cuban ideas of their nation, may have also influenced a tendency to avoid the issue of race or to see it as a nonissue. In addition, learning that African Americans are stigmatized in the United States, Cuban exiles may have wanted to avoid "guilt by association" with African Americans by avoiding attention to Cuban blackness. The silence on race reflected in the newspaper then belies the problematic ways blackness is regarded in Cuba coupled with the insidious but perhaps less overt "color-blind" racism of the neoconservative 1980s United States (Gray 1995). A close look at the case of La Familia Casanova allows for an interrogation of the silences about race and blackness, and allows a view into the contradictory ways Afro-Cubans have been positioned both inside and outside the larger Cuban identity.

Moreover, we hear directly from black Cuban Mariel refugees as profiled in the newspaper. Juan Casanova; his wife, Natividad; and her eight-year-old son from a previous marriage are first introduced to us through the words of Juan Casanova. Juan had been a journalist in Cuba, and *El Miami Herald* provided him with the opportunity to write about his family's experiences. His story, titled "Ten Thousand Were Looking for Refuge and Found Hell," a top front-page story on June 1, 1980, tells of the preparations they took to leave Cuba, such as getting clothes together, saying good-bye to relatives, and consulting the Santos, or the gods, for a safe journey.[40] He documents their harrowing experiences at the Peruvian embassy and the details of the journey until their arrival in the United States on April 30, 1980. Subsequent stories about the family were written by an *El Miami Herald* staff writer, who gives a blow-by-blow account of their daily lives and the little victories and setbacks they encountered. The family brought very little money with them from Cuba and did not have relatives in the United States to help them settle in. After moving from camps to churches for shelter, a North American family took notice of their plight and rallied others to help them with housing, furniture, and food. Nevertheless, their struggles continued. Juan had trouble holding onto his job as a gardener because of transportation problems: the family could not afford a car and relied on bikes that kept getting stolen. Natividad could not find work comparable to the scientific information-processing work she did in Cuba because she did not have the equivalent certificate in the United States. They both struggled to pay their bills.

The staff writer's articles focus on the family members' optimism as they sought to incorporate themselves into U.S. society despite these hardships. This optimistic focus is evident in the titles of the articles—"Exiles from Mariel Have a New Life,"[41] "In Spite of Problems the Family Is Not Discouraged and Is Adapting Little by Little,"[42] and "The Casanova Family Are Adapting to Exile"[43]—and in captions to the accompanying pictures (such as "Casanova refuses to let instability discourage him").[44] In addition, after accounts about their difficulties, the next paragraph would often begin with a statement like "nevertheless the family is optimistic." The last article in the series, written four months after they first arrived, ends their story on a high note. It begins, "It could be a success story." It continues, "After the nightmare of the Peruvian Embassy in Havana, the trip from Mariel to Key West and the first days without a home in Miami, the family seems to be adapting to life in the United States."[45] The stories' accounts frame the family's adversity as the obligatory struggle immigrants undergo to earn the privileges of the American Dream.

By and large the stories leave out the tremendous stigma attached to the Marielitos by the U.S. public and the discrimination many black Cubans faced. By focusing on a mother, father, and child, the series appealed to the immigration policy ideal of family and family unification. The Casanovas are depicted as a generic Cuban family; unlike for other Marielitos, their blackness is of no consequence. They have suffered, but their optimism has allowed them to find some success. They are good immigrants—they do not complain, nor do they wish to impose on the U.S. government.[46] For instance, Juan is recorded as saying, "I'm crazy for not receiving food stamps. [But] I refused to depend on them"; and "I think they could give that to someone else who needs it more."[47] Juan demonstrates proper moral values by expressing his discontent with having to rely on the government for assistance. The family is slowly but surely becoming a part of the American family—their acquisition of a washing machine, which the reporter asserts is a symbol of independence and freedom in the United States, and the son's love of hot dogs, Coca Cola, and children's television programs are all cited as evidence. Although they arrived as "Marielitos," a group stigmatized because of their blackness, association with Castro's Cuba, and supposed criminality, the stories depict them as refugees who redeem themselves and succeed because of their hard work, struggles, and attitudes.[48] Thus, Los Casanovas are able to be represented within the newspaper as exemplars of the good immigrant ideal, wherein their embrace of capitalism and their desire not to be a burden to society allow their blackness to be of no consequence. Their blackness need not be acknowledged.

Yet a closer look at the stories and Los Casanovas' own words demonstrate a greater complexity. The family is indeed optimistic about their chances in the United States, but they are not naive. Like exiles from the earlier generations, they criticize the Cuban government, but they also make comments that represent a critique of the United States. For instance, Juan speaks of the fact that all societies have their problems and does not demonize Cuba. Juan makes a sophisticated critique of both the United States and Cuba, saying, "In Cuba, shortages create an unsatisfied consumer society. It translates into a psychological hunger." He goes on, "Here, it all comes down to people buying things, but some people are against that. But on the other hand, you know that there will always be goods available."[49] His assessment of the United States is mixed. He comes from a society where he lived in extreme scarcity, and the extreme abundance in the United States can be overwhelming. It is clear that one does not have to worry about basic needs in the United States. But he hints at the possible cynicism that can come after the "psychological hunger" is satisfied in the United States—an experience many new immigrants go through after they are confronted with the new hardships that living in a capitalist system entails. One is always chasing the dollar, and this makes for another type of dependency, where survival relies on one's ability to pay for goods.

Though the staff writer's articles about the Casanova family do not make note of the fact the family is black, in his own article about his family's experiences, Juan is not silent about their adherence to Santería, a religion with African origins practiced in Cuba but often maligned in the United States, especially during Mariel. He writes of consulting with Ochún (described in the article as an incarnation of la Vírgen de la Caridad), and he talks of waiting for his wife at her home in Cuba, where her relatives were playing Santería drums.[50] He also recounts that after he and his wife made the decision to leave, her brother-in-law consulted a *babalao* (Santería priest) about the decision. He does not hide the importance of his faith or this African aspect of his culture.

The Casanova family is also noteworthy in how they disrupt the common depiction of the Marielitos as uneducated and unskilled. It is true that a larger percentage of Mariel refugees were lower skilled than in previous waves, but many were professionals and intellectuals in Cuba, as were Juan and Natividad. They were equipped with the social capital many pre-1980 refugees had, yet they still struggled to achieve in the United States. Juan and Natividad sought to continue the intellectual pursuits that may have been stifled in Cuba, but the hardships of taking care of their basic needs in the United States hindered those plans. They aspired to middle-class stability and to own the possessions that symbolized capitalist success, while still offering a sophisticated critique of capitalism. The reports on the Casanovas provide a view into how one black Cuban family confronted the questions of what it means to be included in the American family. Their story is hopeful that full inclusion or "success" is possible for them but also presents an indictment of the United States' exclusionary practices. The stories on the family catch them in the early months of entry into the United States, and we and they cannot see what is coming down the pike. How might they evaluate the United States in terms of racial issues and their treatment? Did race-based discrimination come into play for them, contributing to some of their struggles? If the voices of the Mariel refugees were privileged and they were given more opportunities to express themselves publicly, we might be able to see a fuller picture of the situation surrounding the Mariel exodus and the conditions in the United States that made the incorporation of Marielitos more difficult. Studies in which Marielitos have been interviewed conclude that there is no uniform

Mariel voice (see Portes and Stepick 1993). But if *El Miami Herald* had listened more closely to their voices, we might find a picture of the Mariel crisis more critical of U.S. racism, imperialism, and capitalism. Furthermore, their voices could present a challenge of the divisions between black and white Cubans (and African Americans and white Cubans for that matter) that we see reflected in other *Herald* stories. Subsequent chapters allow further insight into these questions, as black Cuban immigrants discuss their experiences with race in the United States.

Conclusion

The Mariel exodus became a "racial crisis" because public citizens and political elites were up in arms about the real logistical problems of accommodating such large numbers of people, and government officials were concerned about quelling public fears over the perceived threat these purportedly criminal, mentally ill, homosexual, and black bodies posed. In contrast to the treatment of previous Cuban waves, the U.S. government was unprepared to decide how it would process the Marielitos; thus, many Marielitos suffered from being put into a holding position for months. With no sponsors or families to take them in, they languished in detention centers, military bases, and tent cities, with no jobs or financial support. *El Miami Herald* did express criticism of the role of the federal government in making it more difficult to incorporate the Marielitos into U.S. society. But a close look at the coverage of stories reflecting the response of the local Anglo and Cuban exile community to the Marielitos reveals that more often the blame for the Marielitos' difficult incorporation was placed on Fidel Castro or on their own behaviors.

As evident in the newspaper, the distinction between the "real" Cubans and the newcomers did not directly implicate blackness, and the fact that many Marielitos were black was rarely acknowledged. *El Miami Herald* did officially recognize that Mariel Cubans included more blacks than previous waves in early reports on the newcomers.[51] Still, little attention was paid to the role of blackness in their stigmatization. Instead, as I have argued and the evidence suggests, according to a black/white frame, blackness was more covertly implicated in the production of good and bad immigrants to differentiate the exile community and the good, worthy Marielitos from the bad, unworthy ones. The blackness of bodies among the Marielitos caused alarm for some, but regardless of the actual skin color of the migrants, the Marielitos were "blackened" through the use of tropes already clearly utilized in the United States to establish African Americans as nonnormative citizens (including discourses about laziness, dependency, and criminality). Cubans' preexisting prejudices against blackness, carried over from Cuba itself—a prejudice especially pronounced in the culture of wealthier Cubans, those likeliest to emigrate—only compounded the issue.

One could surmise that the inattention to race in the newspaper is a product of the Cuban view that "a Cuban is a Cuban," regardless of race.[52] But the experiences of Cuban interviewees tell a different story; testimonies of black Marielitos we saw here and will see in coming chapters, which include such things as not being taken in by white Cuban sponsors and receiving backhanded compliments from white Cubans when black Cubans did not conform to stereotypes, disrupt the "big happy family" image. Their experiences and the tropes in the newspapers that utilize the black/white frame to indicate which immigrants are "good" and which are "bad" speak to the need to continue to challenge anti-black racism in the hemisphere—calling attention to the fallacy of racial democracy discourses in Cuba but also placing emphasis on how the U.S.-based requirements for citizenship (based on proving worthiness) intensify the need to make claim to whiteness. These discourses reflected in the paper, which worked to prove the worthiness of the Cuban exile community, ultimately serve the reproduction of the white-dominated racial hierarchy.

This discussion about the framing of the Mariel refugees in *El Miami Herald* illustrates the ways race, and blackness in particular, functions as an organizing principle of how citizenship is conferred or denied in the United States. Thinking about today, the discussion further underscores how far the nation is from being "post-race," and how racism, although clearly continuing in overt manifestations, also often comes disguised in the definitions of worthy citizens. The findings in *El Miami Herald* highlight the role of media in disseminating these discourses and the effects of these ideals on how traditionally underrepresented groups receive new immigrants. The staunchly conservative politics of the Miami Cuban community makes the Cuban claims to a white identity as oppositional to a black identity appear more intense than similar claims (or pursuits) made by other Latino groups. Yet in reality, the issue of making claim to the U.S. nation and the impulse to demonstrate how one's own group is more deserving also comes into play for other traditionally underrepresented groups in their reception of new immigrants. In this chapter we saw different perspectives voiced in *El Miami Herald* that illustrate the complexities of Cuban American struggles as they both deployed and resisted predominant nativist and racist U.S. discourses in depictions of the Marielitos, whose negative treatment in the United States disrupted idealistic views about the "inclusion" of their group within the definition of "American." In the Miami case, material conditions and the requirements of worthy citizenship increased inequity among black and white Cubans and encouraged ways of thinking that, as we will see in coming chapters, intensified negative relations among generations of Cuban immigrants and African Americans.

Chapter 3

And Justice for All?

Immigration and African American Solidarity

Just a month before the Mariel exodus, Miami was shaken by a major African American uprising. The immediate cause was the police killing of a black motorist, thirty-three-year-old Arthur McDuffie. On December 17, 1979, McDuffie was chased by police officers after he came to a rolling stop at a red light and reportedly made an obscene gesture to a nearby cop. While in handcuffs, McDuffie was beaten to death by at least six white officers, one of whom was Cuban.[1] Police claimed that the death stemmed from accidental injuries during the chase and were acquitted of his murder. In response, outraged black citizens rose up in what came to be known as the McDuffie Riot, which started May 17, 1980, and lasted three days, resulting in eighteen dead, $804 million in damages, and 1,100 arrests (Dunn and Stepick 1992; Porter and Dunn 1984). For African Americans in Miami, the police brutality and subsequent release of the perpetrators in this incident was testament to the continued need to fight against white domination. In this context, when the Mariel boatlift began in April, some African Americans became worried that the shifting focus of politicians onto the Mariel wave of Cubans and to the question of immigration would cause local institutions to lose sight of the continued subjugation of blacks. These worries were clearly communicated in the reporting on Mariel in the *Miami Times* weekly, Miami's leading African American newspaper since 1929.

In this chapter, I turn our focus onto African American reactions to the 1980 Mariel boatlift through a close examination of the coverage of the boatlift in the *Miami Times*. In Chapter 2, we observed that some Cuban Americans were threatened by the criminal stigma attached to the Marielitos, fearing it could affect their image and good standing in the United States. Even without overt references to blackness in terms of biological race, the stigmatization of the Marielitos relied on a black/white division, and "good" or "worthy" (white) Marielitos were distinguished from "bad" or "unworthy" (black) Marielitos by some Cuban Americans in an effort to preserve the good standing of the Cuban exile community as a whole. Projects of dissociation from blackness, such as the ones enacted by white Cuban exiles, further illuminate the antagonistic climate African Americans and others with black skin live in in U.S. society.

In this chapter, I examine the dual dilemmas faced by some members of the African American community as they grapple with how immigration and the United States' greater diversity changes their conceptualization of "blackness" and the political position of African Americans. As newer immigrants entered the Miami area in 1980, including Mariel Cubans and also Haitians, "native" African Americans faced these dilemmas as they worked to address the problems they were experiencing—problems that they viewed as partly caused by the profound growth of the Cuban population—while also upholding the closely held ideals of the civil rights movement. Upholding these ideals would mean defending all marginalized groups and connecting their struggles to black struggles. As the newcomers in 1980 were arriving, African Americans would draw upon pan-African idealism to embrace Haitian newcomers, but the powerful force of native/foreigner ideologies would ironically constrain an African American embrace of the Cuban migrants.

Previous scholarship has drawn attention to conflict between African Americans and Cubans and to evidence of this in the *Miami Times*, but it has not offered explanations or specifically focused on black reactions to the Mariel exodus. I explore how African American citizens, disenfranchised due to continued realities of police brutality, black unemployment, and other forms of anti-black racism, responded to the new Mariel immigrants in the context of their own tenuous claim to the United States. Examining this response helps us think about the current racial context and about how African Americans can continue building on the civil rights era–inspired impulse to align with other aggrieved groups to fight larger societal problems.

In 1980, less than a generation removed from the civil rights movement, with its promises of better days, African Americans held a precarious position, particularly in Miami, and sought to hold onto this position in the face of changing demographics. Indeed, "The [McDuffie] riot highlighted the frustration of blacks in Miami, who suffered the ongoing effects of an economic recession and watched as a white Cuban elite formed partnerships with a white Anglo elite for control of the city" (Sawyer 2006, 154). African Americans felt doubly marginalized, first by white Anglos and second by the incoming group. Given the precarious position of African Americans in Miami, one might expect that scarcity can explain ensuing forms of interminority conflict. Yet this chapter underscores the argument that despite real concerns over the scarcity of jobs and other benefits of citizenship, ideologies rooted in white dominance played a critical role in shaping the terrain of interminority conflict between African American citizens and new immigrants. Because of the economic, political, and social instability experienced by people of color, they are compelled to worry about and try to reassert their standing in the face of potential new threats. In this context, they may choose strategies in relation to discursive frames that have long been used to reproduce white dominance and powerfully shape debates on race and belonging in the nation. These discursive frames may be used simultaneously as groups such as African Americans seek to *resist* dominant frames (Feagin 2010).

Three themes predominate in the *Times* coverage and illustrate this simultaneity: native-born blacks as Americans versus (Cuban) foreigners or immigrants; black Haitians versus white Cubans; and the necessity of support for all oppressed peoples. The first two themes do demonstrate a disdain among African Americans for Cuban immigration. The first is steeped in the native/foreigner frame, which states that those most worthy of citizenship are those who have a longer history of contributing to U.S. society. The racializing frames that attach worthiness to factors like the length of time a group has made contributions to the nation relative to another become useful as groups seek to prove they truly belong, but they are also exclusionary. Indeed, newspaper reports supported the idea that in contrast to Cubans, black Americans and white Americans were the "real Americans." These sentiments illustrate how African Americans made claim to the nation by affirming an idea that they were "natives" being displaced by "foreigners." The second—and most prominent—theme similarly communicates discontent with Cuban immigration by drawing attention to how "white" newcomers from Mariel received preferential treatment denied Haitians, another controversial migrating group seeking refuge in south Florida at the same time. The black Haitians versus white Cubans theme also demonstrates the African American population's pressing desire to challenge white supremacy and promote greater equality and acknowledgment of blacks in the larger sphere of U.S. culture. The *Times* coverage suggests that African American evaluations of the Mariel exodus were not simply about competing for scarce resources but were shaped by their attempts at a deeper ideological critique of U.S. immigration policy and the ways it upholds white dominance. The limits of the critique stem from the fact that it continued to draw on the black/white binary in ways that fomented conflict rather than solidary between Haitian and Cuban immigrants and African American citizens and Cuban immigrants.

The greater presence of Afro-Cubans among the Mariel Cubans had the potential to challenge the African American framing of Cubans as "whites," forever divided from African Americans, while also highlighting the instability of "race" for building solidarity. To investigate how well the *Miami Times* coverage captured this potential for challenging exclusionary racial frames in this case, along with analyzing African American reactions to the Mariel newcomers as a whole, I examine whether and how the greater presence of black Cubans among them was acknowledged. Interspersing the findings from the newspapers with testimonials from Afro-Cuban interviewees— which offer a view from a liminal perspective that both combines and goes beyond the experiences of both other actors in this controversy—the chapter concludes by underscoring the ways the Afro-Cuban migrants who are blacks *and* "foreigners" as well as blacks *and* Cubans offer a challenge to the native/ foreigner divides advanced in the newspaper.

African Americans in Miami in 1980

By the end of the 1970s, deindustrialization in the United States had caused the nation to experience an economic downturn. Lower-class African

Americans in Miami were hardest hit. Although in the 1970s the black middle class in Miami had a higher average per capita income than other African American communities nationwide, by 1980 they were the poorest blacks in the country and the most frustrated of Miami's residents. Blacks were 24 percent of Dade's unemployed in 1980 compared with 17 percent in 1970, with a poverty rate (29.8 percent) more than triple that of whites (8.3 percent) and almost double that of Hispanics (16.9 percent) (Dunn and Stepick 1992, 47). Nor did their problems begin with the 1979–1980 recession. In the 1960s, urban renewal programs had destroyed thriving black cultural and business centers, and middle-class blacks left these areas for the suburbs, concentrating Miami's poorest blacks in the inner city (Dunn 1997, 2016; Grenier and Pérez 2003; Grenier and Stepick 2001). A major "accomplishment" of Miami's urban renewal programs was the construction of Interstate 95, which cut right through Overtown and displaced twelve thousand people (Connolly 2014).[2] The highway became a new way of maintaining racial and class-based segregation. Low-income housing was built on west side of I-95, in areas such as Liberty City, which became Miami's "second ghetto" after the decline of Overtown. Whites would live on the other side of the highway (Connolly 2014, 265). The highway and racist zoning practices such as eminent domain, which allowed for "the taking of private property for public use," all operated to disenfranchise poor and working-class African Americans and enforced the separation of the races (Connolly 2014, 5).

All these changes made it more difficult for blacks to mobilize politically and raise new black leaders. With members of the black middle classes moving out of the area, split from inner-city blacks, this, along with spatial changes in the city, made it difficult for blacks to create solid voting blocs compared with Cubans (Grenier and Pérez 2003). Furthermore, Miami-Dade County has a metropolitan governance system that has at-large elections for the commissioners, a practice that suppresses the sort of neighborhood forums that, in other cities, can benefit minorities (Grenier and Pérez 2003). Given that residential segregation is one of the primary enforcers of black–white division in the United States, black neighborhoods frequently emerge as one of the only concentrated black power bases. Thus, a form of government that cuts off power at the neighborhood level will pose unique challenges to black people. But despite the difficulty in electing leaders, African Americans knew they still needed to fight. Racist practices in the allocation of space, the pervasiveness of negative stereotypes about blacks not only in the local but the national media in the 1980s, and a string of cases of police brutality, of which the McDuffie incident was just the latest, offered confirmation that local institutions were not committed to ensuring the welfare of African Americans.

Even as it coped with a serious recession, the United States of the early 1980s began to show the effects of major demographic shifts driven by the post-1965 growth of immigration from Latin America and Asia among other regions of the world. The new changes would contribute to a new public focus on concepts like "diversity" and "multiculturalism," with the United States seemingly moving away from a bipolar black/white divide. But the 1980s would also usher in a nativist backlash as whites feared being "conquered" by all these people of color. The logic of this nativism was seductive because it cloaked itself under the mantle of "national security," a cause that sounds more legitimate on its face than "racial exclusion" or "maintaining white supremacy." Despite the fact that U.S. elites in reality want immigrants because they provide cheap labor that enriches corporations, nativists argued they needed to preserve scarce resources for their own families, who they believed had more rightful claim to those resources because they had been here all along. Thus, the powerful native/foreigner dichotomy that has been utilized over and over in U.S. history gained renewed power in the 1980s, even as "multiculturalism" was becoming a household word.

Despite there being a long tradition of African American political organizing that is not only inclusive toward immigrant groups but has actively advocated for them, African Americans would also get caught up in such zero-sum reasoning. In the 1980s and beyond, many African Americans would continue their tradition of pro-immigrant organizing. Yet, at the same time, some would worry that the new immigrants might compete with them for jobs and other resources and that the new immigrants, particularly those who were nonblack, would not be motivated to join with them in their fight for equal justice.

These conflicts were most visible in Miami, a city that in the 1970s had experienced much white flight and by 1980 was already a "majority-minority" city (Connolly 2014; Shell-Weiss 2009). The black population in Miami had always been heterogeneous, but this heterogeneity intensified as more and more black immigrants began to arrive from the Caribbean. Until 1980, most black Caribbean immigrants would go to New York, avoiding the Jim Crow

South. But in the post–civil rights era, black Caribbeans were coming to Miami in larger numbers and arriving in a post-Jim Crow climate in which they could more readily maintain their ethnic distinctiveness (as opposed to assimilating into the category of "African American"). While the black Caribbean population was increasing, the Latino population exploded. By the late 1980s, Hispanics were 60 percent of the population of Miami and 50 percent of the population of the Miami-Dade metropolitan area (Miami-Dade Planning Department 2009). Cubans were by far the largest and most influential of them.

As we have seen in previous chapters, African Americans had worried since the 1960s that Cuban newcomers would shift local and federal political attention from the concerns of blacks. The United States' rhetoric and policies, especially during and after the missile crisis in 1962, gave these fears grounding in reality. Accordingly, Cuban immigration or Cubans are not in and of themselves the "cause" of black disenfranchisement; rather, government programs—the choice not to address both groups' concerns seriously—exacerbated the perception of inequality (López 2012). For instance, between 1968 and 1980, the Small Business Administration disbursed 46.6 percent of its loans to Latinos and only 6 percent to blacks (Grenier and Stepick 2001, 156). This disparity in aid caused some black leaders to argue that Hispanics should not be included in minority set-asides (Grenier and Stepick 2001, 156). These government programs contributed to the great success Cubans were able to achieve. By the end of the 1980s, 42 percent of all Miami-Dade enterprises, for instance, were Hispanic-owned, with three-fourths of these businesses controlled by Cubans (Grenier and Castro 1999, 280–281). The deteriorating situation of blacks in Miami stood in dramatic contrast to the strengthening position of Cubans in the city.

When Cubans began to arrive after the Cuban Revolution, they were viewed as possible allies at first. In the spirit of the black civil rights agenda, Martin Luther King took note when some blacks showed concern that Cubans would infringe on them, and he warned against actions that would work to create division between blacks and Cubans (Dunn 1997). Moreover, scholars have illuminated an important historical relationship between African Americans and Cuban blacks in which they came together to oppose American imperialism and anti-black racism in both the United States and Cuba in the nineteenth century (Brock and Castañeda Fuertes 1998; Greenbaum 2002; Guridy 2010; Hellwig 1998; Mirabal 2003, 1998). However, the imperatives of Cold War–era anti-communist efforts would pit Cubans (conceptualized as a homogenous group) against African Americans. And since so few Afro-Cubans arrived with the first waves of Cuban exiles, Cubans were read as "white." As discussed in Chapter 2, some exile Cubans themselves promoted their own whiteness, and drawing on the idealization of whiteness in Cuba as well as the United States' brand of white racism and anti-blackness, they set up divisions between not only themselves and African Americans but also between themselves and Afro-Cubans. Consequently, as Cubans gained power in Miami, they came to be viewed by African Americans as rivals when they did not clearly align themselves with blacks. In 1980, as blacks endured continuingly volatile race relations with white Anglos, tense relations with some members of the established Cuban community, and a depressed job market, many of them were not happy to see a new group of Cubans when they began to arrive in April 1980 as the Mariel boatlift began to get under way.

The Haitian Counterframe

During the time of massive Cuban immigration from Mariel, Haitians were also seeking asylum in the United States. Their numbers were much larger than the numbers of other migrants coming from other regions of the black Caribbean. Between 1977 and 1981, fifty thousand to seventy thousand Haitians arrived in Miami (Stepick 1992). Haitians began fleeing to the United States when the dictator Francois Duvalier ("Papa Doc") assumed power in 1957. Duvalier and his son, Jean-Claude ("Baby Doc"), to whom power was transferred in 1971, had a complicated relationship with the United States. Seeking to maintain Haitian political stability in order to protect U.S. economic, political, and military interests, the U.S. government alternated in its support and disapproval of the Duvalier regimes. When Jean-Claude Duvalier condemned communism early in his presidency, cooperation between the United States and Haiti was renewed (Ferguson 1987). The complicated relationship that had been established between the two countries set up profound economic and political inequities. These inequities allowed Duvalier to brutalize his people, directly affecting Haitian immigration.[3] Yet, the United States' history of supporting the Duvaliers, and Jean-Claude Duvalier's anti-communist stance during the Cold War period, made it difficult for the U.S. government to fully demonize him as it had Castro. As a result, while U.S. immigration policy had historically allowed Cubans to be classified as "good immigrants"—refugees seeking asylum—Haitians, who also sought to flee a dictator, were generally sent back or contained in the U.S. naval base in Guantánamo, Cuba. Classified as economic immigrants, Haitians were viewed as a drain on society (Greenhill 2002).

Given these disparities in the U.S. deployment of foreign policy, much of the reporting in the *Miami Times* on Mariel would be driven by stories that contrasted Haitian and Cuban immigration. African Americans had been fighting against anti-black racism as it affected African Americans locally, and now it appeared the United States was continuing to perpetuate the denigration of black peoples in its favoritism for Cubans over Haitians. In the tradition of pan-African idealism that allowed African Americans to fight together for their own civil rights, African Americans rallied behind the Haitians as they sought to challenge anti-blackness as it manifested in U.S. foreign policy. As the first black independent nation in the world, Haiti has been a powerful symbol of black redemption for proponents of Afrocentric thinking. The emancipation of the Haitian slaves and the country's independence on January 1, 1804, inspired black struggles for independence and slave emancipation across the diaspora (Pamphile 2001). This history, and the fact that a majority of Haitians had darker skin, would allow African Americans to view them as unequivocally black in contrast to Cubans.

The Mariel Boatlift in the *Miami Times*

The local African American newspaper, the *Miami Times*, operated as a space for African Americans to monitor the mainstream press and provide alternate readings of newsworthy events (Jacobs 2000). As we saw in Chapter 2, the vast numbers of Cubans arriving during Mariel and the tensions between the Cuban regime and that of the United States made the Mariel crisis a top story in the *Miami Herald* and in *El Miami Herald*. My analysis of the coverage of Mariel in news stories, op-eds, editorials, and letters to the editor in the *Miami Times* reveals that, in contrast, the exodus actually received little attention in this paper except in reference to Haitian immigration occurring at the same time (to which the paper dedicated much space and coverage). A search for articles in bound newspaper archives and on microfilm covering the 1980 Mariel exodus and its aftermath between the months of April and October 1980 yielded only thirty articles: news stories, editorials, and letters to the editor.[4] What the *Miami Times* did cover, however, provides important insight into the tensions in the black community regarding the entrance of refugees from Mariel and their view of U.S. immigration policy more broadly. Below I discuss the three predominant themes that emerged in the coverage: native-born blacks as Americans versus Cuban foreigners or immigrants; black Haitians versus white Cubans; and the necessity of support for all oppressed peoples.

Black "Americans" versus Cuban "Foreigners"

The native/foreigner frame emerged as a prominent discourse in the newspaper, reflecting—and shaping—African American responses to the Mariel boat lift. In the native/foreigner frame, groups claim to be more entitled to citizenship on the grounds that their group has a longer history of time or investment in being included in the United States. The *Miami Times*'s news stories and editorials painted Cubans as "newer" foreigners who should not receive privileges over African Americans, who are "natives" to the United States, entitled to the privileges of citizenship and standing closer to whites. For instance, an editorial titled "America's Partiality to Cubans" asks the readers to consider whether the United States should draw the line in helping Cubans. It argues that African Americans were getting the short end of the stick and that the racialized experiences of African Americans were worse than those of Cubans. The article claims that Cubans suffered less scrutiny than African Americans and that Cubans were rarely falsely accused of crimes, as were African Americans.[5] This analysis failed to recognize that, as discussed in Chapter 2, the new wave of Cuban immigrants from Mariel (many of whom were black) were depicted as criminals within both the Cuban and U.S. press (Masud-Piloto 1996).

Stories in the paper firmly establish African Americans as part of the "we"—American citizens who, along with white Americans, believe in preserving the economic and political interests of the nation. An editorial written later that summer, "Government Should Accommodate Those Cubans Wanting to Go Back," reads, "It is inexcusable that American citizens are being victimized by the federal government's shoddy handling of the

Cuban boat flotilla. . . . It's time we remind Castro that he's not dealing with the thirteen original colonies."[6] The editorial lays claim to the U.S. nation and its "greatness," as it criticizes the federal government for "sidestepping its responsibility" toward U.S. citizens and leaving a mess for the local government to clean up. This criticism of the federal government reflects a stereotypical "get tough" opposition to Castro that is similarly expressed in the editorials of other local Miami newspapers such as the *Miami Herald* and *El Miami Herald*. But using a native/foreigner frame of reference, the editorial's support for allowing Cubans to go back to Cuba demonstrated a sentiment that was not just about supporting the United States' anti-communist stance but also about advocating for the end of Cuban immigration. The Mariel exodus is depicted as problematic not only because it meant accepting people Castro had sent to the United States but because the acceptance of the refugees and the drain on the local government meant that "real," more deserving American *citizens* would be disenfranchised on the refugees' behalf.

A prominent way of establishing African Americans as more deserving, "real" Americans was through an emphasis on the controversies of language. For instance, a top front-page news story titled "'No Habla Español' Costs Black Maids Their Jobs" reports that a hotel manager fired black maids because he wanted to hire Spanish-speaking maids to better cater to the Latin American tourists who frequented the hotel. The article expresses the fears found in several other stories and editorials that Cubans were taking jobs from blacks and that blacks should fight against linguistic discrimination by Spanish speakers. Indeed, the hotel manager did tell the paper that a large volume of his patrons were tourists from Latin American countries and that some guests complained that the maids could not understand Spanish. As Cubans became more influential in Miami and as Cuban-owned businesses expanded, African Americans seeking employment would very likely encounter Cubans as employers, and the discrimination the article speaks of was not unheard of. Hence, this article and the sentiments it reflects is indicative of a greater fear held by African Americans that this new immigrant group was set on adopting the anti-black attitudes of white citizens. The article ends by linking these firing incidents with the larger controversy going on at the time over an anti-bilingualism proposal that was being circulated.[7] The support for the ordinance by some African Americans demonstrated a view among them that, as English speakers, African Americans, like white Americans, held a more rightful claim to America's resources than did "foreigners."

This sentiment was expressed in a letter to the editor, "Bilingualism an Excuse for Discrimination," which complains that bilingualism has been used by Spanish-speaking people to justify discrimination against blacks. In the letter, which was in response to an editorial published September 11 that advocates that blacks learn a second language, the author asks, "Why should our people waste their hard earned money and time to learn a second language? Giving in to such a measure would show our people to be weak and passive."[8] The letter calls for members of the African American community to stand up for themselves in the face of cultural change. Moreover, the critique being advanced was that by accommodating newcomers rather than fulfilling its responsibilities toward African American citizens, the federal government was continuing to fail them.

One of the most scathing letters to the editor regarding Cuban immigrants and bilingualism, "Cubans Should Not Be 'One up' on Blacks," sets up a fierce native/foreigner opposition:

> Spanish should not be crammed down Americans' throats whether Black or White. When refugees are invited into a person's home (America), they shouldn't rearrange the furniture (English language), after getting here, but they leave all cultural ties either at home or in that foreign country that they come from in order to adapt the culture of America namely, an appreciation for an English speaking society. They are both minorities but Cubans should not have one up on language whereby it is a liability not to speak Spanish.

The writer presents the metaphor of the United States as a house, a house where both African Americans and whites belong, in part because both groups speak English.[9] The stance that newcomers can be accepted only if they are willing to give up their own culture and adopt the culture of the United States reiterates the traditional assimilation imperative and the Anglo nativist stance, firmly planting African Americans as the indigenous minority of the United States.

Another prominent argument that emerged in the newspaper was the idea that the new immigrants were benefiting from all the contributions African Americans had made as builders of the nation. The letter to the editor about bilingualism and the use of language as an excuse to discriminate against blacks captures this view:

> It seems as though our people have been discriminated against more so since America has adopted an open door policy. Europeans, Asians, Latins, etc. can come to this country and produce on a grand scale at the expense of a people whose blood, sweat and tears are part of the foundation that makes this country what it is.[10]

This letter and those like it complain that Cubans and other immigrants were forcing their way of life on everyone else.[11] African Americans, having worked hard to establish themselves in the United States and to secure the civil rights that benefit other groups, were being run over and taken advantage of. The authors advocate that blacks should "stand up for what is ours." The idea here is that African Americans had earned a rightful place in the nation through their own efforts and thus should be rewarded and acknowledged as rightful worthy citizens of the nation. These critiques demonstrated that this African American perspective, which seemed to target Cubans as rivals, was also about an African American view that the federal government was responsible for the unequal treatment of African Americans and Cubans. Thus, in many stories that utilized a native/foreigner frame, we see an embedded acknowledgment or assertion that the division between Cubans and African Americans was actually an outgrowth of the federal government's mishandling of its responsibilities toward its African American citizens.

To some African Americans, the differential treatment of the two incoming refugee groups—Haitians and Cubans—amounted to a perpetuation of the United States' tradition of privileging white over black among the native-born. A letter to the editor, "South Florida's Goal: Keep out Haitians," illustrates how African American concerns about the differential treatment of Haitians and Cubans was related to their exasperation about the city's treatment of African Americans and neglect of their needs. Haitians are in fact mentioned only in the first sentence—the rest of the letter complains about the advantages and discriminatory behavior of Cubans toward African Americans:

> Why is it that the news media are always aligning the Cubans with Haitians, or for that matter with us blacks. Nonsense!! South Florida will do anything to keep out Black [*sic*] illegally at random. The only time the Cubans align

themselves with blacks is when it is to their advantage. It has become part of
the criteria for getting a job to speak Spanish. This takes jobs away from
blacks. Must we always be last. . . . I'm sorry but the "Cuban love affair is over."
Every black voter should vote against bilingualism because it is only the beginning! The other South American countries do not welcome the Cubans—
why should we?[12]

Ironically, while the letter criticizes the United States' plan to keep Haitians
out, it advocates keeping out Cubans. Stating that because Cubans jeopardize African American jobs, they should not be allowed to enter the United
States, it presents an argument often put forth by white nativists against all
immigration. The letter also makes reference to the ongoing bilingual debate
described in previous news reports and editorials. By November 1980, voters
had successfully passed the ordinance that repealed the Bilingual-Bicultural
Ordinance, making it now against the law to use Metro funds for any non-
English-language programs (García 1996). The passage of this ordinance
was testament that African Americans and Anglos in the local community
as a larger whole would come together to pass detrimental anti-immigrant
policies when inspired by nativist feelings of "threat."

The strong stance taken against bilingualism by some members of the
African American community is incongruous, given the paper's wide support
of Haitian immigrants. Haitians were also not English speakers (over 90 percent
are monolingual in Kreyol, a language without the number of speakers or the
international scope of Spanish), yet there was little mention in the newspaper of
conflict over language between Haitians and African Americans. Arriving in
such large numbers, Haitians were also potential competitors for jobs. Only one
article in the sample, by nationally syndicated columnist and civil rights leader
Bayard Rustin, acknowledges in passing that conflict also existed between African Americans and Haitians.[13] Besides this one acknowledgment, the majority
of the newspaper articles demonstrate an assumption that the blackness of Haitians represented a kinship between them and African Americans—a natural
alliance that erased economic, linguistic, and other lingering conflicts. The contradiction here of African American support of Haitians, who were also immigrants, illustrates the fact that while the immigrant/foreigner frame emerged
as a prominent ideological trope in the newspaper, it was not immigration per
se that African Americans were opposed to. Rather, they mounted a critique
of U.S. immigration policy on social justice grounds because they believed it

to be racially biased policy. The critique was fundamentally problematic, however, as it drew from and remained constrained by the white dominant black/white binary and "race" as the dominant frame.

Black Haitians versus White Cubans

Black activism strongly supported Haitians following a tradition of Pan-African idealism. Historically, early black leaders such as Booker T. Washington and Marcus Garvey emphasized connections between various black communities to rally people of African descent to fight their common oppression. Afrocentric thinkers such as Molefi Kete Asante have argued for the need to define a separate African identity because, as Asante asserts, "an African renaissance is only possible if there is an African ideology, distinct from a Eurocentric ideology, that allows African agency, that is, a sense of self-actualizing based upon the best interests of African people" (2003, 1). Such ideologies have circulated among African Americans, inspiring a common identity and social action. These ideologies rallied African Americans behind the Haitian migrants, not only to castigate the United States for its treatment of African Americans, but also to support Haitian migrants themselves. Thus, in the *Miami Times* (black) Haitians versus (white) Cubans emerged as a prominent theme.

The insistence on black Haitians over white Cubans makes sense when we consider how American black people are forced to live, and thus to use, the fiction of race. Race has been paramount in the U.S. political arena in struggles for economic, social, and cultural power. Thus, in a critique of the coverage of Mariel in the *Miami Times*, I do not wish to imply that the concept of race is or should be done away with; minority groups understandably cling to "race" as they seek to bring about change. As Stuart Hall argues, "[race] is also the principal modality in which the black members of that class 'live,' experience, make sense of and thus *come to a consciousness* of their structured subordination. It is through the modality of race that blacks comprehend, handle and then begin to resist the exploitation which is an objective feature of their class situation. . . . Thus it is primarily in and through the modality of race that resistance, opposition and rebellion *first* expresses itself" (1978, 347). Blacks learn that race matters through the ways they are treated, and then race (in the form of clinging to and affirming a black identity) becomes a primary way to resist that treatment, as we can see in the *Miami Times*.

The seeming preferential treatment of Cubans over Haitians strengthened African American opposition to Cuban immigration. Politicians, responding to negative stereotypes about Haitians (as AIDS carriers, for example), worked hard at keeping them out. But black churches, civil rights agencies, and human rights organizations galvanized strong support of Haitians and helped defeat some government efforts to restrict Haitian immigration and incorporation into U.S. society (Stepick 1992).[14]

The first reference to the Mariel events in the *Miami Times* was an op-ed by Ricky Thomas on April 17, 1980, during the same month that Mariel began, which reflected the strong African American community support for Haitians and set the tone for future reporting that conformed to a black/white binary. The author begins with a forceful statement about government favoritism for "white" immigrants: "The immigration policies of this nation are prejudicial and anti-black." He points to the widespread support the Cuban immigrants had from the exile community, which mobilized demonstrations, raised money, and collected food to help those at the Peruvian embassy. "On the other side of the immigration coin, while the Cubans were demonstrating, the lowly black Haitian refugees were in federal court fighting deportation, fighting for survival and the right to remain in this country as political refugees just like the Cubans." Thomas does not clearly explain why one should believe it is the government's fault that the exiles were supportive of the newcomers, but he aligns the Cuban exile community with the U.S. government—portraying the exile community as helping to support or influence immigration policy, while the Haitians have no supportive community (and thus African Americans should take on that role).[15]

To convince readers further, the columnist provides stories and testimonies of the harrowing experiences of the Haitian refugee seekers. For instance, a man recounts that Haiti's secret police, the Tonton Macoutes, had forced him to stand for four days in a cell, where all he had to drink was his own urine. With such testimonies, the columnist seeks to convince readers that the Haitian condition was horrible—arguing here that it is worse than that of the Cuban refugees:

> I don't buy the U.S. government's answers about one nation is communist and the other a dictatorship. If you are killed by the forces of a dictator you are just as dead as if it were by communist forces. . . . I am not against Cuban, Nicaraguan, Vietnamese or any other refugees who are admitted to this na-

tion. What I am totally against is the lilly white immigration policies of these United States which has an unwritten code which states, "if you're white you're right, if you're black go back." Write our U.S. representatives and tell them to stop treating our Haitian brothers and sisters unjustly.

The article calls into question the main defense used by the government for accepting refugees from communist countries over those seeking refuge for economic reasons. The author paints the Haitian situation as a human rights issue, asserting that the oppression experienced by groups seeking refuge should be what determines offers of asylum. The columnist seeks to expose a racist policy, but the larger climate of the Cold War and the ideology that supported it is reduced to mainly a racial issue. For instance, racism is discussed as if it is experienced only by those with black skin (and not by Cubans, Nicaraguans, and Vietnamese who fled communist regimes). Cubans are deemed to be "whites" and therefore favored by the U.S. government, whereas Haitians are constructed as the "brothers and sisters" of African Americans. The columnist speaks directly to the African American community: "So you see my people" and "So black folks, we must bring forth pressure upon our U.S. representatives." The piece calls for African American activism around immigration issues in solidarity with Haitians as members of a black diaspora.[16]

In "Cuban Sealift Illegal," another op-ed by the columnist Thomas, the author further indicates the belief that the Cubans are considered white immigrants and that Haitians were not receiving the same welcome in the United States because they are black. He complains about the many Cuban American citizens who took boats to pick up their compatriots leaving Mariel. He argues that even though "our" laws prohibit such actions and illegal immigration, "our governments from the national, state, county and cities are aiding and abetting them in the breaking of our American laws to illustrate the two kinds of justice which is practiced by our governments." The two types of justice Thomas refers to depend on whether the defendant is white or black. Besides stopping the boat lift, he advocates the following:

The other immediate thing which the federal government needs to do is to declare the Haitians political refugees, so they could come under the Federal Migrant Refugee Act and receive political asylum in this nation just as all other white refugees have received with open arms.

Thomas accuses the U.S. government of being willing to break its own laws to privilege whites and whiteness. The columnist contends that government officials would not take the appropriate actions to mobilize federal assistance for both the Cuban and Haitian refugees or stop the boat lift because they did not want to anger Cuban American voters. He petitions members of the black community to become involved, voice their concerns about U.S. immigration laws, mobilize, and put pressure on the government to listen to African American voices.[17] In his critique of Cuban American mobilization, Thomas depicts the concerns of Cubans and of African Americans as being directly oppositional to each other. As such, the op-ed adheres to a black/white binary that makes it impossible for Cubans and African Americans to be on the same team.

An editorial published a month later establishes an official newspaper viewpoint on the matter that corroborates the views of the columnist. Titled "Haitian Refugees Finally Noticed," the editorial maintains that the Mariel influx may have had the unintentional benefit of forcing leaders to deal with the Haitian refugees. The article opens with "It took an inflow of 24,000 new Cuban refugees in the past week to bring attention to the 25,000 Haitian refugees who have been here among us for two years." Although the piece calls for the equal treatment of both groups, the wording of the headline, lead sentence, and much of the article downplays the Cuban immigration in favor of a focus on Haitian immigration. This indifference toward Mariel Cubans is ironic, given that the article is about the indifference of the federal government toward the Haitian cause. The article reports that a coalition of Miami-Dade leaders voted to demand changes in the 1980 Refugee Act and more equitable treatment of Cuban and Haitian refugees.[18] The new attention to the Haitian case is viewed as a positive development for African American and local government relations: "It was a good move by the Dade County Coordinating Council because it comes at a time when many black citizens in this community are beginning to wonder if the county really gives a damn."[19] By underscoring the comparison between the plight of Haitian refugees and government inattention to African American concerns, the newspaper continually frames the Haitian issue as an African American issue. Government attention to the Haitian cause would amount to, finally, an affirmation that the concerns of African Americans truly mattered to the country. As the editorial illustrates, the concerns expressed in the newspaper over immigration policy are not about mounting a critique of the United States' treatment of immigrants and refugees in general, because little concern is displayed about the Cuban refugee situation and the obstacles they were encountering. Instead, the article implies that the contrast between the Cuban refugees and the Haitians is part of the same old story of white discrimination against blacks that African Americans have been experiencing for hundreds of years. As the paper depicted, race, and anti-blackness in particular, was at the heart of the differential treatment of the Haitians and Cubans. Rallying behind the Haitian cause, African Americans could continue their fight against anti-blackness as it took on new forms.

An op-ed written by prominent black leader Vernon Jordan, whose syndicated column appeared regularly in the paper, echoes the predominant sentiment of the *Miami Times*. The op-ed begins with the assertion that the government had been wishy-washy about its policy on the Marielitos, "but for those who managed to reach our shores, America has welcomed them, in the President's words, with 'an open heart and open arms.' But the Haitians [*sic*] refugees are the 'invisible boat people.'" As in other articles in the *Times*, Jordan questions the U.S. policy of assisting refugees from communist countries and not from others, such as those under the Duvalier dictatorship. He notes that "denial of basic human and political rights is hardly a monopoly of communist countries." Invoking the black/white frame in a reaction against it, Jordan asserts that race was most likely the reason for the differential treatment of Haitians:

> While immigration authorities implemented a deportation plan for Haitians, there was no such plan to deport Asians or Cubans as a "deterrent." Why? It is hard to escape the conclusion that race is a factor. Many white Americans may harbor prejudice against Asians and Hispanic people, but those feelings flower into brazen racism when they are confronted with blacks.

Jordan speaks to a hierarchy among racialized groups, arguing that although other minorities were discriminated against in the United States, the treatment was not as blatant as anti-black racism. Jordan's piece, like many of the other editorials and news stories related to Mariel, stands within a black and white framework, in which black oppressed "brothers and sisters" are pitted against other immigrants, particularly Cubans, or "foreign whites."[20]

The history of black disenfranchisement by whites in Miami had created a strict black/white binary opposition. As can be seen here, African American criticism of the United States' immigration policy was a predominant concern in the *Miami Times*—and the stark difference between how Cuban and Haitian migrants were treated helped feed into the conclusion that immigration policy mirrored domestic racism. The *Miami Times* critique was limited, however; a closer look at the case of the Marielitos would have revealed that it was not only Haitians who were being deported but also those deemed undesirable among the Cuban newcomers. Furthermore, the differential treatment of Afro-Cubans disrupts the idea that Cubans are simply "whites." Although race was a factor in the treatment of refugees, the predominant themes in the *Miami Times* did not capture the fact that other issues were at stake that influenced immigration policy, such as the fact that Duvalier was a puppet of the United States, whereas Castro was its avowed challenger. Seeing how the United States' treatment of the Cuban refugees was also part of a greater imperialist project is important to break down the black/white frame.

Overall, the views expressed in the *Times* allowed Haitians to be included within the African American community but expressly excluded Cubans. Ironically, seeking to fight against a black/white frame that positions whites as true Americans and blacks as unworthy to be citizens, the newspaper reaffirmed a politics of racial division by painting Cubans as "whites" with whom solidarity could not be built. Framing the racial politics of Miami in these strict black-versus-white terms followed a model that had been set up long ago, as whites enforced a strict separation between the races. What we see going on in the *Times* illustrates how oppositional relationships between minority groups stem from the fact that as they seek to affirm their place in the nation, they can get caught up in a web of zero-sum reasoning firmly entrenched in the culture of the U.S. nation.

Call for Unity among All Oppressed Peoples

Although the majority of the articles in the *Miami Times* covering Mariel and the influence of Cubans in Miami are generally negative, about a fourth of the articles also voice positive opinions. These articles express the civil rights agenda to preserve alliances between minority groups and to explain conflicts between the two groups with a critique of white racism. This more positive coverage demonstrates that the newspaper did not have one singular stance on the issue of immigration and Mariel. Indeed, studies indicate that, nationally, African Americans were generally supportive of immigrants in the 1980s and 1990s. Some scholars have argued that black support for immigration during this time reflected the ideals of black leaders and not of the general black public (Fuchs 1990). Yet, other studies demonstrate that black publics and not just black leaders also saw how the disenfranchisement of immigrants is related to that of African Americans (Jaynes 2000; Pastor and Marcelli 2004; Thornton and Mizuno 1999). For instance, analyzing data from the 1984 and 1988 National Black Election Study data sets, Michael C. Thornton and Yuko Mizuno (1999) found that African Americans who felt less economically secure were more likely to feel affinity with immigrants than African Americans who felt more secure, perhaps due to feelings of empathy. In addition, the study found that blacks who believed immigrants were in competition with them felt less close to whites, a sentiment that, according to Thornton and Mizuno, indicates a sophisticated assessment of how power works in society and a belief among African Americans that white racism may be the cause of the inequalities between marginalized groups. From their analysis of 2003 Gallup poll data demonstrating more positive black than white attitudes toward immigration, Manuel Pastor Jr. and Enrico A. Marcelli (2004) similarly argue that African Americans believed that the gains that could result from political coalitions with immigrants outweigh the other problems that could result from increased immigration. In their view, black values about equality and humanitarianism, more than economic realities, may shape opinions.

However, in the *Miami Times*, the voices of black leaders were prominent in supportive articles. The writings and actions of black leaders have been influential in swaying African American public opinion and political behavior concerning immigration throughout the twentieth century (Pastor and Marcelli 2004). In the 1980s, the *Miami Times* reports included stories about the NAACP's stand on immigration issues, and the paper ran regular or guest columns by leaders such as Vernon Jordan, Jesse Jackson, Bayard Rustin, and renowned African American scholar Manning Marable. Such articles about the stance of black leaders or columns from black leaders were much more supportive of the recent Cuban immigrants and the ideals of social justice for all. In his column titled "Bayard Rustin Speaks," the civil rights leader argues that the major political problem in Miami was the pitting of one oppressed group against another. He provides a wide view of some of the problems plaguing Miami at the time—the barbarism of white hate crimes; the African American response to racial inequality, including the recent McDuffie Riot; black unemployment and the depressed economy; and black fears about the Cubans arriving during Mariel. Rustin argues that:

> the widespread hatred and animosity of blacks toward the Cuban and Haitian refugees demonstrates that our economy of scarcity has at least succeeded in breaking the natural bonds linking the oppressed, the old strategy of "divide and conquer" has been resurrected, and black people have been distracted from the real sources of their problems by those who use refugees as convenient scapegoats.

Including Cubans along with Haitians, Rustin asserts a "natural" affinity between African Americans and other oppressed peoples, regardless of color, based on issues of social justice. He points to an outside source of conflict between the groups: the "powers that be" that manipulated and divided the groups, using immigrants as scapegoats. Rustin implies that the white power structure had not taken care of African Americans' concerns, which were exacerbated by the 1980s depression. According to his ideals, blacks and other oppressed groups should not feed into the divide-and-conquer tactic but instead work together to bring about the changes that had not yet come into fruition.[21]

A September 18, 1980, news story presents a similar view promoted by the greater Miami chapter of the NAACP. In "NAACP Decries Anti-Bilingual Petition," the NAACP argues that such an ordinance would affect not just the groups targeted (such as Spanish speakers) but also African Americans and jeopardize events celebrating Kwanzaa, for example. The NAACP contends that anti-bilingualism efforts support white supremacy, something blacks have been fighting against for centuries. The reporter of this story spoke to Dr. Bill Perry, president of the greater Miami chapter, who "compared the proposal to eliminate Dade's bi-lingual status with the way African slaves arriving in America had their native language taken away from them—'the first step in destroying us.'" The report shows how the NAACP situated the suffering of several minority groups within a larger context of white racism and aligned the black community with other minority communities.[22] An editorial, "Bilingualism Is Here to Stay," echoes some of these ideas, maintaining that blacks should accept the reality that (at the time) Dade County was close to 50 percent Latino, suggesting that bilingualism could be an asset, and advocating that black kids learn Spanish as well. Although the *Times* included some editorials supportive of the Mariel Cubans, no letters to the editor—that is, voices from the public—presented arguments supportive of Cuban immigrants. It is not clear whether the newspaper was not receiving such letters or if the paper chose to publish only those letters that represented the dominant opinion. Still, articles written by black leaders and other articles supportive of immigration demonstrate the complexity of African American–Cuban conflicts and serve as a reminder that there was no simple unified African American stance on the issue. The reception of the Marielitos was shaped by African American civil rights principles, the United States' historical treatment of African Americans, and local black experiences with Haitians and Cubans. Additionally, class differences may have influenced the extent to which members of black communities were supportive of immigrant communities (Gay 2006; Marrow 2011; Thornton and Mizuno 1999).

Cuban Brothers and Sisters?

Interviews conducted with Afro-Cubans currently living in Miami and the attention to Afro-Cubans in the newspaper point to the reality of a more complex picture when thinking about African American and Cuban relations. The larger presence of Afro-Cubans among Mariel refugees presented a challenge to the newspaper's simple binary between black and white and complicated the native/foreigner divide. As discussed in Chapter 2, between 15 and 40 percent of the Marielitos were black or mulattos (García 1996). Marielitos received intense scrutiny and were criminalized by other Miamians because they were perceived as fitting stereotypes commonly associated with blackness or African Americans (Hamm 1995). Although the Marielitos came from the same country with the same leader as the members of the exile community, their welcome by the federal government was not the same. On the whole, the *Miami Times* did not account for this complexity, asserting that the main reason for the difference in immigration policy toward Cubans and Haitians was racism rather than political ideology or economics, because Cubans were viewed as white. What to do, then, with black Cubans? If Cubans were white but black Cubans were benefiting from the same "liberal" polices toward white Cubans, could U.S. policy toward Cuban immigrants be attributed simply to racism?

Despite the predominance of the depiction of an African American/ Cuban divide in the *Miami Times*, the newspaper also exhibited a Pan-African idealism in stories that picked up on the fact that some of the Mariel newcomers were also black. The newspaper did acknowledge the existence of black Cubans, pointing out that "the new Cuban refugees are bringing a far larger number of blacks than the original freedom flights of 10 years ago."[23] When discussing black Cubans, the paper demonstrated more sympathy than it did toward "white" Cubans and pointed out the racism they experienced. Each time the paper reported on black Cubans, a photo was included, perhaps to demonstrate the dark color or "black look" of these Cubans.

The paper first took notice of black Cubans in an op-ed, "Reflection," by Haiba Jabali, who connects black Cubans to a black diaspora and declares that the concerns of black Cubans should also be the concern of African Americans. Discussing important current events in the international black world in the previous month, she critiques the oppression of blacks by other blacks:

> The suffering of Haitians are [*sic*] no different from the suffering of South Africans or the Afro-Cubans or the Jamaicans, or the Afro-Americans. Like the Cubans who jammed the streets of little Havana in Miami in support of their fellow countrymen, blacks too should rally behind supporting each others' efforts to break forth with human dignity, justice and freedom, and the basic necessities needed to live a decent life in today's world.

The op-ed paints Cuban American activism in support of Mariel as a positive phenomenon that should inspire African American action. The author advocates the unity of a larger black community beyond the United States. Her final thoughts affirm a reevaluation of Pan-Africanism, proclaiming, "together we will win."[24] The following month the same author wrote a feature story more directly focused on Afro-Cubans, titled "Afro-Cuban Refugee Point of View." The feature discusses how becoming resettled in the United States had been more difficult for Afro-Cubans than for their lighter-skinned compatriots. The author recounts what happened when she and an Afro-Cuban friend were shopping in downtown Miami. Her friend reprimanded some white Cuban women in Spanish because they had assumed that the Afro-Cuban friend was an African American and had warned that the two black women should be watched closely because they might steal something. The recounting of this story helps bring to life the similar experiences blacks regardless of national origin have in the United States.[25]

The editorial "Cuban Refugees and Haitian Refugees," discussed earlier, similarly acknowledges that blacks existed among the Cuban refugees and that they were discriminated against in the same ways as other blacks. While the editorial focuses on the differential treatment of Cubans and Haitians by the government, it also notes that very few black Cubans could be found in Miami because they were often singled out as having criminal records. A larger proportion of them were sent to federal correctional institutions or refugee sites such as the Elgin Air Force Base in Florida and Fort Chaffee in Arkansas. By making these connections about the similar criminalization of various black peoples in the United States, the author makes space for black Cubans to be joined with other blacks and for African Americans to support them.[26]

The idea that nonblack Cubans were rejecting black Cubans was also picked up by the *Times*. In a letter to the editor, "South Florida's Goal: Keep out Haitians," the writer was unsympathetic to the Cuban case except in critiquing the differential treatment of black and white Cubans. In a discussion of city plans to take down the tent cities and house unemployable Marielitos in African American neighborhoods such as Opa-locka and Allapattah, the letter writer asks, "Why not build housing in Hialeah [a Cuban neighborhood] or around 701 SW 27th Ave? It appears as if the nonblack Cubans are shunning the black ones that were brought here. They certainly are not getting the assistance and placement that their non-black brothers receive." Although the author does not find resemblance among African Americans and white Cubans, she points to the ways the local government and the exile community appeared to be making choices to place the people they found to be undesirable, who were also black, in African American neighborhoods. Such moves, according to the letter, demonstrate white disdain of African Americans and of black Cubans.[27]

Although African American and Cuban exile relations have been strained in Miami, the long history of amicable relationships between

African Americans and Cubans on the island could be drawn upon to promote solidarity. Nineteenth-century African Americans were aware of racism in Cuba and supported black Cuban struggles (Guridy 2010; Hellwig 1998). Before the Cuban Revolution, many prominent African Americans opposed U.S. involvement in Cuba in solidarity with Cuban blacks. This sentiment was reflected in the African American anti-imperialistic press (Brock and Castañeda Fuertes 1998). Cubans also have historically aligned with African Americans—in the 1930s, famous black Cuban poet Nicolás Guillén and other black Cuban voices sympathized with the plight of African Americans, criticizing U.S. imperialism and racism (Guridy 2010). Afro-Cuban immigrants who arrived in the United States in the nineteenth century and during the Jim Crow era found solace from white racism among African Americans as they built relationships with them (Greenbaum 2002; Guridy 2010; Mirabal 2003, 1998).

My interviews with Afro-Cuban immigrants reveal a continued tendency for Afro-Cubans to align themselves with African Americans to some degree in the present day.[28] The majority of respondents reported being mistaken as belonging to other groups—mostly African American, Puerto Rican, or Dominican but also Jamaican, Belizean, Brazilian, Panamanian, Trinidadian, Bahamian, Guyanese, Haitian, and African. Because they are often thought to be from these groups that share significant African heritage, Afro-Cubans are aware of their inclusion in a larger African diaspora. Contrary to research on immigrants of African descent, which highlights their desires to dissociate from African Americans (Bailey 2000, 2001; Duany 2005; Landale and Oropesa 2002; Waters 1999), these respondents seemed to look at this connection as a matter of fact and were not offended when people associated them with other black peoples.

For example, forty-one-year-old Lucy, who lives in Los Angeles and came to the United States in the early 1990s, is often mistaken as a member of other ethnic groups, based on her color. She said that in Cuba she would be considered a *mulata*, but in the United States people often think she is Puerto Rican or African American. She says, "That does not offend me [when people confuse me with another ethnicity] either. Because where did all black people come from? We are descendants of our ancestors who were slaves and through our past relatives." For the most part, many respondents distinguished black *Cuban* pride, but, like Lucy, they also acknowledged a brother- or sisterhood with other blacks because of their perceived racial features.

Some respondents spoke about preferring to socialize with African Americans rather than white Cubans or other Latinos because they felt more accepted by them or felt they had more in common with them. Ariane, a then twenty-two-year-old living in Los Angeles who came to the United States in 2004, noted how African Americans respond to him when he walks on the street and that they address him as they would a fellow African American. When they hear his accent, however, they are caught off guard and categorize him as not truly "black." Despite this, he explained, "I feel more comfortable with black Americans 'cause, I don't know if because it's the skin or I don't know but I feel, you know, we go out, we hang out, we talk, you know. It's almost the same [as with Cubans], you know." Ariane was hard at work earning his general equivalency diploma (GED) and working at a local Japanese restaurant, but when he is not working he enjoys playing basketball and dancing at a local dance club, where he often "shows off" his dance style. He complained about the freedom that is lost in the United States because one must always be preoccupied with work to be able to pay the rent and have basic necessities; he sees other groups as caught in that trap. He relates to the lifestyle of many of his African American classmates in his GED class who also include music and dance in their socializing. A voluntary association with African Americans could also be seen among interviewees who adopted African American Vernacular English (AAVE) in their speech.[29] As we will see in Chapter 5, using terms of endearment that made African Americans and Afro-Cubans part of an "us," such as referring to an African American potential coworker as a "brother" or criticizing nonblacks for being racists while still going after black "sisters" also signifies moves by some Afro-Cubans to align themselves with African Americans.

Nancy, the only interviewee who arrived in the United States before 1980 (in the late 1960s), illustrated how Afro-Cubans can also draw on African American cultural symbols along with Cuban ones to fight against the psychic challenges that come from bring denigrated for being black. She talked about how she responded to her U.S.-born granddaughter about the racism the child experienced at school:

One day, my granddaughter told me what happened to her in school . . . and [my granddaughter] replied that "I met another kid that told me that I was black." And . . . I told her . . . "Remember the greatest ones in our lives, how many were black?" "What was Martin Luther King?" He was not green. He was black but still he was Martin Luther King. "And, then, there's [Celia Cruz]. Look at the people who are legends, Nat King Cole. . . . . You are black, sweetie! Being black is not a problem unless people make it into one. Even blacks have come out with songs about being black and using the term. There are no good songs about the "white Blondie"; it's always about blacks—"La Negra Tomasa." We even dominate in that. Tell me where are the songs about the whitey with the green eyes or the spicy whitey, or the freckled one. But, there is "La Negra Tomasa." Then, Celia [Cruz] came out with the song "La Negra Tiene Tumbao" [The Black Woman Has Rhythm]. Take note: there are no songs about the white woman with punch or musical style. None.

Nancy's humorous response to her granddaughter draws on the connections between people of African descent as well as the assertions of pride that come through in songs by Latinos where "la Negra," or the black woman, is praised. In her response, she also reclaims figures of sexualized black women's bodies from the songs and imaginations of white Cuban men, advancing a black/ Afro-Latina feminist politics. Nancy shows the kinds of connections Afro-Cubans and other Afro-Latinas make to navigate the U.S. racial system that vilifies blackness, regardless of country of origin.

As history as well as the current context shows, bonds are forged between African Americans and Afro-Cubans (and black Haitians) as a matter of surviving anti-black racism, as a matter of principle and notions of pride, and because of interpersonal affinity. In the *Miami Times*, the majority of articles that brought readers' attention to black Cubans similarly express the idea that all black peoples in the African diaspora should unite, or at least they imply a natural link between black peoples. These connections disrupt the Cuban/black binary and also attest to the realities of anti-black racism, which fosters Pan-African idealism. Cubans complicate the idea of race alone being the factor for creating political bonds because in reality Cubans are white, black, and "mixed." Yet, in the *Times*, only identifiably black Cubans were included within the Afro-diasporic family. Appeals to Afro-diasporic identities that bonded African Americans with Haitians were not, for the most part, extended to all Cubans. Thus, the African American stance toward Cuban newcomers as depicted in the newspaper was limited by the black/white racial frame. Still, we are reminded that the desire and need for black Americans and black immigrants to bond together on the basis of a black identity is due not to a simplistic embrace of race as an organizing principle in society but to the fact of anti-black racism and discrimination that black people from various national origins experience in the United States.

Conclusion

The hard-fought battle for equality and justice for African Americans continues to this day. In Miami, the government's handling of the Cuban refugees helped divide Cubans from African Americans—by differences in aid and differences in the treatment of Cubans and Haitians. Such distinctions reinforced black sentiment that the United States' tradition of privileging white over black was perpetuated during Mariel. The century-after-century stability of the position of African Americans at the bottom of the racial order—their continued status as the "ultimate other" against which whiteness is constructed—contributes to African American "defensiveness" (Feagin 2010; Jordan 1977; Kim 2000; Noguera 2003). To overcome such positioning, some African Americans may invoke the construction of worthy citizenship or the native/foreigner frame. This stance is problematic because it relies on dominant exclusionary nativist ideals central to the creation of the U.S. nation. Yet the stance also points to the persistent need for the country to address the disparities blacks continue to experience.

In the Miami scenario, African Americans sought to overcome white denigration by organizing around and celebrating a black identity along with connections to other Afro-descendent peoples, like the Haitian newcomers. Organizing around a black identity has been historically important to African American conceptualizations of solidarity. Percy Claude Hintzen and Jean Muteba Rahier contend, because black identity has been "taken for granted" as a product of the politics of race in the United States, African American representations and practices "constitute *political* challenges to the Manichean juxtaposition of whiteness as superior and blackness as inferior" (2003, 2). Thus, by including other non-"native" blacks into the newspaper's identification of what constitutes the U.S. black community, the *Miami Times* invokes the black/white racial frame in its reaction against the mainstream view. It also acknowledges and attacks evaluations of whiteness and blackness such as those promoted in *El Miami Herald* coverage. In Chapter 2, I argued that *El Miami Herald* constructed the idea of "belonging" according to the black/white racializing frame. In this frame, ideas of behavior were racialized as white equals "worthy" and black equals "unworthy." This stance promotes the idea that groups can be proper and worthy citizens of the United States only when they achieve whiteness by conforming to sanctioned behaviors and adopting legitimized ideals. These ideals reflected those of the Anglo community in Miami and of the Cubans exiles who clung to the same ideals. In the *Miami Times*, we again see the strength and endurance of the black/white frame, but it is employed in a very different way as Africans sought to fight against it.

Ironically, the *Times*'s stance reaffirms dominant ideas about race by conforming to rigid constructions of a binary racial structure that leave out other complexities that determine immigration decisions, such as the United States' political relationships with other countries. In an effort to attend to the needs of the black community at the time of Mariel, African Americans included Haitians in their community and excluded Cubans. Such exclusion does not allow space for racial ambiguities, mixtures, and non–African American constructions of blackness, particularly as conceptualized by people from Spanish-speaking countries—such as the Afro-Cubans from whom we heard in this chapter. Furthermore, it denies the ways Cubans of various colors are linked, which makes strict separations between black and white Cubans impossible. Likewise, the political, economic, social, and racial problems in Miami are too interlinked to use a simple black/white binary as an explanation.

Afro-Cuban voices through their inclusion in and contributions to the newspaper as well as through my interviews illuminate some of these complexities. Indeed, the presence of Afro-Cubans among the Marielitos presented a challenge to the African American community's construction of Cubans as white and as competition. Still, the newspaper's overwhelming construction of Cubans as monolithically "white" and of Haitians as "black" erased possibilities for new alliances and sites for protest in Miami. Such constructions also erased the fact that all refugee issues are linked to black concerns of justice, although there are, indeed, specific differences between Haitian and Cuban waves that include but go far beyond, race. A more complex study on the actual plight of the Marielitos—and on Afro-Cubans and their relationships to other Cubans, African Americans, and the U.S.–Cuban political conflict—allows a closer look at the broader contexts of racism and imperialism affecting local conflicts.

Although there were far fewer supportive than antagonistic articles relating to Cuban immigration found in the *Times'* Mariel coverage, the supportive articles acknowledge the possibility of African American and immigrant coalitions and highlight the presence of Afro-Cubans. These articles point to the encouraging fact that many African Americans see that building coalition with immigrants can offer a solution to problems faced by black communities. In this coverage, the newspaper points to the agency African Americans (and immigrants for that matter) can exert to resist dominant racial orders such as the black/white binary and the native/foreigner frame. Negative ideas about Cuban immigration predominated in the *Times*, but there were still opinions that demonstrated a concern for the historical civil rights agenda and commitment to achieving solidarity with aggrieved groups regardless of color. In the next chapter, we return to these issues, as they relate to African American/Latino divides, and explore the role suffering plays in the mainstream framing of the worthy citizen narrative when another wave of Cuban exiles entered Miami fourteen years later.

Chapter 4

FRAMING THE BALSERO CRISIS

The Racial and Moral Politics of Suffering

In the years following the 1980 Mariel exodus, smaller numbers of Cubans were still making their way to the United States, but it was not until the summer of 1994 when the movement of people from Cuba to the United States was again conceived of as a crisis. During the Balsero, or "Rafter," crisis, more than thirty-five thousand people fled the harsh conditions of Cuba brought on by the fall of the Soviet Union. But rather than being viewed primarily as criminals and anti-socials sent by Castro, the Balseros were depicted as brave souls who fled Cuba voluntarily, on rafts they painstakingly made with their own hands. The risks taken by this group was portrayed in the nationwide media as the ultimate proof that the newcomers were indeed worthy of U.S. asylum. In contrast to the Marielitos, who had been viewed as a criminal threat, the Balseros retained the "anti-communist freedom fighter" image in large part because their intense suffering was made visible as they made their way across the sea.

Examining news coverage in the Cuban-run *El Nuevo Herald* and in the African American *Miami Times* between the dates of July 1 and December 31, 1994, within the context of the broader discourse about the Balsero crisis, this chapter explores the role suffering plays in the mainstream framing of the "good immigrant" and worthy citizen narrative. It sheds new light on the extent to which, for racialized native-born and immigrant communities alike, citizenship is implicitly understood as conditional, earned through suffering. I contend that this assumption establishes the grounds for interethnic conflict as different racialized/marginalized communities compete to improve their community's position by demonstrating their greater claim to suffering. As can be seen in the U.S. history of racism and in contradictory immigration policies, the government has placed value on the role of suffering for gaining the reward of U.S. national belonging, but this varies in particular political and historical moments. It also depends on who is suffering. While the citizenship of whites is often taken for granted, an unspoken requirement of U.S. citizenship for racialized groups has been that they suffer to prove their worthiness. As such, conflicts between racialized groups such as African Americans and Latinos nationally, and African Americans and Cubans locally, often turn into competitions over who has suffered the most. Such a competitive stance framed the discourse about the Balsero crisis found in *El Nuevo Herald* and the *Miami Times*.

The ethnic media coverage examined in this chapter, which centers on the differential treatment of Haitian "boat people" and Cuban Balseros, offers a lens through which to analyze not only the ways in which Cuban Americans and African Americans evaluated U.S. immigration and foreign policy but how they assessed the relative positions of their respective communities within the racial hierarchy of U.S. society. In Chapter 2, we saw that in 1980 a black/white frame more overtly racializing the Marielitos by distinguishing good/white immigrants from bad/black ones was prominent in *El Miami Herald*. During the Balsero crisis, however, a framing of the Balseros according to a worthy/suffering good immigrant narrative predominated in the renamed *El Nuevo Herald*. In response to the crisis, the government had made a dramatic policy decision that signaled it would continue closing the historically open door to Cuban immigration. Cuban exiles had further reason to believe their standing as worthy citizens was being eroded. The empathetic framing of the Balseros in *El Nuevo Herald* then reflected Cuban American support for compatriots who were newly affected by U.S. government moves that would become codified into more restrictive Cuban immigration policy. The newspaper's depictions of the newcomers' suffering also reflected a strategic move by some members of the Cuban American community to recapture their own position as "good immigrants" in the nation.

In contrast to the positive depiction of the Balseros in the *Herald*, the *Miami Times*'s Balsero coverage was similar to its Mariel articles in tone and subject matter. Reflecting African American sentiments, the newspaper continued the characterization of the newcomers as white immigrants being favored over black Haitians. Fourteen years after Mariel, the enduring high rate of poverty among Miami blacks and the growing political influence of Cuban leaders in contrast to the diminishing political clout of black leaders painted a bleak picture. As the *Times* coverage illustrates, even more so than during Mariel, moves by members of the community to invoke a native/ foreigner frame relied on the idea that the longer length of time of African American suffering casts them as more deserving of citizenship than Cubans. Though these frames are limited, African Americans strategically drew on the native/foreigner frame to resist the white/black racializing frame that has historically cast African Americans as noncitizens.

While a main goal of this chapter's analysis is to emphasize the problems inherent in accepting a white dominant exclusionary framing for asserting collective identities and community belonging, the chapter also underscores the underlying critiques being advanced by both communities as they turned the lens onto the U.S. government, indicting it for its own moral failures. The establishment of an identifiable "human rights regime" made the political climate in 1994 quite different from the Cold War climate of 1980 during Mariel. In this context, calling out the United States for rejecting morally upright Balseros who were the "good type" of immigrants who eschewed deviant behaviors and were willing to suffer for freedom, *El Nuevo Herald* demonstrates that in reality members of the Cuban American community understood the conditional nature of U.S. American citizenship. The *Miami Times* further uncovered contradictions in the idealization of suffering for worthy citizenship by pointing out that, despite having struggled as "true" or "native" U.S. citizens for ages, African American suffering continues in the present day without bringing about ultimate rewards.[1] Furthermore, African American concerns as they also took on the cause of black Haitians reveal the truth about the U.S. racial framework—that is, that blacks, whether foreign-born or native-born African Americans, cannot escape their constructions as "other" in some shape or form when compared to whiteness or "Americanness."

When we examine how Afro-Cubans figure in the polarization of African Americans and Cubans, we can start imagining ways to undo that polarization. The media discussions of the struggles of Afro-Cubans, both Balseros and earlier arrivals, were limited but nonetheless point toward alternative ways to understand the Balsero crisis and the racial origins and consequences of U.S. immigration policy and to generate new potential for collaborative rather than competitive relations between Cubans and African Americans. I focus on the instances when Afro-Cubans were included in the coverage and find that, by including Afro-Cuban voices, the papers did provide alternatives to the zero-sum characterization of Miami race relations. Indeed, the papers reflected greater recognition of the overlaps between the communities than they had during the Mariel boatlift. Afro-Cuban journalists' voices figured prominently in both *El Nuevo Herald* and the *Miami Times* in the months covered in this analysis. Including the contributions of Afro-Cuban journalists, specifically those of Dora Amador, an award-winning contributor to *El Nuevo Herald*, and Rosa Reed, an Afro-Cuban businesswoman who wrote her own column in the *Miami Times*, contributed to a more complex analysis of the interethnic conflict in Miami and of the meaning of the social, economic, and political change occurring in the nation as well as the local community.

The Economy of Suffering

The end of World War II, which saw the United States promoted to the status of "superpower," also saw the creation of a narrative in which the United States was not a racist empire but a savior and spreader of freedom to lesser nations (Espíritu 2006). We see this benevolent recasting not only in efforts to redeem the United States for war atrocities by painting war efforts as rescue missions, but the idea of U.S. benevolence is also prominently showcased in its "nations of immigrants" narrative (Espíritu 2006, 2014; Oxford 2008). Indeed, the inscription on the base of the Statue of Liberty, part of which reads, "give me your tired, your poor, your huddled masses yearning to breathe free," provides a strong narrative of national benevolence and care about human suffering associated with the identity of the nation (Espíritu 2014, 93; Oxford 2008). That the United States could have the capacity to take on the world's poor points to the nation's wealth, strength, and dominance in the world. But as we know, the United States does not take in all the world's tired and poor. Rather, it first ranks degrees of suffering to decide who is most worthy of inclusion. In this process, immigrants and refugees have had the burden of proving that they are indeed poor and needy and that they are the right type of immigrants who will eventually become good citizens (Espíritu 2006, 2014; Loescher 1986; Oxford 2008; Ticktin 2011).

As Yen Le Espíritu points out in the context of war, a narrative in which U.S. soldiers are always benevolent rescuers also requires some assumptions about the character of those rescued. Rescued "others," such as the Vietnamese refugees of the Vietnam War, are the embodied evidence of the justness of the war (Espíritu 2006). The co-optation of "the rescued" is also problematic because along with being used to legitimize state violence, it perpetuates the subordinated positioning of the "other" (Ticktin 2011). As Miriam Ticktin argues, the humanity of those seeking care (such as asylum) from powerful nations often goes unrecognized unless they can prove they are "morally legitimate suffering bodies." As such, they become subjects of care only as long as they remain disabled (Ticktin 2011, 4). Because of such conditions, an economy of suffering is born—for those seeking inclusion in the nation, suffering becomes an oddly desirable condition (Ticktin 2011). And since the United States rank orders suffering, it creates conditions wherein immigrants and minorities must vie for their place within a hierarchy of suffering. The tendency in the United States to rank suffering (and worthiness) is problematic not only because it obfuscates the fact that inequality is structurally enforced, but because the resulting hierarchies are anchored in a binary racial frame that holds conceptions of blackness (or unworthiness) as the extreme negative end and worthiness (whiteness or near whiteness) at the other. As such, the hierarchy makes (human) rights a zero-sum game.

Yet, the establishment of an identifiable "human rights regime" by the time of the Balsero crisis helped provide for disenfranchised groups a legitimized language for holding nations responsible for inattention to their suffering. In 1948, the United Nations drew up a document setting out the idea that human rights should be the concern of all nations and that nations should work together to ensure that human rights are universally protected. In 1994, the abolition of apartheid in South Africa would be a major milestone illustrating worldwide commitment to these aims. The end of apartheid, negotiated in part by Nelson Mandela, came also because of sustained pressure from various nations, including the United States, in the form of sanctions, among other pressures. For African Americans looking on at the victory in South Africa, the same human rights narratives used to argue against apartheid could be used to indict the United States for its continued disenfranchisement of African Americans. In the 1990s climate, Cubans too increasingly began to use the narrative of human rights in their political organizing to remind the United States of its obligation to work toward the defeat of Castro (García 1996). In reality, such narratives already underlay the designation of Cubans as being worthy of rescue in the first place. Throughout the 1980s, the Cold War efforts to fight communism had led to U.S. decisions to invite refugees from communist countries in Southeast Asia as well as continuing its open-door stance toward Cubans. Notwithstanding that such moves were less about care for these refugees than U.S. imperialist projects in these regions of the world, these decisions gave the message that political repression had a sort of value in terms of who was worthy of U.S. inclusion— political repression has been ranked higher than other forms of oppression in terms of how legitimate suffering is defined (Espíritu 2006, 2014). In the Cuban case, by deeming the Castro government more oppressive than others with the Cuban Adjustment Act of 1966, the United States had made Cuban suffering both desirable and normative. In the context of the circulating narratives about human rights, Cuban Americans ramped up this line of logic in their political organizing around their fight for Cuba and for their incoming Cuban compatriots (García 1996).

Still, in spite of the prominence of "human rights" as a political narrative, U.S. internal racial issues belied a strong contradiction. Since the 1980s, the United States had begun rolling back the civil rights victories meant to help African Americans, such as affirmative action and programs designed to fight poverty (Lipsitz 2006; Steinberg 1995). In the early 1990s, under George Bush Sr.'s leadership, it continued with these efforts. The continued power of anti-black racism in the United States was also made overt in the 1991 beating of Rodney King, an African American male, by four white police officers in Los Angeles, California. That the beating was captured on film for all to see served as a "wake-up call" for a nation perceiving itself to be getting closer and closer to a postracial society. In 1994, the country was still reeling from this event, as well as from the aftermath of the notorious 1992 Los Angeles Riot, which was in response to the acquittal of the officers involved. At the same time, while the increasing diversity of the nation due to immigration had been cited by some as evidence of the nation's growing racial tolerance, there was also a profound backlash. The economy had shifted after the deindustrialization of the 1970s, and during the 1980s and 1990s, there was increasing demand for low-skilled labor. Yet at the same time, anti-immigrant sentiments rose, as evidenced by the 1994 passage of Proposition 187, a bill seeking to deny undocumented immigrants in California social services and education, and by the proliferation of nativist discourses in the public and media as society reacted to the growing presence of Latinos (Lipsitz, 2006; Santa Ana 2002). The continued opposition to African American civil rights gains and the backlash against immigration illustrate that while liberal democracies claim to care about human rights and refugee protection, human rights codes end up becoming difficult to implement as humanitarian goals become incompatible with other national interests. Public concerns about national security and the impact of incoming refugees and immigrants on limited local health and social services can turn political leaders against those seeking care from powerful nations (Greenhill 2010; Stedman and Tanner 2003).

The contradictions inherent in the United States' national myth recur in the contradictory treatment of Cuban and Haitian boat people. As African Americans and Cuban Americans looked at the inconsistencies in foreign policy decisions as well as local racial politics in 1994, it became increasingly clear that the United States was not fully on the side of African Americans nor of Cuban Americans. Still, the contradictory treatment of the Haitians and Cubans seeking U.S. refuge was the basis for contentions between Miami Cubans and African Americans during the Balsero crisis as human rights became a zero-sum game. In the next sections, I discuss three primary contradictions in relation to the Cuban and Haitian influx that framed these local opinions: shifts in foreign policy that differentiated previous waves of Cuban exiles from the incoming Balseros; the differential mainstream views of Marielitos and Balseros; and the differential immigration policy and views of the mainstream public with regard to Haitians and Cubans.

1994 Policy Shifts and Cuban Political versus Economic Migrants

The Balsero crisis signaled the closing of the historical open door to Cuban refugees. The U.S. government had begun reversing its open-door policy shortly before Mariel with the Refugee Act of March 1980, which made

Cuban acceptance into the United States less automatic and determined on a case-by-case basis (Masud-Piloto 1996). On August 18, 1994, in a historic move, President Bill Clinton went even further: he announced that Cuban refugees found at sea would no longer be brought to the United States, and he ordered twelve navy and coast guard vessels to patrol the seas and transport incoming Balseros back to Cuba (A. A. Fernández 2000).

The Balsero crisis happened at a time when Cuba was going through a period of extreme economic deterioration, known as the "special period."[2] In response to conditions wherein food, water, electricity, and medicine had to be rationed due to profound economic scarcity and political instability after the fall of the Soviet Union, discontented Cubans set out en masse for the United States in *balsas*, or homemade rafts. The rafts, made of inner tubes and various kinds of scrap material, were crafted with great ingenuity and creativity. But trusting the safety of these *balsas* in the unpredictable sea was a dangerous endeavor. Still the Balseros kept coming; in January 1994 the U.S. Coast Guard rescued 248 people; 1,010 in July; and 21,300 by August (Ackerman and Clark 1995). In an effort to avoid "another Mariel," wherein uncontrolled numbers of people streamed to U.S. shores, the Clinton administration brought the Balsero crisis to an end by instituting a policy known as "Wet Foot, Dry Foot," which allowed only those Cubans who made it to dry land without being discovered by the U.S. Coast Guard to remain in the United States. Those Cubans who did make it to U.S. shores would be sent immediately to the Krome Detention Center in Miami for processing or a hearing, but Cubans caught at sea would be sent to Guantánamo, the U.S. naval base in Cuba, or "safe havens" in other countries (Henken 2005; Soderlund 2003). The impact of the crisis on the local Miami community was lessened by the government's actions to stop the exodus, as 55 percent of the Balseros caught at sea were taken to Guantánamo (Soderlund 2003). Cubans in Guantánamo, Clinton decreed, would be held there indefinitely (Greenhill 2002). In May 1995, President Clinton loosened his stance and agreed to gradually allow the Guantánamo refugees into the country over the next nine months. But his hard line against immigration directly from Cuba remained; unless Cubans seeking refuge made it directly to U.S. soil on their own, any Cubans caught at sea would be taken back to Cuba (Henken 2005).

Researchers speculate several reasons for the new hard-line stance against Cuban refugees. By the 1990s, the Cold War had ended and the United States had less reason to be concerned with Cuba and fighting communism (Nack-erud et al. 1999; Soderlund 2003). Under George Bush Sr.'s leadership, the United States had moved on to the war in Iraq and a focus on the Middle East. Now, in September of 1994 under Clinton, the United States had a focus on reinstating Haiti's ousted leader, Jean Bertrand Aristide, and was gearing up to invade that country. Clinton also desired to avoid the backlash he experienced when, as governor of Arkansas, his welcoming of Marielitos to Fort Chaffee and his responses to the riot there cost him reelection (Henken 2005). As president, he could not ignore the fact that, although mainstream media generally depicted the Balseros positively (Ackerman 1996; Soder-lund 2003), public sentiments opposing the newcomers also ran high (Masud-Piloto 1996). Whatever the reasons for the new policy moves, for Cubans, the government's dramatic and official declaration that they were no longer auto-matically "good immigrants" proved that their community's welcome was more tenuous than the previous open-door policy had suggested. The Balse-ros came to be viewed as economic immigrants rather than political refugees, and the new restrictive Cuban policy positioned earlier Cuban arrivals as more worthy of asylum than recent arrivals, despite that they were all fleeing the same country and the same leader.

Marielitos and Balseros in the Public Eye

A second primary contradiction can be seen in the differing public attitudes toward the 1980 Mariel entrants and the 1994 Balseros more specifically. Given that the media had depicted the previous wave of Cuban migrants, the Marielitos, so negatively, how can we understand the more positive main-stream media image of the Balseros? As mentioned earlier, despite the government's official stance, the mainstream media (in contrast to the local Miami Anglo media) were more supportive of the Cuban point of view re-garding the Balseros and more critical of Clinton's foreign policy. Media schol-ars offer a possible explanation; when political elites are in conflict, the media is more likely to be less affirming of their ideals and can even be highly critical of the political establishment at such times (Hallin 1986; Robinson 2002). Conflict between political elites with regard to Cuba and Haiti was highly visible in that the government's foreign policy (restrictions on Cubans and moves to invade Haiti) was unpopular among both Democratic and Republican party politicians.[3] The parties' position was in line with the sentiments of the general public. As Piers Robinson (2002) argues, the media framing of news relies on the ideals of the public to produce a product that increases its profitability because it connects with their commonsense ideals. Toward the goal of staying in step with the buying public, it is likely that the dominant framing of the events by the mainstream media echoed the ideals of the public as well as the political dissatisfaction with President Clinton's foreign policy (Girard 2004; Soderlund 2003).

Along with this explanation, I contend that empathetic media framing (Freedman 2000; Robinson 2002, 28) of the Balsero crisis was effective because, unlike Mariel, when the arrival of thousands of criminalized Cubans in Miami had a profound economic and social impact, the relative distance from actual Balseros (resulting from their containment on Guantánamo) allowed the public to view this influx as less of a threat. The smaller overall local impact of the Balseros as compared with the Marielitos demonstrated that the Balseros would not be a drain and created an opening through which the public and politicians could jump on a humanitarian band wagon and criticize the government for being restrictive in its immigration policy. As a result, the media and politicians could affirm a public impulse to reclaim the narrative of the United States as a nation of immigrants—the ideal and welcoming haven for the world's tired, poor, and needy. Despite the fact that U.S. interest in Cuba was waning with the winding down of the Cold War, the long-held sentimental view of Cubans as anti-communist freedom fighters still had currency, affirming an idealized view of the U.S. nation.

Differing Public Perceptions on Haitians and Cubans

The third major contradiction is the same that manifested during Mariel, the different views and policies toward Cubans and Haitian refugees. In 1994, the United States was still in the middle of a debate over the handling of the Haitian and Cuban refugees. By 1994, political unrest and poverty in Haiti had reached stunning proportions, causing some Haitians to leave on rafts for the United States.[4] Thus, the arriving Haitians were also "Balseros" because they were attempting to come to the United States on rafts. But the fact that they were being taken to Guantánamo and not accepted into the United States received much less vocal opposition from the U.S. public.[5] Images of human suffering, risk, frustration, and tragedy that provoked primarily empathetic depictions in pictures and video footage of the Cuban Balseros did not seem to provoke the same reactions in the public when the sufferers were Haitians. Moreover, Congress and the general public disagreed with President Clinton's Haitian invasion plan, not seeing Haiti as a priority. Nevertheless, Clinton moved forward with his plan to stave off a mass exodus from Haiti and boost his personal and foreign policy credibility (Girard 2004).[6]

As they had in 1980, African Americans continued to be vocal in their support of Haiti and Haitian immigrants. Some political scientists maintain that Clinton's new policy was a response to the Congressional Black Caucus's accusations of discrimination against Haitians (Girard 2004; Vanderbush and Haney 1999). Clinton actively developed strong relations with his African American constituency after they played an essential role in electing him president in 1992, when 82 percent of blacks voted for him. He maintained a high approval rating among African Americans throughout his presidency; it was even at 90 percent during his impeachment (Girarad 2004; Vanderbush and Haney 1999). Clinton leaned on black leaders for advice and recognized that he owed much of his success to the black community. Clinton's policy change, which would treat Haitians and Cubans more equally, and his decision to invade Haiti were viewed as positive moves to attend to the African American voices that had been largely ignored by past presidents. For his African American constituents, the new developments under Clinton would be a small victory, but the differential view of the worthiness of Haitians and Cubans by political elites and members of the public provided another reminder that the tired and poor narrative did not extend to all suffering groups.

Reports in *El Nuevo Herald* and the *Miami Times* captured some of the views of members of Miami's African American and Cuban American communities, as they evaluated the contradictions in U.S. foreign and domestic policy that affected their own communities' standing in the nation during the Balsero crisis. In the context of the rise of an identifiable human rights regime, both groups realized suffering was an unspoken requirement of "worthiness" for citizenship and that, perhaps, identifying themselves with suffering could give them a better chance at acceptance.

The Morality of Citizenship in *El Nuevo Herald*

The United States' new policy moves reawakened the "us versus them" or "reactive ethnicity" impulse that stimulated Cuban unity during Mariel (Portes and Stepick 1994). Rallying to support their compatriots, Miami Cubans staged mass protests.[7] *El Nuevo Herald*, which by 1994 had become an independent paper led by Cuban writers and editors and had become more accepted as the voice of Cuban Americans (Soruco 1996), supported such actions by taking on the function of a sounding board for frustrated Cuban Americans. Functioning much like today's social media, the *Herald* acted as an advocate for Cuban Americans and refugees in many ways—including things like providing lists of names of arriving refugees, soliciting help, and allowing people to make pleas for help finding their relatives. Thus, in contrast to the marked ambivalence the paper exhibited in its depictions of the Marielitos in 1980, the *Herald* depicted overwhelming support of the Balseros.[8] The positive reports are primarily human-interest stories with a sympathetic focus on individuals' lives and stories reporting on community efforts to help the newcomers. The stories describe the separation of family members, the anguish of the search for their relatives, and the joys of family reunification.

A popular sentiment among Cuban Americans, expressed in *El Nuevo Herald*, was the idea that the United States had turned its back on them and their cause. The United States' actions were framed as a moral failure that privileged "national interests" over human lives:[9]

> Almost overnight, the alliance between Washington and the anti-Castro Cubans began to unravel. In the same way that the drama in Cuba is reaching a critical stage, the nation that has taken in so many Cuban immigrants looks as if it's closing its doors, pockets, and heart.[10]

The Cuban critique pointed out that nothing had changed in Cuba to make Cubans less worthy of asylum—Castro was still in power. What had changed were U.S. interests, not the reality of Cuban suffering. Thus, because the United States' original promises were predicated on its acknowledgment of Cuban suffering, Cubans drew on these criteria to affirm the idea that their status should not be changed. In the reports, Castro remained demonized for his role in creating conditions Cubans would need to flee. But President Clinton also emerged as a traitor and a new enemy of the exile community.[11]

The focus on Clinton as an individual actor worked to shift the blame from the nation as a whole. Yet Clinton's moves were far from an aberration; they were in line with a historical pattern of governmental decisions designed to satisfy U.S. imperialist needs. Indeed, in the context of the United States' investment in the Cold War, Cubans functioned as important "political weapons" for discrediting the Castro government (Greenhill 2010). As Ted Henken points out, "The U.S. would continue to readily accept Cubans as political refugees because their exit was symbolic proof both of the repressive nature of Cuban Communism and the attractiveness of U.S. democracy" (Henken 2005, 396). Furthermore, Clinton's Cuba policy change matched the increased anti-immigrant sentiment that could be felt in 1994 among local Anglos and in the nation as a whole. The government's response to the Balsero crisis, like the Mariel exodus, exposed the reality that Cubans were not exempt from being used as pawns of the United States. Hence, as during the Balsero crisis Cubans came to be depicted as "aliens" attempting to enter the United States illegally for the first time (Masud-Piloto 1996; Pedraza 1996), the Balsero crisis forced the exile community to come to terms with the fact that despite their suffering, they were no longer exceptional or favored. According to the logic of worthy citizenship, during Mariel, the "evidence" of deviance among some Marielitos had "rightfully" required explanation, and *El Miami Herald* demonstrated how a "blackening" of deviant Marielitos was enacted by some members of the Cuban American community to distinguish them from the good Marielitos and from the members of the established exile community. But in the absence of "evidence" of deviance among the Balseros, the fact that the U.S. government was now criminalizing "innocent" Balseros was too much of a contradiction for many Cuban Americans.

Strategically, depicting the Balseros as suffering and courageous figures who braved great dangers to escape Cuba could possibly convince the public that automatic refugee status should be restored. As such, *El Nuevo Herald* focused on the pain and suffering the Balseros endured as they set out on the high seas through the dramatic retelling of the exodus in news articles and editorials. In this example, the courage of the Balseros is highlighted:

> Not even the possibility of death in the Florida straits nor an uncertain fate in the refugee naval base daunted the Cubans. A nation's general sentiment is repeated. "It is preferable to die at sea or end up someplace else than in the prison that is Cuba." And the rafters continue arriving.[12]

Portraying Castro's regime as so horrid that Cubans would risk all to come to the United States, the paper's stance was a reminder to the U.S. government that Castro remained an enemy of the United States. News accounts paint pictures with words to make the newcomers' suffering and passion to start a new life palpable. For instance, a news story about a woman who lost her son at sea captures the refugees' intense desire. The woman recounts, "The United States was his passion. . . . More than once he told me that he preferred to be eaten by an American shark because in Cuba there was one that was devouring him slowly."[13] Using the metaphor of "political sharks" (which brings to mind the oceanic sharks that claimed the lives of many of the Balseros who did not make it) and characterizing whatever dangers or mistreatment the Balseros might encounter in the United States as preferable to Castro's regime, the stories reaffirm the idea of the obligation of the United States to put an end to this suffering and continue to serve as a place of refuge.

In addition to the dramatic retelling of events, the newspaper invoked even more sympathy by focusing specifically on the children involved in the crisis. For example, an article titled "With Every Raft That Leaves, Cuba Is Bled Dry" describes the plight of an eight-year-old child who was the only one in his group to survive the voyage to freedom:

> On Monday, an eight-year-old child by the name of Daniel Bussot was the only survivor of a vessel on which six persons traveled. Moments before the child witnessed the way in which a storm spilled the others into the sea, his mother placed her only life vest around his body, and his father placed him on the other accompanying boat. There have been other children like Daniel since the exodus defined as another "Mariel." But their stories, like the tales of those arriving, have come to us in undefined and impacting waves. Meanwhile, as the survivors blend in with the population, we prepare for another Mariel.[14]

The image of the boy's parents sacrificing themselves to save his life and the thought of his parents and the other travelers all losing their lives is heartbreaking. The words used to describe the story encouraged the community to mobilize to help the newcomers as they did during Mariel. The reference to the fact that other children have similar stories of tremendous loss or of being the lone survivor reinforced the magnitude of the risks involved in the

Balseros' journey and the impact of the journey on the most innocent people caught in the fray—children.

News reports utilize stories about children to criticize the governments of both Cuba and the United States. The poverty of Cuba is highlighted by emphasizing the prosperity of the United States in this story of a child and her mother rescued by the Coast Guard:

> Bravo and her two-year-old daughter were taken to the hospital, Lower Florida Keys Health System, so that the child could receive medical attention. Aboard the Coast Guard vessel, the *Monhegan*, she suffered a small wound to the head. In front of various members of the press, the child, restless and hungry, said, "Mommy, milk." Out of habit, her mother responded, "There is no milk." But, Arturo Cobo, director of the Transit Home for Cuban Refugees, near Key West, interrupted, "Yes, there is milk. There is milk in abundance.[15]

The image of the mother from Cuba finally being able to ease her child's hunger in the United States, where "there is milk in abundance," offers a heartwarming portrait of the United States as a safe place for children and indicts Cuba for its abuses of the most vulnerable of its population.[16]

The plight of children was also used to demonstrate the inhumanity of Clinton's policies. In one news story, a spokesperson for the Valladares Foundation, an organization that helped the Balseros, argues that the Clinton government was using children as sacrificial lambs: "'That is criminal,' said Valladares. 'They are using [the treatment of] these children to discourage others from leaving Cuba.'"[17] It is noteworthy that rather than indicting the parents for child abuse for risking their children's lives at sea, the governments of the United States and of Cuba are criticized in these articles. Instead, the parents are depicted as people who should be praised for saving their children from a worse fate: life in Cuba.[18]

In later months, numerous news stories focusing specifically on the plight of the Cubans held in Guantánamo continue the theme of suffering, advancing a harsher view of the United States and the new policy change. The stories depict the horrors of Guantánamo, documenting the heat, sickness, shortages of food and supplies, and unmet needs of the elderly and children being held there. In one story, the plight of children is underscored, as a doctor there emphasizes the fact that Guantánamo is no place for children:

"This is a military base. Here we have medication for war-related emergencies, not for children."[19] Other stories point to the good character of the detainees in Guantánamo to criticize the new policy change as unjust. The very act of holding the Balseros at a military base is viewed as an insult because it suggests that they are criminals:

> The wake-up call needs to be sounded loudly in face of the agony of thousands of rafters who throw themselves into the sea and who today are held at Guantánamo Naval Base or in Panama. The exile community, with its force in numbers and influence, has to make its presence felt in favor of those brothers subjugated to an inhumane confinement they don't deserve because they are not criminals; they're men, women, and children who risked their lives in the pursuit of liberty.[20]

The implication here is that if the Balseros were truly criminals, they might deserve exclusion, but they seek only freedom, a goal that does not merit punishment and should instead be rewarded. The stark difference between the image of the Balseros and the criminal "bad immigrant" is driven home here and also in other stories that emphasize that many of the twenty thousand adults held in Guantánamo were professionals and many held university degrees; they included doctors, teachers, sculptors, artists, engineers, carpenters, dancers, electricians, and plumbers.[21] The sympathy shown in *El Nuevo Herald* for the "brothers and sisters" of the Cuban American community—regular people with education and skills who were being mistreated in Guantánamo—expresses the Cuban American disappointment and anger that the worthy Balsero immigrants were being wrongly excluded from the United States and denied access to the American Dream and the immigrant success story.

Reports on the tireless efforts of Cuban Americans from all walks of life to help the Balseros portray a Cuban community unified in their welcome. With the expression "at least you are helping your own," a Cuban American service agency employee working to help incoming Balseros settle in Miami poignantly captures the message emanating from articles on Cuban American efforts to support the Balseros:

> "I am tired, very tired," a 57-year-old employee, who declined to give her name, said as she walked home at noon on Thursday after a tiring workday.

The woman said that she began to work on Wednesday at 8 a.m., the day that 225 rafters were processed, without going home. On Thursday, a larger number of refugees were to be processed. But she did not complain. "It's lovely to do this work," she said. "At least you are helping your own kind."[22]

Such stories reveal that members of various segments of the Cuban American community, including high-profile Cuban American stars, singers, athletes, and politicians, along with ordinary citizens and children, helped the Balseros. For instance, through descriptions of pictures drawn by the youngest members of the exile community for the refugees at Guantánamo, an article elucidates several factors that promote Cuban American unity—a shared disdain for Fidel Castro; the idea that Cubans, regardless of immigration status, are part of a cohesive family unit; and the music of popular Cuban American singer Willy Chirino:

> Some students drew small vessels, peace symbols, or American and Cuban flags. Another made a map showing the distance between Havana and Miami. Another drew happy faces and cited verses from a popular song by Willy Chirino: "And, still they are arriving." One child, specifically, drew Fidel Castro, within a circle intersected by a line, in the style of the "no" icon, made popular by the film, *Ghostbusters*.[23]

In this story and others illustrating the high level of Cuban American involvement in rallying to the Balseros' cause, the newspaper reinforces the view that the new immigration policy and the plight of the Balseros was, and should be, the concern of every Cuban American.[24]

But despite the fact that the Balseros are depicted as worthy of help simply because they are fellow Cubans, an underlying message in several articles, such as those described earlier that eschew a criminal image and argue that the Balseros were potential assets to the United States, is that this value depends on the extent to which the newcomers conform to moral notions of worthy citizenship. A story about how a recently arrived Balsero directly benefited from the support of the Cuban American community suggests that the Balseros would not be a liability for the United States because they had a bootstrap mentality. In the story, the Balsero, named Mojena, highlights how he fits the U.S. ideal for citizenship: "'After arriving, I did not take benefits or anything. Not Medicaid or anything else,' confirmed Mojena, who is from Marianao, a suburb of Havana. 'If one looks around, one finds work because there are jobs to be found here. One has to begin little by little, doing anything while you move ahead.'"[25] Ironically, Mojena boasts that he did not need social services, but the article focuses on how he benefited from the intense mobilization of Cuban American organizations on behalf of the Balseros. Such resources and support from the strong Cuban American enclave and their network of community aid put him in a position where he could avoid requesting welfare and Medicaid, unlike other poor immigrants or racialized groups without U.S.-based networks. Nevertheless, his statements about coming to the United States and starting from the bottom without public aid affirm the idea of the good immigrant who arrives willing to work at anything to succeed (Espíritu 2006, 2014; Saito 2001). Hence, this and other supportive articles invoke a morality frame by implying that the Balseros are the right "type" of immigrants. The language in the paper also points to what characteristics would make one the "wrong" type of immigrant—criminals and those merely seeking handouts. The right type not only shares the proper moral characteristics but also has the skills that can ensure upward mobility. Most of all, as their voyage has proven, they are worthy because they are willing to suffer to become Americans.

The *Herald* coverage affirmed white Anglo elites' moralistic framing of the requirements of worthiness, but it also continued to raise questions about the nation and its failures to meet moral obligations to its citizens. Here, a Miami lawyer is cited who argues that the United States should have already intervened in Cuba, as advocated by the Cuban exile community. He argues that Haitians in 1994 were in a better position than Cubans. This, he argues, is because the United States planned military intervention in their country, which would allow Haitians to return home, but was not moving to overthrow Castro:

> "The legal situation of the Cubans held at the Guantánamo Naval Base is different than that of the Haitian refugees, and the solution to the rafters' dilemma lies in the political pressure that members of the exile community may exert," said Miami lawyer, William Allen. "Haitians have a realistic chance that the government of their country will change. . . . At this moment, there is no hope for Cubans. That is why their asylum requests would be very different."[26]

This story points out contradictions in foreign policy toward Cubans and Haitians, yet the position advanced contrasts sharply with views expressed in the African American *Miami Times*, where Cubans are portrayed as having the advantage. Notable here is that a politics of division is invoked as the criticism being made is constructed by setting up an oppositional relationship between Cubans and Haitians.

An editorial pointing out that Cuban Americans have often been accused of being *una minoría mimada*, or "a spoiled minority," criticizes the United States by insisting that it must reaffirm its commitment to its citizens who have already proven themselves through suffering and contributing as "good immigrants." The article portrays the Cuban American identity as inextricably tied not only to the idea of exile and possible return to Cuba but also to being American and "favored" in America. The author argues that the "spoiled" stereotype has always been false because the United States' stance toward Cuba and Cuban Americans is the appropriate and just response to a "despotic regime." Further, he insists, the allegation that Cubans are a spoiled minority overlooks the fact that Cubans work hard and make sacrifices and that their conservatism stems from their gratitude for the nation that took them in. The detention of the Balseros in Guantánamo, the author argues, is further proof against the stereotype.[27] Articles such as this demonstrate an embrace of the idealized requirements of U.S. citizenship. That the country could betray them, however, exposes the limited benefit of embracing such requirements of whiteness and moral superiority.

Cubans could see that the nation-of-immigrants narrative did not consistently hold true in the U.S. treatment of them and that their suffering would not always be rewarded. The United States was motivated by something other than humanitarian concerns. During the Balsero crisis, some members of the wider public followed an impulse to reaffirm the white mainstream idea that when the right people were suffering from the right conditions, the United States would respond. Furthermore, the United States had established the rules by which the Cubans were required to play when it declared their government dangerous and Cubans as worthy suffering immigrants with the Cuban Refugee Adjustment Act of 1966. But unlike European immigrants, who could by the third generation become whites or generic "Americans" (Waters 1990), Cubans found that even after having suffered for citizenship, their whitened status could be revoked as the imperialist goals of the United States shifted.

"What About Haiti?" The Politics of Suffering in the *Miami Times*

> The names of Cuban rafters detained at the Guantánamo Bay Naval Base can be found posted on bulletin boards at Radio Mambi and grocery stores in Little Havana and published in Spanish-language newspapers. But no one knows the names of the nearly 15,00 [*sic*] Haitians detained at the base—and for a longer period.[28]

As the above quote illustrates, the differential attention to Haitians versus Cubans continued to be a major point of contention for African Americans in 1994. In the years between the Mariel boatlift and the Balsero crisis, the economic situation for African Americans had not much improved, and this would also shape how the *Miami Times* framed the Balsero crisis. From a national perspective, blacks had made some important gains; for instance, the percentage completing high school rose from 51 percent in 1980 to 63 percent in 1990. But at the end of the 1980s, the national unemployment rate among blacks was at 13 percent, slightly higher than it was for blacks in 1979 but more than twice that of whites (5 percent). Because of economic recessions, the poverty rate had decreased only slightly between 1980 and 1990, from 29.9 percent to 29.5 percent (Dunn 1997). In Miami, conditions for poor blacks were worse than for those across the country. Although many blacks were making it into the middle class, the gap between poor and higher-income blacks had widened so that they had the highest poverty and unemployment rate of all ethnic groups in Miami (Dunn 1997). The median family income for African Americans was $13,897, compared with $44,092 for Anglos and $19,801 for Latinos. Whereas 18 percent of Anglo families and 23 percent of Latino families lived below the poverty line, 43 percent of African American families fell below it in 1990 (Martinez 1997). In 1994, African Americans were in better jobs and were better educated than ever before, but black business growth lagged far behind that of whites and Latinos. In contrast, by the 1990s, 42 percent of all Miami-Dade enterprises were Cuban owned (Grenier and Castro 1999). In the 1980s, Miami was torn apart by several urban conflicts, including black uprisings against three incidents of police brutality, two of which involved Latino police officers (Portes and Stepick 1993). Black concerns about poverty and racism expressed during the riots, and the continuing interethnic conflict between Cubans and

African Americans, carried into the 1990s (Portes and Stepick 1993; Martinez 1997). These matters provided the background context for the reporting in the *Miami Times* during the Balsero crisis, wherein writers looked at their own "native" African American suffering (as well as "black" suffering more generally as exemplified in the treatment of Haitian migrants) and questioned why it had not been rewarded.

An op-ed feature taking up about three-quarters of a page and written by a member of the community elaborates the local concerns of some African Americans. The title, "We Are a Community Controlled by Others and Failed by Our Leaders," puts forth the reasons, the author believes, that African Americans remain disenfranchised. The op-ed primarily expresses that African Americans are not in positions of power where they can make their own decisions about what happens to their community, the children do not see themselves represented in the curriculum of the educational system, and black Miami leaders are not as visible as Cuban and Jewish leaders. The main problem, the columnist says, is that blacks are too concerned with helping all: "Whites for Whites, Jews for Jews, Cubans for Cubans, Blacks for everybody!"[29] The author advocates black self-reliance and the ideas of racial uplift with a critique more in line with the sentiments of members of the public, which diverges from the civil rights rhetoric of coalition building and general social justice and equality endorsed by prominent black leaders such as Jesse Jackson.[30] By the beginning of the 1990s, Cuban economic and political power had become clear (Portes and Stepick 1994). In 1980, only a few Cubans had held elected office and they generally stayed out of U.S. local politics as they focused on efforts to facilitate changes in Cuba and a return to the island. But "by mid-decade, the mayors of Miami, Hialeah, West Miami, and several smaller municipalities in Dade County were Cuban born, and there were ten Cuban Americans in the state legislature—quite a step up from the one or two envisioned in the 'embryonic organization' plan outlined by the Cuban American Dade County official in 1981" (Stepick et al. 2003, 37). When African Americans ran for office in the 1980s and 1990s, the Cubans who ran against them almost always won. Thus, blacks seemed unable to gain any real political ground (Stepick et al. 2003). The real "on the ground" problems faced by Miami's blacks gave credence for some African Americans to the idea that when immigrants and other groups win, African Americans lose.

A predominant idea portrayed in the *Miami Times* was that the underlying cause of the disparities between Miami's ethnic groups was anti-black racism, and congruent with this, when the paper turned its lens on immigration and the Balsero crisis, its writers took on the cause of Haitians as an African American or black issue, as they had during Mariel. As in 1980, the *Miami Times* gave less space to the coverage of Cuban immigration in 1994, and the infrequent reports it printed were mostly in contrast to Haitian issues, with editorials setting the tone. Two of the themes predominant in the paper's coverage of Mariel remained salient in this context and they greatly overlapped: (1) black Haitians versus white Cubans, which draws on the black/white racializing frame in a reaction against it (but also positions Haitians as potential "good immigrants" while depicting Cubans as detrimental to society); and (2) native-born blacks as Americans versus (Cuban) foreigners or immigrants, which affirms a predominant U.S. nativist stance. The category of the "necessity of unity among all oppressed peoples" prevalent in the Mariel reporting was less salient.[31] The zero-sum oppositional framing of the issues was problematic because it affirmed the idea that worthiness could be measured on the basis of suffering. Furthermore, placing blame on other minority groups and immigrants obscures the underlying causes of racial disparities imposed by the nation's white power base. But the discourses in the *Times* also helped turn attention to moral obligations back onto the United States, as it raised questions about the nation's contradictory foreign and immigration policy.

Because African Americans perceived a rank ordering of Cuban and Haitian suffering by the U.S. government and the public, the *Miami Times* reflected an effort to revise this view by reordering the groups so that Haitians now would come up on top and Cubans on the bottom. One of the earliest editorials in the *Miami Times* commenting on the larger influx of Cubans that year, "the biggest since 1980," immediately brought the issue of race into focus by arguing that it was the main factor in the differential treatment of Cuban and Haitian immigrants.[32] The opinion voiced in the editorial is echoed in letters to the editor, such as "President Clinton's New Cuba Policy Is Welcome," written by a woman who says that the United States is racist against Haitians and that Cubans should be locked up just like the Haitians. In her view, the United States has done more than enough for Cubans: "We have paid our dues with the Cuban people. . . . We welcomed the Cubans with open arms and slammed the door in the Haitian people's face because our great country has had a fixation with race, meaning if the Haitian people were White, we or, say, the White people, would have welcomed them with open arms too. But since their skin is dark, they don't deserve the same consideration as others."[33] The writer includes herself within the definition of American by saying that "our great country" and "we" let the Cubans in with open arms, but she then corrects herself by noting that the real decision makers are "the White people." It is about time, she argues, that Haitians also get their due. Speaking as an "American" responding to immigration and as an African American who has less of a say than "the White people," the letter writer provides a prime example of the DuBoisian notion of African American double consciousness and of its duality in Miami and in the national framework.

Other stories drew attention specifically to the suffering of Haitians to contest what they argued was the government's favoring of Cubans over Haitians. An editorial, "What about Haiti?," written after Clinton's policy change, asks, "Why is Clinton working so hard to avoid another Mariel and so slow on Haiti?" The editorial begins, "The rapidity with which President Bill Clinton is moving to confront the Castro regime in Cuba over the threat of another Mariel boatlift stands in sharp contrast to the foot-dragging that has come to characterize the Democratic administration's response to the nose-thumbing and atrocities of the military government in Haiti."[34] Like other stories in the paper addressing Haiti, this article make the point that the atrocities happening in Haiti are the same if not worse than those in Cuba and thus Haitian suffering should not be devalued.

Despite the progressive stance of seeking to undermine a U.S. tradition of racism that would negatively affect both native and foreign-born blacks, the opinions expressed in the *Miami Times* were often nativist in tone with anti-immigrant sentiments similar to those expressed in the mainstream. For instance, in a feature titled "Street Talk," where reporters from the *Miami Times* connect with people "on the street" and ask their opinions about particular questions, members of the general public corroborate the newspaper's predominantly negative evaluation of the new wave of Cuban immigration. An installment written before the enactment of "Wet Foot, Dry Foot" asked, "What should the U.S. do about Mariel II?" All the respondents (four men and two women, all African American) commented on the inequitable treatment of Haitians compared with Cubans, arguing that both groups should be treated the same. All the respondents also asserted that there were too many "illegals" and that the Cubans in particular (though not truly fitting the term "illegal") should be shipped back to Cuba. One respondent argued that

America should worry about itself instead of other countries. She said, "We've got enough people here; there are too many now. They still put the Haitians down—and the Cubans get what the Haitians should get. I've been here all my life and Miami's still the same to me as before the first Mariel boatlift. I think they are going to let them in, I sure do. They let anybody in . . . the Cubans, anyway."[35] The language used, such as "too many," "illegals," and "ship them back," mirror the nativist discourses identified by Otto Santa Ana (2002) and Leo Chavez (2001) as circulating in the general public about Latinos during the 1990s. Thus, such coverage illustrated an African American embrace of a narrative positioning themselves as "natives" against foreigners.

This opposition expressed in the *Miami Times* is further illustrated in that, at times, Haitians were also included in the "immigrant threat." For instance, in another installment of "Street Talk" that asked, "What effect will the Cuban crisis have on the black community?," of the six African American people polled (three men and three women), five argued that the crisis would make it more difficult for African Americans to get jobs, and two of the six respondents argued that not only would Cubans hurt African Americans' ability to get jobs but Haitians would too. As we saw in Chapter 3, in the 1980 coverage of Mariel, Haitians were almost exclusively discussed as the "brothers and sisters" of African Americans. However, during the Balsero crisis, the coverage in the *Miami Times* reflected a move toward grouping Haitians into the idea of "illegal" as well. As evidenced in some of the "Street Talk" installments, though many members of the African American public were generally for the acceptance of Haitians, some argued simply for equal treatment; either both groups should be excluded, or if the Cubans were included, then so should be the Haitians. Clearly, African Americans, continuing to idealize Pan-African sentiments, had taken on the cause of Haitians immigrants. Yet, as expressed by one man on the street, the real stake for other segments of the African American community was that "as we divide the pie between more people, our [African American] slice of the pie keeps getting smaller."[36]

Linked Fates: We Suffer Together?

The findings discussed so far demonstrate discourses emanating from African American and Cuban exile communities that set at odds the various Miami

populations. We could see in the newspapers that the predominant arguments utilized for reclaiming or situating one's own community or race in a
more favorable position in the U.S. hierarchy centered on declaring one's
own group as having suffered and thus being deserving of U.S. inclusion.
However, these were not the only sentiments in the newspapers, and certain articles in both papers show more awareness of the overlaps among
communities. Such coverage captures a more complex view of the politics
of race in Miami by illuminating links between the fates of various Miami
communities.

El Nuevo Herald acknowledged similarities in the plight of the Balseros
and of other racialized groups as it recognized that the "special pact" between
the U.S. government and the Cuban community was eroding. For example,
a news article picks up on the idea that Cubans previously deemed "model
immigrants" were also being caught up in an overall anti-immigrant backlash in the country. It reads, "From Los Angeles to El Paso, and Miami, with
a fervor, according to some analysts, not seen since the 1920s, Americans are
faulting excessive immigration for the erosion of the quality of life in the
United States." As the writer goes on to explain, "Suddenly, the official U.S.
opinion viewed Cubans as no different from mere poor and hungry foreigners, including the Mexicans who dream of reaching California and the Haitians huddled in tents at Guantánamo."[37] The sympathetic framing of the
Balseros in this article serves as a strategy to preserve and bolster the former
"Golden" identity in the face of a policy that equated Cubans with Mexicans
and Haitians. However, the language also introduces the idea that, now
lumped with other economic refugees, Cubans could no longer count on their
image as the brave souls who fled communism for democracy to ensure
their position atop the hierarchy of Latinos and other immigrants in the
United States. Such observations illuminate that U.S. immigration policy
had instituted the hierarchy in the first place and that all immigrant groups
were, in reality, subject to the whims of the government.

In contrast to the *Miami Times*, only a few stories in *El Nuevo Herald*
directly compared the plight of Cubans with that of Haitian migrants, and
the limited discussion of Haitians in Balsero-related stories underscored the
fact that various members of the Cuban American community simply did
not connect the experiences of the two groups. This article, however, takes
the stance that the public should have the same concern for both Haitian and
Cuban detainees in Guantánamo:

On Wednesday, in a labor of love accomplished mostly by Hialeah Cubans and NE Miami African Americans, and that lasted the whole day, 40,000 pounds of clothing, shoes, and toys stored in a cement warehouse were catalogued and packed. "This is not only for Cubans but for Haitians," said Cuban exile Oscar Torres, owner of the warehouse. "We are all human beings."[38]

The report of the efforts of Cuban American and African American communities to work together is noteworthy, given that, for the most part, the local Miami newspapers depicted African Americans as being concerned about the needs of Haitians and not Cubans, and Cuban Americans were depicted as being concerned with Cuban migrants but not Haitians. In this exemplary case, the group that packed forty thousand pounds of donations was organized by a Cuban exile who believed that "we are all humans," implying that ethnicity should not matter when distributing aid and when recognizing suffering. This example of cooperation is rare, but it reveals the shared interests that could unite the two communities.

Another article in *El Nuevo Herald* captures the shared interests of Cuban and Haitian refugees in its reporting on the news in mid-November that Cuban children held at Guantánamo were being allowed into the United States in response to humanitarian concerns. A person quoted makes the point that all the refugees should be treated equally: "All children everywhere are the same. . . . I would like them to release all the children on the base, not just Cubans." In the same article, however, activists for the Haitian cause claim that Haitians were not being allowed to leave because they were being punished for racial as well as political reasons. A lawyer at a Miami refugee center explains: "We think it's wonderful that Cubans are being allowed to come here," he says. "Our only complaint is with the Clinton Administration, which believes that the Statue of Liberty's whiteness does not apply to black Haitians."[39] The lawyer takes the position voiced by many members of the African American community, that color was a major determinant of the (preferential) treatment of Cuban immigrants that allowed their suffering to be ranked higher than the suffering of other groups. The few *Herald* articles that discuss the plight of both Cubans and Haitians show that, overall, the concerns of Cubans, Haitians, and African Americans are viewed as being unaffiliated with one another, if not in opposition. Still, by including stories such as this that do not only affirm the predominant stance (which elevated Cuban concerns and ignored Haitian ones), *El Nuevo Herald* provided some space for debate on the issues faced by Cubans, Haitians, and African Americans.

A focus on Afro-Cubans could potentially further complicate the framing of these three groups' concerns as being in opposition. But Afro-Cubans are the focus in only three *Herald* stories about the Balsero crisis. Although the percentage of blacks among the Balseros was smaller than among the Marielitos, it was more than double the amount that arrived with the pre-1980 exiles.[40] Still, no articles in this sample focus on the racial background of the Balseros as a group or make any racial distinction between this group and earlier waves.[41] It is notable, however, that an Afro-Cuban voice was prominently heard in this period of coverage in the voice of Dora Amador, an award-winning journalist for *El Nuevo Herald* who self-identifies as a black Cuban.

Amador provides her perspective on the Haitian/Cuban immigration in an op-ed that begins by addressing the response to one of two articles she wrote on black Cuban experiences with white Cuban discrimination in the United States. But as the opinion piece develops, Amador shifts to the issue of Cuban and Haitian immigration and, in her evaluations, mirrors the predominant perspective of the newspaper. It is apparent that, despite her concerns about the stigmatization of blackness in the Cuban American community, she does not promote a Pan-African connection between Haitians and Cubans. She compares the case of the Balseros to that of the Haitians and argues that Haitians have a better deal than Cubans and that African Americans have not shown any concern. In her view, "Today, we are the beggars and pariahs that a whole continent rejects, those herded in detention camps in whose defense not one voice is raised, not by Anglos, Afro-Americans, or other Latin Americans." She ends by saying, "Today I am envious of the Haitians. At least in their country, the marines have landed."[42] Amador paints the Cuban community as being alone in their struggle because other Americans—Anglos and African Americans—are silent. Alleging government discrimination against Cubans, her words are in sharp contrast to rhetoric that praised the United States for its welcoming stance toward Cuba and the Cubans. Her words corroborate the opinions expressed by some members of the Cuban American community, in opposition to African American arguments in the *Miami Times*, which insisted that Haitians were the ones being discriminated against, not the Cubans. In Amador's opinion, Cubans have been situated by "native" Americans within Miami's racial order as forever foreign.[43] As public opinion polls and articles in the *Miami Times* reveal, her contention that Anglos and African Americans were not supportive of the Balseros and the Cuban community as a whole had some credibility.

Amador is concerned with the political conflicts between the United States and Cuba on the one hand and the United States and Haiti on the other, and she reaffirms the role of the United States as the arbiter of freedom and democracy, without acknowledging how her concerns may reflect her (black) Cuban American subjectivity. While Amador makes no connection between black Cubans, African Americans, and Haitians, as the *Miami Times* often did, her black Cuban subjectivity does come into play; in another section of this op-ed (and in other stories that she writes), she makes an important contribution through addressing racism against black Cubans by white Cubans. But Amador does not have be overt in addressing black concerns to make a contribution; that a black Cuban writer such as Amador is given a prominent voice in the newspaper serves to remind the public of the multiracial nature of the Cuban community.

The *Miami Times* coverage also showed more acknowledgment of the overlaps between the Cuban and African American communities during the time of the Balsero crisis. The new multiculturalism in the United States presented complex new challenges for the directions African Americans would take to resolve lingering inequality and forced a recognition that like native-born African Americans, immigrants also suffered from racialization in the United States. In the *Times* coverage, voices of leaders and some members of the public worked to complicate the mainstream African American view that placed African Americans and immigrants, especially Cubans, in opposition.

Two op-eds speak to the new diversity and endorse an African American response more affirmative of the strategy of coalition. "Immigrant as Scapegoats" by Mohamed Hamaludin argues against placing blame on immigrants for the U.S. economic and social problems: "There should be a natural alliance between immigrants and African Americans and other non-whites in America because of the similarities of their history of exploitation. Those who seek to set them against each other should be thoroughly rebuffed." Further, he argues, "The anti-immigrant lobby carefully disguises its real intent, which is to be a part of the current effort to make American [*sic*] decidedly Anglo-Saxon at a time when there is a growing clamor for the country to move away from just such a bigoted position and acknowledge diversity in all aspects of American life and culture."[44] The author's critique is similar to that argued in this book—that at the heart of interethnic conflict between African Americans, other minority groups, and immigrants there are the workings of racial power to keep the United States white. But the assumption of a "natural" alliance between African Americans and immigrants because they are denied access to whiteness would also assume that this denial is equally allocated.

In his regular column "Across the Color Line," African American political scholar Manning Marable similarly argues for alliances between blacks and Latinos. He talks about how the population of Latinos is now surpassing that of blacks in some cities but does not view this phenomenon as negative, merely as a matter of fact. He ends the article with a statement recalling DuBoisian themes: "The problem of the 21st Century is the problem of 'the new color line'—whether blacks, Latinos and other people of color can overcome their differences to construct a new democratic, multicultural majority for America."[45] Writing in 1994, when the major demographic shifts that have now occurred across the country had become profoundly evident, Marable spoke to the inevitability that African Americans would need to go beyond a binary analysis of racial problems. Viewpoints expressed by people like Marable, Jesse Jackson, and Hamaludin allowed the *Miami Times* to present alternative evaluations of the Balsero crisis and of the significance of increased immigration on the African American community, offering a challenge to the predominant negative view of the impact of immigrants in the United States. Their statements also acknowledged the suffering of various groups as equally legitimate.

The *Miami Times* articles involving Afro-Cubans offer another view into the complexity of the issue of immigrant–African American relations and, more specifically, the interethnic relations between Cubans and African Americans. In the articles collected for this period, six of them cover Afro-Cubans in the form of a news story, an op-ed, and a column written by Rosa Reed, an Afro-Cuban woman. A July 14 news story, "Afro-Cuban Dissident Takes Refuge in Miami," demonstrates the African American press's interest in the concerns of Afro-Cubans but also reports on Cuban American awareness that their community was being criticized for receiving preferential treatment over Haitians. The article reports on the arrival in Miami of Angele Herrera, who left Cuba because of the threat of imprisonment. She was president of the Cuban Democratic Coalition (identified in the article as the largest human rights organization in Cuba) and founder of the Afro-Cuban rights group Maceo Movement for Dignity. In the article, Cuban American leader Jorge Mas Canosa, director of the Cuban American National Foundation (CANF), explains that the arrival of Herrera was significant for the Cuban democratic movement: "[It is] symbolic because it shows that Black and White Cubans fight for a common cause. . . . It destroys a common notion that the Cuban community holds something against Black people." The article also states that the CANF recently paid $20,000 to $30,000 to reunite Haitian children in Haiti with their families in the United States.[46] Mas Canosa, the notoriously conservative Cuban American leader, includes both black Cubans and Haitians in the category "Black people" by referring to the usefulness of Herrera's arrival and CANF's efforts for the Haitian community to undercut criticism that white Cubans, and more specifically white Cuban American organizations, are racist. Although Mas Canosa's actions and statements may be viewed as opportunistic and insincere by some, particularly by members of the African American community, the article displays how attention to Afro-Cubans brings a complexity to the racial conflicts in Miami, between blacks and white Anglos, black and white Cubans, Haitians and Cubans, African Americans and Cubans, and so on, and points to areas of overlap, such as mutual concerns about immigration and possibilities for coalitions. The presence of Afro-Cubans forces Cuban Americans to see race and pushes African Americans to acknowledge that Cubans are more than "white."

In an op-ed, "Race at Heart of Cuba Crisis," Ricardo E. Gonzalez tackles the subject of race and racism among Cubans referred to by Mas Canosa by informing the African American community that the issue of race and the stigma attached to blackness is not only an African American concern (or a Haitian concern for that matter) but also "is at the heart of Cuba's crisis." The op-ed focuses on the "conspicuous" absence of blacks among the Cuban immigrants. Although studies have characterized the two most recent immigration waves from Cuba as containing a higher percentage of blacks than the pre-1980 waves, Gonzalez notes the high percentage of blacks in Cuba (65–70 percent, according to his estimates) and claims that 90 percent of exile Cubans are white. Gonzalez's op-ed is concerned more with race in Cuba; he argues that Castro needs to address the issue of race more, and he cites the infamous Malecón riots, of which he says that the majority of the participants were blacks and mulattos, as evidence of black Cuban discontent on the island.[47] Although Castro took action to solve racial inequalities in Cuba, Gonzalez says that blacks in Cuba remain disempowered by white communist elites. The author's focus is not on the experiences of black Cubans in the United States, but he argues that the "powerful, conservative anti-Castro lobby in Miami, whose leaders are itching to switch places with Castro," are taking the racial situation in Cuba into account; they pray for the end of Castro but are apprehensive about the large numbers of blacks there. He continues, "And so the much-tabooed 'racial question,' sometimes timidly addressed but more often ignored, once again feared, is heard on both sides of the Florida Straits through the resurgence of the old paranoid phobia known throughout Cuban history as the 'Peligro Negro' (the Black Peril)!"[48] The racism he identifies as existing in Cuba also translates onto U.S. shores, where the differential treatment of black and white Cubans speaks to the tenacity of white racism against blacks regardless of national origin in the United States. By connecting Cuba's and the United States' racism, Gonzalez's article, written for the African American *Miami Times*, unites the Afro-Cuban cause to that of African Americans.

The newspaper also connected its African American audience to the plight of Afro-Cuban Balseros in two photo essays that include pictures exclusively of black Cubans setting out on their voyage to the United States. One essay, "Thousands Flee from Castro's Failed Revolution," shows a large picture of black Cuban men in the water, saying good-bye to a woman as they set off on their raft.[49] The photo essay is very short, only describing the picture and announcing that the United States and Cuba will begin talks to resolve the disputes over immigration policy. But the next day the paper ran another photo essay, "Rafter Stocking up for Sea Trip," which contains a photo showing black Cubans buying bread to bring with them on their trip and notes that Cubans who leave Cuba are now being brought to Guantánamo naval base as a result of changes in immigration policy.[50] In contrast to the supposed whiteness of the Cuban Balseros, the photos allow the reader to see that some of the refugees are black, providing an alternative interpretation of the events revolving around U.S. policy toward Cuba—that this policy affects black peoples. Yet given the overwhelmingly predominant depiction of Cubans as whites in the newspaper, and with little discussion in the newspaper about the significance of the fact that some Cubans are black, the pictures may not have had much impact in revising negative reactions to the crisis.

Still, the newspaper did open a major channel for readers to connect to Afro-Cubans and, perhaps, white Cuban Americans, by running a regular op-ed column by Rosa Reed, whose ethnicity was displayed prominently in her byline "an Afro-Cuban businesswoman in Miami."[51] Five op-eds by Reed were published during the period investigated. Perhaps to offset the fact the *Miami Times* did little reporting on Cuban Americans, her articles discussed U.S. immigration policy and Cuba, along with other Cuban American concerns. In "Support the President on His Tough Stand against Castro," Reed takes a stance contrary to a large proportion of Cuban Americans, most of whom were against Clinton's policies. She argues, "We Cubans should stop criticizing Clinton. . . . We must also make sure that all Cuban refugees are processed fairly, whether Black or White, rich and influential Miami relatives or not."[52] Reed supports the stronger sanctions against Cuba proposed by Clinton, although she is opposed to Clinton's decision to send Cubans to Guantánamo. The article does not explore at length the differential treatment of black and white Cubans, but her plea that all refugees be processed fairly implies she believes that race and class have been factors. Like the Afro-Cuban writers for *El Nuevo Herald*, Reed's voice demonstrates that Cuban Americans did not all agree, even on issues that were viewed as what unified the Cuban American community. Her contribution then had the potential to provide a wider view of Cuban Americans among members of the African American community.

In another article, Reed directly addresses black American leaders, requesting that they also involve themselves in issues affecting black Cubans because, just as Haitian issues were considered African American issues, African Americans should also care about the concerns of Afro-Cubans. In "Black Cubans Need Friends, Not Defenders of Castro's Regime," in which she criticizes Jesse Jackson's argument that the United States should suspend its trade embargo with Cuba, she also draws attention to the fact that Afro-Cubans have specific concerns and claims and that they are puzzled by Jackson's stance when he does not try to represent those who "have no representation in exile and are politically invisible."[53] By looking to African American leaders to take on the Afro-Cuban cause, she affirms a connection between the two communities and states that this connection should exist on the basis of their shared racial background. Although she shares an anti-Castro stance with other Cuban Americans, her comments also highlight the fact that race makes her and other Afro-Cubans invisible, even though it distinguishes them from the majority of the exile community.[54]

In "Cuban Power in Miami," Reed brings further attention to how race comes between black and white Cubans and puts forth a firm criticism of the powerful white Cubans in Miami in a discussion of a local political race that polarized the Cuban and African American communities. County commissioner Arthur Teele, a black Republican, was pushing for his candidate, Cynthia Curry, for the position of county manager, but "the so called 'Latin bloc' flexed its muscle" and the Latino candidate, Armando Vidal, won.[55] The article goes on to detail rumors about a physical confrontation between Teele and another politician and the move by some Latino commissioners to oust Teele. Reed is highly critical of the Latino power base and asks, "Have the Hispanics decided that Teele's power trip is now over, he has served his purpose and it's time for him to move to the back of the bus?" With the "back of the bus" reference she calls forward a collective black memory of Miami's Jim Crow history and equates powerful Latinos with white Anglos. She also alludes to her own siding with African Americans. White Cubans are trying to take over, she says; "We have a white Cuban public schools superintendent, we have a white Cuban county manager. What's next? . . . Are the white Cubans salivating at the prospect of absolute power?"[56] The specific political context Reed describes offers a fascinating look at a concrete contest over power between African Americans and Cubans. It is also interesting how she, a black woman and a Latina, positions herself so firmly with African Americans. Reed's critiques indict Cuban Americans for deploying the notion of white supremacy to elevate themselves or to exclude "others," particularly African Americans, Afro-Cubans, and other blacks, whom they see as threats to their own livelihoods.

Reed's articles demonstrate that she thinks of her blackness in a diasporic sense and aligns herself closely with African Americans, though she is still concerned about issues affecting the Cuban American community. In another of her articles, she labels herself and other groups of African descent living in the United States as African Americans. She says, "African Americans regardless of their roots (Cuban, Jamaican, Panamanian, Nicaraguan, Haitian, Nigerian, etc.) are not asking for handouts, welfare or more social programs. We are asking for solid jobs, quality and affordable healthcare . . . housing, less tax increases and less bureaucracy." She says that "we" must vote for politicians who will work with "us" to have the opportunity to share the

American Dream.[57] She affirms the overall stance of the *Miami Times* that race can be a unifying factor for people from various countries of African descent but does not make the leap to necessarily include powerful white Cubans in the "us." The fact that she was given a column in the newspaper demonstrates a move by the newspaper to connect to the Cuban American community but affirms that this connection is made only on a basis that reaffirms the binary between black and white. The situation in Miami, in which Cubans and African Americans held so much tension against each other, may have constrained any efforts to go beyond this reasoning. Still, the voices of Afro-Cubans and acknowledgment of their presence by the paper was a start toward connecting the two communities, affirming their mutual suffering, and linking their fates together.

Conclusion

El Nuevo Herald and the *Miami Times* clarified the new political, economic, and racial stakes of Cuban Americans and African Americans in light of the 1994 Balsero crisis. As we read the discourses in *El Nuevo Herald*, we find an embedded critique of the national project of exclusion even in a climate of enhanced worldwide attention to the importance of universal human rights. The larger national frame of anti-immigrant backlash, which showed itself in restrictive immigration policies, provided a context where immigrant groups knew they were under more intense scrutiny, and "native" groups were provided with the discourses they could accept or reject about the threat immigrant groups posed for them. After thirty-five years of maintaining an open-door policy, the Clinton administration responded to the Balsero crisis by instituting its "Wet Foot, Dry Foot" legislation, a move that allowed Cubans to acknowledge the conditional nature of whiteness and the reality that the motivation for U.S. policy decisions is to protect U.S. interests rather that fulfill moral duties. In the *Herald*'s use of the worthy suffering immigrant trope, we see the strategic nature of such framing; rather than merely being an effort of members of the Cuban American community to decide who is worthy and who is not, the use of racializing frames is a testament to the fact that it is actually the dominant group that imposes these restrictions and requires the suffering of marginalized groups. In the *Miami Times*, we gain perspective on views among African Americans. With the economic, social, and political standing of the Miami black community hardly improved fourteen years after Mariel, the Balsero crisis to them was merely another Mariel. Another mass immigration from Cuba was viewed as a disruption for the African American community, which continued to suffer and struggled to make gains. Overall, both newspapers affirmed the idea that in the United States suffering is required of racialized groups and thus these groups must compete with one another to benefit from their suffering being recognized and rewarded above other groups. Although I critique this zero-sum reasoning, ultimately the strategies used in *El Nuevo Herald* and in the *Miami Times* contain an important protest because they indict the United States for its own moral failures to fulfill promises it has made that it would respond to and care about human suffering.

The newspapers also provide some encouragement that an oppositional stance is not the only one taken by members of the Cuban and African American communities. As both newspapers illustrate, some links were made between African Americans and Cuban Americans, which open up spaces of possibility that could help toward resolutions of interethnic conflict. In *El Nuevo Herald*, few articles in the coverage specifically made connections between Cubans and African Americans. But the articles that did exist connected the plight of Haitian and Cuban refugees and discussed Cuban Americans in relation to other Latinos in the United States, demonstrating a realization among some Cuban Americans that their fate was linked to those of other minority and immigrant groups. Furthermore, Afro-Cuban voices in the paper further challenged white Cuban Americans by emphasizing a need to acknowledge race. The *Miami Times* also demonstrated the fact that not all African Americans were against the Cubans, and, through the voices of prominent leaders and thinkers, some articles in the paper challenged African Americans to support interethnic alliances. The paper incorporated Afro-Cubans more than it did during Mariel (owing largely to the articles written by Reed). The move to include Afro-Cubans under the African American umbrella affirmed the Pan-African philosophies of the newspaper but also served in a small way to connect African Americans to the Cuban American community and to Latinos in general, a connection that would be all the more crucial as the numbers of Latinos across the country rapidly began to surpass those of the African American population.

The next chapter focuses more specifically on Afro-Cubans, who were marginally included in Cuban American and African American newspapers, to attempt a deeper engagement with their voices and to hear how they speak to the continued rigidity of race in the United States. Their experiences illuminate how white Cubans, African Americans, and other communities make claim to the nation by promoting the exclusion of other minority groups, particularly those who do not fit within any dominant racial paradigms. The chapter provides greater insight into how people placed "in between" present a challenge to dominant racial frames and offers insights useful for promoting the alleviation of interethnic conflict between various racialized groups.

Chapter 5

Afro-Cuban Encounters at the Intersections of Blackness and Latinidad

This chapter expands our discussions relevant to the Miami context and the previous chapters by shifting our focus onto the experiences of Afro-Cubans living in the United States today.[1] Drawing from in-depth interviews, the chapter explores how Afro-Cubans confront the exclusions they encounter as they navigate the intersection between blackness and Latinidad. In previous chapters, we examined how the presence of larger numbers of black Cubans among the 1980 Mariel and the 1994 Balsero migrants complicated how race and social membership was conceived of for white Cuban exile and African American groups in Miami. The Afro-Cuban presence highlighted the anti-black racism that played out among white Cubans in contests over power and recognition. Their presence also brought into question the African American strategy of mounting their support of Haitian immigrants and of themselves in opposition to (white) Cubans by emphasizing blackness as a requirement for solidarity. The moves made by members of these communities are related to the fact that the United States' white-dominated system creates conditions that require racialized groups to manage the stigma of race strategically. This book has underscored that while the social meanings of race originate from white elites, they become common sense and may be adopted by people of color (see also Feagin 2010). Straddling the borders between black and Cuban identities, Afro-Cubans can disrupt the logics behind the exclusionary ideals of worthy citizenship held by some members of Cuban and African American groups in the Miami scenarios discussed in the previous chapters, revealing the breaks in the lines that had been drawn around social membership in African American and Latino communities.

In this chapter, I provide further examples of how Afro-Cubans straddle these boundaries and examine how Afro-Cubans negotiate identity and community belonging among white Cubans and African Americans in Miami and among African Americans and people of Mexican descent in Los Angeles today, to think about broader questions related to divisions between these groups. Although Miami is the preeminent Cuban enclave, Afro-Cubans settle all over the United States, in part due to U.S. resettlement efforts, and also in part due to the rejections they experience from white Cubans in Miami (see Aja 2016). Given the specific ways Los Angeles, another primary immigrant destination site, has exemplified the dramatic diversity of the "new" America both historically and currently, many scholars have taken a keen interest in Los Angeles as a key site for investigating black–Latino relations in particular and for examining the extent to which the United States' growing diversity challenges rigid racial notions more broadly. Thus, in this chapter, while maintaining a focus on Miami, I extend the intellectual conversation outside of it by also exploring how Afro-Cubans navigate the context of Los Angeles, where because of the high percentage of people of Mexican descent, Latino identity is most often defined as "Mexican."[2] As it is the intention of this book to take lessons from the past—through an examination of historical racial dynamics in Miami—so that they can be utilized to illuminate current problems and solutions, this chapter brings our discussion closer to the present. Thinking about Afro-Cuban negotiations of the broader categories of blackness and Latinidad as well as the binary divisions of worthy citizenship in Miami and in Los Angeles, we not only gain a better perspective on how post-1980 Afro-Cuban immigrants experience race in the larger United States but extend our scholarly conversation about the ways race works in multiethnic America today.

Along with these goals, I also take the opportunity in this chapter to address a key tension that has emerged from the past chapters' discussion of between-group boundaries and the tactics that can be used to overcome them. I have argued, and I illustrate further here, that Afro-Cubans, like other Afro-Latinos, multiracials, or others often placed "in between," have a multiple positionality that allows them to disrupt and cross the United States' rigidly policed ethnic/racial boundaries. They disrupt such boundaries because they simply cannot "choose one" identity but must inhabit several identities concurrently (Jiménez Román and Flores 2010). They also illuminate the ways people in power, threatened by their multiplicity, furiously work to maintain previously existing boundaries. Yet my acknowledgment of the resistive potential of multiplicity and in-betweenness is not the same as the exaltation of "mestizaje" or racial mixture that we see in some Latin American countries, nor is it a move toward the color-blind idea that "race doesn't matter" or "we need to get rid of racial categories" that we see in "postracial" United States. Some scholars have argued that the greater racial complexity of the United States today, with so many people now falling in between black and white, can in and of itself challenge race. Instead, I contend, the resistive potential of "in-between" identities lies in the fact that they further illuminate the strength of hegemonic power dynamics that dictate the idea that one's placement in particular categories makes them more or less worthy of social membership and national belonging. In other words, they do not fix our racist cultural situation, but they do demystify and clarify it. I argue that the Afro-Cuban negotiations of race we see here help resist the "postracial" celebration of multiplicity because in Afro-Cubans' responses to rejections, they not only undermine a U.S. discomfort (and fascination) with multiplicity but also make visible the cost of being raced by strategically challenging the stigma attached to black identity.

Caught in the Middle

In the racial terrain of twenty-first-century United States, Afro-Cubans, like other Afro-Latinos, not only negotiate what it means to be black and African American in the United States but must simultaneously grapple with the many meanings that hide within the single term "Latino." The respondents report being frequently questioned about their identities, and this questioning is related to the fact that, like others with perceptibly mixed identities, they do not fit nicely in census boxes. Yet, they are not allowed to be "more than black," as Cuban patriot Jose Martí had envisioned, because their blackness constructs them as the "ultimate other" (Gosin 2010; Noguera 2003, 193). Their identities are called into question also, because black and Latino identities are often viewed as discrete. The questioning of their identities by people who are simply curious, as well as the "micro-level rejections" they receive from others who feel they are "too black" or "not black enough," occur within a white elite dominance system that continues to operate from a politics of division.[3] This system emphasizes strict divisions between whiteness and blackness, and it attempts also to create other discrete racial categories.

Mariela's and Caridad's cases provide illustration. Mariela is a well-traveled dancer who moved from Cuba to Miami in 1991. Every day, she encounters fellow Cubans who assume she is African American and address her in their accented English:

> When I go to the market, people ask me if I am American. Other Cubans do in English. . . . It's the way I look or something. . . . It's funny—they come with a funny accent, "May I help you?" You know? I know it's an English-speaking country, but most of the time they speak Spanish in the stores, so you know, why me? But they were singling out the fact that I was black.[4]

Caridad, who was thirty-six at the time I interviewed her and who came to the United States in 1980 as a child, similarly recalls being misunderstood, even rejected by other Cubans in Miami. In grade school, her schoolmates did not accept her as either African American or Cuban. Caridad was caught in the middle—among white Cubans she stood out because of her color and among African Americans she stood out because of her language:

> I couldn't talk to them, to the black American kids. Because I had no ways of communicating [because of limited English proficiency]. . . . For the born Cubans I was the black, you know, the black student or the black girl. For the black students, I was not a true black. I was not a true "sister" so to speak. And they always, they never understood why it is that I hung around people who didn't look like me.

Like many of the other Afro-Cubans interviewed in this book, these women found, in navigating the racial climate of the United States, that they do not fully fit into groups that they might perceive themselves as belonging to, such as Cuban, black, or Latino groups, because of how rigidly other U.S. Americans interpret these categories. Mariela offsets her annoyance at the predicament of being singled out because of her blackness in her activist work by educating people about the importance of black culture and religion in Cuba. Caridad defaulted to hanging out with other Cubans because of the language barrier, but as her English proficiency improved, she was offered more choices. Today, she is married to a man from Spain and has a very diverse group of friends. Mariela's and Caridad's cases illustrate that finding community in this U.S. context can be difficult. However, Afro-Cubans locate ways to insert themselves into U.S. society—such as directly challenging anti-blackness as Mariela did, or, like Caridad, they use their status of being "in between" to traverse various communities.

When discussing scenarios where they have found a welcome and created spaces to belong, the Afro-Cubans in the study help break down boundaries as they illuminate the overlaps where coalitions between groups such as African Americans and Latinos are possible (Gosin 2010). At the same time, they put forth direct challenges to rigid racial notions and anti-black attitudes as they embrace their blackness—but with a Cuban emphasis. Previous research on black immigrants has underscored a tendency among those of the first generation to dissociate from African Americans and black identities in order to avoid being stigmatized, yet here we see a different outcome. We might expect Afro-Cubans to work especially hard to distance themselves from blackness because of their status as phenotypically black but ethnically Latino and because they come from a country with a color-blind racial ideology into a context where they perceive their co-nationals to be more anti-black than in their home country. Instead, what we see is a sense of pride in both their blackness and in the Cuban national idealization of racial fraternity.[5] But in their deployment of Cuban racial democracy idealism, they capture the original philosophical intent, to challenge, rather than excuse, anti-black racism.[6] Drawing upon their Cuban identities, they also insert themselves into a larger African diasporic community to challenge moves made by some African Americans to limit what it means to be black. In their challenge to the idea that because they are black they cannot also be "Latino," they allow for a larger critique of anti-black racism in Latin America and the ways white supremacist notions from Latin America and the United States intersect and intervene in the lives of Afro-Latino immigrants. Thus, as they move between and challenge the boundaries set up between the various communities they inhabit, they enact shifting identity processes not unlike those of phenotypically ambiguous mestizos and multiracials. Yet their manipulations of their multiplicity suggest not a simplistic exaltation of multiplicity or the call to get rid of or expand categories. When thinking about the way race functions in the United States today, we can gain from looking at Afro-Cuban negotiations of their placement "in between," because they allow an intervention that provides a conscious challenge to the anti-black notions foundational to binaries of worthy citizenship.

Why Racial Multiplicity, Alone, Is Not Enough

Despite a long history of racial mixture in the United States, many everyday U.S. Americans continue to believe that black and white represent an "essential and unbridgeable difference" (Bailey 2007, 158). Indeed, the United States has worked hard to maintain distinct racial categories in the service of preserving the power of whites (Davis 2001; Omi and Winant 1994). From the "one-drop rule" to the enforcement of miscegenation laws until 1967, the United States has enforced these divisions and constructed race as a simple dichotomy: full (white) citizens, and black/"Others" (Bailey 2007; Davis 2001; C. E. Rodríguez 2000).[7] Because of the importance of preserving white racial purity, people with known African ancestry have historically been considered black regardless of phenotype. As such, being "in between" was made problematic. Black/white biracial individuals would be subject to great scrutiny as whites looked to racial cues such as skin color, hair texture, and facial features to ascertain racial difference. This scrutiny belies both a fascination with racial mixture as well as the repulsion of it (Joseph 2013).

Significantly, Americans today are more frequently identifying with multiple racial categories; the total multiple-race population grew nationwide from 6.8 million in 2000 to 9 million in 2010 (Jones and Bullock 2012). This illustrates a major shift among the population in that interracial marriage and relations have become more acceptable. Yet, despite these trends, a common denominator of the multiracial experience is that people are constantly questioned about their identities because other U.S. Americans exhibit a strong desire to place them in distinct racial categories according to "normative" phenotypic distinctions (Brunsma 2006; Deters 1997; Harris and Sims 2002; Jones 2011, 147–148; Khanna and Johnson 2010). U.S. Census categorizations have changed over time, illustrating that, in actuality, racial hierarchies and identifications have never been truly fixed in the United States. Still, the white/black paradigm has been resilient, and there is no category for an intermediary racial categorization, such as "multiracial" or "mulatto," as there is in other countries such as Cuba and Brazil.[8]

Although multiracial individuals now have more of a voice or, at least, presence in the United States, the color line has been more resistant to shifting for people who are phenotypically black (J. Lee and Bean 2004). If one looks like the surrounding community's idea of "black," an alternative identity (such as Latino or biracial) is often not accepted in U.S. society (Khanna and Johnson 2010; Waters 1996). Post-1965 black immigrants soon learn that there is often an expectation that they choose between their multiple identities and to privilege an identity as "black" over their national identities (Bailey 2000, 2001; Gosin 2017; Waters 1999, 2001; Landale and Oropesa 2002; Torres-Saillant 2010). Today, the population of U.S. Afro-Latinos of various national origins—Dominicans, Puerto Ricans, Colombians, among others— has grown, making them more visible in some regions of the country. Yet, in many other regions, an African American speaking unaccented English continues to be the prevailing social norm of what is "black." Thus, when a person who is visibly black manifests an accent or other markers of foreignness, their blackness is often "othered" (Jiménez Román and Flores 2010; Torres-Saillant 2010).[9] In part due to this othering, black immigrants engage with race, ethnicity, and identity in ways similar to multiracials in that, in many contexts, they are constantly asked to explain their identities. But they differ from multiracials because while phenotypically they are assumed to be "black," the combination of their blackness and "foreignness" prompts questions about their identities (Bailey 2000, 2001; Gosin 2017; Jiménez Román and Flores 2010; Landale and Oropesa 2002; Waters 1999, 2001). As blacks and foreigners, black immigrant positioning provides potential for disrupting (black) native/foreigner divides. Further, when they affirm their multiplicity, black immigrants create a space for troubling U.S. discomfort with racial/ cultural ambiguities.

Disrupting the racial boundaries put in place in U.S. society is important because these boundaries exist to empower whites, in part by giving them control to dictate who is most worthy to belong and "who goes where." Yet an uncritical celebration of multiplicity or of racial/cultural hybridity as the solution for racial essentialisms in multicultural societies would be problematic (Gosin 2016; Puri 2004; Jiménez Román 2005). Such celebratory language comes through in U.S.-based assertions that, due to mid-twentieth-century demographic change and its greater diversity, the nation is becoming "postrace" (Bonilla-Silva 2010; D. Rodríguez 2014). This would mean that compared to the pre–civil rights era, racial discrimination and other forms of racism have greatly diminished and racial distinctions between groups of people are no longer consequential. Racially charged events in the first decades of the twenty-first century make it clear that overt forms of racism continue to plague the nation. But in the blinded eyes of proponents of the idea that we are postrace, people who fall between black and white, such as multiracial individuals, get made into exceptional symbols of progress, "a bridge between estranged communities, a healing facilitator of an imagined racial utopia, even the embodiment of that utopia" (Joseph 2013, 2). As Ralina Joseph (2013) argues, in the supposed "postracial" moment, the "exceptional multiracial" is able to help us achieve a postracial ideal because she or he transcends blackness—if she or he is not quite white, she or he at least avoids the heavy sanctions of blackness, thereby allowing a space to deny the reality of such sanctions. Such an assumption clearly leaves whiteness atop the national racial hierarchy while continuing to position blackness as undesirable and subject to denigration.

The desire to "transcend" blackness also appears in Latin American racial democracy discourses. In Latin American societies that define themselves as racial democracies, it is argued that class, rather than race, is the basis for social stratification.[10] Because of the prevalence of racial mixing in the population, racial categories are also viewed as no longer existing.[11] Racial categorization paradigms in Latin America are generally more fluid than U.S. paradigms because there are many intermediary categories between "black" and "white," but a "pigmentocracy" exists. As in the "not quite white" cases considered in the U.S. context, the whiter one is, the greater is one's claim to honor and privilege, leaving whiteness atop the hierarchy. Darker-skinned people identified with African or Indian groups continue to be stigmatized (Duany 2005; C. E. Rodríguez 2000; Sawyer and Paschal 2009). Scholarship on blackness in Latin

America has duly criticized racial democracy claims, pointing out that while they supposedly celebrate racial difference, these discourses have ironically worked to obscure the racism that exists, even enabling the appropriation of indigenous land and the exploitation of indigenous and black labor (Puri 2004; Rama 1996; Telles 2006). The celebration of racial mixing simply idealizes another form of biological race ("mixed race") and thus does not truly get rid of racial essentialism. What comes from celebrating any biological race (or even mixtures acknowledged as "cultural") as an ideal or sign of progress "is not the recognition and proclamation of ethnic difference or of a heterogeneous identity but the Eurocentric glorification of a cultural sameness, or similarity in identity" (Martínez-Echazábal 1998, 23).[12] In Latin American countries where celebrated mulattos/mestizos are considered a symbol of progress, the white element is often viewed as redeeming or "neutralizing" the black, improving societies by whitening them. All the while a structure of white domination is perpetuated as blackness is treated as something to be transcended or escaped from (Aja 2016; Duany 2005; Joseph 2013; Martínez-Echazábal 1998).

In accordance with current moves within Afro-Latino scholarship to underscore the need to understand Afro-Latinidad as a product of the movements of culture, people, and politics across national boundaries (Rivera-Rideau et al. 2016), I place the scholarly critique of racial democracy in Latin America in conversation with critiques of current manifestations of U.S.-based color blindness and racial progress narratives. The United States has derived specious political comfort from the presence of those who are "between" white and black, such as multiracials but also Latinos and Asians. Moreover, some scholars have interpreted the growing reluctance of individuals to choose traditional racial categories as evidence of racial progress in U.S. society, arguing that racial/ethnic boundaries have become more permeable (Alba and Nee 2005; Fernandez 2008; Hollinger 1995; J. Lee and Bean 2004). Other scholars interpret the high percentage of Latinos specifically identifying as white or "other" on the census as evidence that they are adopting a progressive color-blind racial ideology, deliberately downplaying the significance of race (Yancey 2003). Yet this interpretation does not take into account, as Julie A. Dowling argues in her research on how Mexicans in Texas self-identify, that the "the situational use of labels for both Mexican Americans and immigrants often reflects strategies for dealing with discrimination" (2014, 121).[13] Thus, rather than race "not mattering" as is the case for white European immigrants, for whom race and ethnic identity can be purely symbolic (Waters 1990), racial identification for people of color, such as the people of Mexican origin in her study, she argues, is neither optional nor costless (Dowling 2014, 4). In a similar fashion, I contend that the choices Afro-Cubans (and other people deemed in between) make in regards to race and ethnic identification, wherein they take on multiple identities, is not necessarily evidence of racial "progress." Rather, because these choices are often in response to questioning that tells them they are not viewed as normative, their manipulations of their identities often work as evidence of just how pertinent race and racism continues to be in their lives.

Thinking about how Afro-Cubans negotiate their social environment as they confront rejections from people of various backgrounds is useful for gaining a better understanding of the U.S. racial climate today and the power dynamics that preserve the U.S. white/black binary (and the other binaries of worthy citizenship) despite the nation's increased ethnic/racial diversity. Such power dynamics persist even in areas where the population of white individuals has decreased. When Afro-Cubans experience micro-level rejections from white Cubans, African Americans, and other Latinos, these acts, though not communicated by dominant actors, grow from a culture of white supremacy (Gosin 2017, 11). Anti-black prejudices that developed in the United States (and in Latin America) are the legacies of white colonization. Moreover, "In societies that privilege whiteness and denigrate blackness, identities are scrutinized by people of color in order to distance themselves from stigmatized identities or conversely, to hold fast to those identities in the interest of political solidarity" (Gosin 2017, 23; see also Dowling 2014, 115). When Afro-Latinos embrace their multiplicity, it challenges a politics of division that requires the separating out of identities, while also resisting the hierarchization of white over black. I explore the complex Afro-Cuban negotiations of their "in-between" status next, focusing on Afro-Cuban relations with white Cubans in Miami first, wherein they draw on Cuban idealizations of racial democracy in ways dramatically different from their white peers, to contest white Cuban racism and reclaim a Cuban identity. I then examine their interactions with African Americans and ways they negotiate what it means to be "black" in both cities. I conclude with a discussion about

Afro-Cuban interactions with people of Mexican descent in the Los Angeles context as they negotiate a pan-ethnic "Latino" identification.[14]

Challenging White Cuban Hegemony in Miami and Reclaiming a Cuban Identity

Lucy came to the United States in the early 1990s and currently lives in Los Angeles. She idealizes Miami, a city she has spent time in, because even major retailers like Target sell "Croquetas Cubanas" and "Vaca Frita."[15] Josué, who came to the United States on a homemade raft in 1994, similarly has fond memories about the comfort he felt upon arrival in Miami, where he now lives, because of its resemblance to Cuba. "I will tell you that I feel that Miami is like Cuba but with everything [such as basic material needs and luxuries] that is missing from the island," he says. Like Lucy and Josué, some interviewees idealized Miami because the strong Cuban presence allows a cultural familiarity they cannot find in other U.S. cities. The ethnic composition of the Latino population has been changing, but at more than 50 percent of the Latino population, Cubans still hold power and cultural influence.[16] As a result, Miami continues to be a mecca for Cuban refugees. However, while Cubans of all colors often pass through Miami at some point (as they did during the 1980 Mariel exodus and 1994 Balsero crisis), the population of Afro-Cubans there has remained quite small. Given the current small numbers of Afro-Cubans and the fact that only a small percentage of the Cubans who arrived before 1980 were black, the Miami exile community continues to be recognized primarily as white (Ackerman and Clark 1995; Aja 2016). Among the interviewees for this study, more than half had met some forms of rejection from white Cubans in the area. Thus, despite the idealization of Miami by some of the interviewees because of its Cuban flavor, many Afro-Cubans find themselves grappling to feel completely at home in Miami, and some decide not to stay.

The experiences of Afro-Cubans in the United States are distinct from those of other Afro-Latinos because of the differential racialization of Cuban immigration waves (Aja 2016; Gosin 2010). Because Cuban exiles in Miami fleeing the Castro regime before 1980 have been "whitened," Afro-Cubans coming to the United States after 1959 must negotiate their identities in reference to U.S. Cuban whiteness, as well as in reference to Miami Cuban definitions of proper exile politics (Aja 2016; López 2012; Portes and St-epick 1994). Moreover, as Mariela alluded to earlier, even at the basic level of identification, Afro-Cubans must work to be regarded as Cuban. Given Miami's demographics and the presence of African Americans and other black immigrants, it is perhaps not surprising that upon seeing a black person in Miami, one would not immediately think he or she was from Cuba. However, despite demographic realities, many of the respondents viewed being questioned about their identities or being viewed as not Cuban by white Cubans in Miami not as an innocent mistake but rather as a statement about the worthlessness and noncharacter of blackness (Gosin 2017). In Chapter 2, we heard from some of the interviewees that arrived during Mariel, who expressed their dismay about meeting rejection when they first arrived from *los antiguos*—Cubans who arrived in the 1960s and 1970s. In this expanded discussion, we hear from some of the same respondents, as well as others, whose stories illustrate that the tense relations between Afro-Cubans and white Cubans in Miami are not a thing of the past.

Carlos, a very dark-skinned man living in Miami who arrived in the 1990s, captures a dynamic by which, as Alan Aja (2016) explains, white Cubans exercise cultural hegemony over the Spanish language. It is perceived that black Miamians are supposed to speak English, and thus other Latinos (whites and mestizos) are viewed as having "ownership" of Spanish. Carlos laments that he is addressed in English by other Cubans who assume because of his dark color that he is North American or from Guyana or Haiti. He said, "Cubans approach me speaking in English. . . . So, I respond in English. Of course, they notice that I have an accent and so they ask why I speak to them in English. I reply that, well, 'since you spoke to me in English I responded in English.'" For Carlos as well as others, responding in English is a way of denouncing those making an assumption that that they do not speak Spanish and cannot possibly be Cuban (Gosin 2010, 2017). Although the Spanish language remains stigmatized in the United States more widely, due to the Cuban American and Latino transformation of the city, in Miami the Spanish language predominates, and has gained a sort of prestige, even as the language of business. Thus, with Spanish being so widely spoken, Afro-Cubans take it to be even more of an affront when they are assumed to be a non-Spanish speaker. By denying the possibility that they speak Spanish, white Cubans revoke from Afro-Cubans a (shared) Cuban identity.

Cuba is a multiethnic and multiracial country, so Carlos is outraged that Cubans in Miami seem not to know there are blacks in Cuba. "In Cuba, there are towns that are 90 percent black. These are whole towns . . . and so, for the love of God!," he says, continuing his critique. He theorizes that the white Cubans he encounters actually do know that there are blacks in Cuba but want to deny them: "It's a matter of denial or lack of will to acknowledge these things. In Catholicism there is a type of precondition for sinfulness called 'Culpable Ignorance'—and this is when someone makes up their minds and believes, 'I don't want to know.'" In Cuba, a black person would (of course) be assumed to be Cuban, and given the large proportion of blacks in Cuba, the Miami Cuban denials are hard to explain. Antonio López's analysis of white middle-class Cuban American accounts of their return to the island gives some insight. As he argues, their surprise at finding their previously owned homes now occupied by Afro-Cubans (even their former servants) elucidates a belief that the proper place of blacks in prerevolutionary Cuba was in the background of the lives of the "rightful" white owners. Further, the white middle-class Cuban American narratives expose a deeply held belief that the postrevolutionary Cuban national house is "in shambles," in part due to it now being occupied by blacks who could not properly care for it (López 2012, 189). As such, Afro-Cubans, who were invisible before in that all manner of Cuban life was dismissed, remain regarded as not Cuba's "true" inhabitants (Aja 2016).[17]

The idea of Afro-Cuban nonbelonging in the minds of some white Cuban Americans could also be seen in their deployment of stereotypes about blacks in their interactions with some of the respondents. One way these attitudes were expressed was when white Cubans offered "backhanded" compliments about how Afro-Cuban respondents did not fit stereotypes. Digna, who lives in Miami and came to the United States during Mariel, resented being treated as an exception by white Cubans:

> They say that I am a "very decent black person." You know? So, as you can see, they cannot let go of the stereotype. They cannot let go of the basic image of the black person as vulgar or uneducated. Generally, I cause some sort of "trauma" to white Cubans because of their misguided image of how blacks are—or, how they should be. You know? So, when they meet me their image changes and they think, "What is this?" [They think] that what they see is some type of "exception" or "rare phenomenon."

Stereotypes about blacks being "uneducated" or "uncouth" reflect attitudes that are common among whites in Cuba as well as among white Anglos in the United States, who project these same stereotypes onto African Americans.

The respondents were fully aware of the transnational circuits of race making that intervene in their experiences, and when asked to discuss why they believed some white Cubans in Miami display racist sentiments, respondents presented thoughtful analyses about how racial notions from Cuba intersect with the dominant racial ideologies of the United States. Their explanations pointed to individual attitudes but also to systematic and historical causes. For instance, Luis, a 1990s Balsero, contended that white Cuban racism in Miami can in part be attributed to the lingering racism among white Cubans that exists in Cuba. He says,

> Even today, there are traces of this division [between white and black Cubans].
> There are still mothers that want their white daughters to bring home white
> boys and not men such as myself. Such things have happened to me. The wife
> I left in Cuba was white but from an impoverished and very humble family.
> They think, "A fly fell into the milk." I lived through that.

Luis's description of his in-laws' idea that blackness has the polluting effect of "a fly falling into the milk" is an example of sentiments perhaps not openly acknowledged or commonly voiced in a Cuba that purports to be a racial democracy. Such sentiments are indicative that whiteness still reigns as the ideal in the minds of some living in Cuba.

Although there were some interviewees who, when contrasting their racial experiences in the United States and Cuba, seemed to embrace the idea that Cuba truly is a racial democracy, most felt racism exists in Cuba but operates differently than in the U.S. national context. In Cuba, as in many other Latin American countries, the idea of being both white and black is not a foreign concept; indeed, it is not uncommon for families to have many black, white, and "mixed" members. It is also exceedingly common for blacks and whites to socialize together, and they generally live in the same neighborhoods (Sawyer 2006). Moreover, whereas anti-racist discourses did not become prominently affiliated with the identity of the U.S. nation until the 1960s, discourses emphasizing the idea that national identity supersedes racial identity, attributed to patriarch Jose Martí, have been prominent in Cuba since the nineteenth century. In this, Cuba shares Latin American perspectives that endorse ideals of racial democracy. However, Cuba also differs from other Latin American countries in an important way. In postrevolutionary Cuba, blackness has been officially celebrated as the Castro government took on the project of celebrating Cuba's African heritage.[18] This official recognition, albeit problematic in the ways it folklorized blackness (De la Fuente 2001), could allow some blacks to not view their blackness as a liability. The Castro government also underscored the ideals of racial fraternity as it criticized the U.S. capitalist imperialist system by contrasting the gains in the welfare of Cuban blacks and the continued racism of the United States. Castro's usage of racial democracy discourses was strategic and has served to keep disenfranchised blacks in line because any level of race consciousness, even for organizing against racism, has been deemed "racist" (Benson 2012, 2013; Clealand 2013; De la Fuente 2001). Thus, there are many scholars who would push back from any notion that Castro has actually been successful in diminishing overt racism.[19] Yet the political consciousness that postrevolutionary Afro-Cubans imbibed with the culture itself may have inspired them to ask critical questions about race and politics in the context of the United States (Gosin 2010).

In their efforts to explain differences in how they perceive that race operates in the United States and in Cuba, some respondents made reference to Castro's influence. Pedro, who arrived in 1994 as a Balsero, says:

> Even though there was racism in Cuba, it was very, very, very discrete. Because you just cannot do it in public like that because you're going to jail—Castro don't play that. So it's not like here, you cannot call no one a name, white cracker or nigger, no, no. You go to jail for that.

Mariela offers a similar argument as Pedro that Cuban racism is heightened in the United States and provides an analysis of how white Cuban racism shifts in this national context:

> I think that . . . many of them [white Cubans in Miami] have old prejudice and patterns that people [from the exile community] have in their mind. And yeah, and then what happens is that, you know—do what the Romans do. And it reinforces what they had a long time ago in their minds, that Castro kind of put on hold.

As Afro-Cubans have varied opinions about the nature of race in Cuba (Clealand 2013, 2017), the idea that Castro was actually successful in diminishing overt racism is a sentiment not shared by all interviewees.[20] Still, Mariela's assertion that white Cubans in the United States take their cue from white Americans and "do what the Romans do" was a view also held by several other interviewees. Interviewees expressed the view that Miami Cubans have adopted U.S. American values and have become more similar to white Anglos than to Cubans on the island, who they described as holding more traditional Cuban values of family and culture. In this way, they situate Cuban American whiteness within a specific context related to the United States' history of anti-black racism and its anti-communism and imperialist goals. The distinctions they make between Cubans on the island and in the United States arguably require more nuance to capture how white racism prevails in present-day Cuba and how Cuban anti-black attitudes intersect with what white Cubans learn from white Anglos in the United States. Nevertheless, in their arguments, the Afro-Cubans in this study drew on their own perceptions about how the United States and Cuba differ in order to reclaim their Cuban identities, which are often revoked by white Miami Cubans. Many of the respondents draw on Cuba's racial ideologies to contest the racism they meet in the U.S. context and to grapple with the differences in the ways race is lived in the two countries.[21] As official discourses such as "all men are created equal" have been used by African Americans and others in the United States to fight injustice (despite the fact that the nation itself does not actually treat all people equally), Afro-Cuban immigrants, who may be well aware that Cuba does not uphold its official anti-racist discourses, may still invoke these discourses to critique the racism they experience in the United States.

While several respondents expressed disappointment, even anger, over their treatment by white Cubans, other respondents were pragmatic about being assumed they were not Cuban because they were black, even drawing upon their positionality as being in between to have a bit of fun at their questioner's expense (Gosin 2017). When asked whether he gets upset when white Cubans do not recognize that he is Cuban, Charlie, a thirty-eight-year-old who lives in Miami and arrived in the United States from Cuba as a child during Mariel, responds:

> No. I just feel like, good, 'cause I'm more a chameleon; it's good that you don't know what's going on in here. You know what I mean? I'd rather know . . .

like put it that way, [it's] smarter for me to know what's going on and make
them think—make other people think, oh, yeah, they know it—they think
that they know what's going on, but I really do.

Charlie expresses the pleasure of possessing a multiple or Afro-Latino "triple
consciousness" that Flores and Jiménez Román (2009) argue allows for the
embracing and celebrating of all the dimensions of oneself. He knows what
it is to be black, to be Cuban, American, and foreign, breaking down boundaries between native and foreigner, black and white, and good and bad immigrants. He emphasizes that by playing the chameleon, he can blend into
various identities, which allows him to be one step ahead of the people that
he encounters on a daily basis. By playing along with people's assumptions,
he inverts a hierarchy in which white Cubans seek to make determinations
about who qualifies as good/bad immigrants. By establishing the idea that
he is the one who is actually more knowledgeable about who he is and about
who others are, he can challenge other Cubans who make themselves into
the arbiters of proper Cuban identity. Being in between, Charlie and others
like him can traverse various communities, allowing for small victories in
everyday life (Gosin 2017). But this is not to say that simply being in between
means one is automatically better at overtly resisting dominance than others.
Rather, the identity negotiations of people who inhabit the spaces "in between" make even more clear the "increased complexities of the 'color
line' in light of the transnational nature of present day social experience"
(Jiménez Román and Flores 2010, 15).

The respondents' positioning not only in between the United States and
Cuba but in between identities that in the United States are viewed as being
discrete allows them to make spaces for themselves to belong despite meeting rejections. As Caridad indicated, she chooses to associate with other
"othered" people, while Charlie situates himself among Cubans and among
African Americans, moving seamlessly between communities. Mariela challenges anti-blackness in her work but also speaks passionately about the connections between Cubans of all colors, as did the other respondents who expressed a love for Cuba and for Cubans. As she says, "we Cubans have our
problems at home, but you don't mess with us, you know? We have problems
in our family, but you don't mess with them." Racism among Cubans is a
very complicated issue, but much like African Americans with a "double
consciousness"—those who cling to an American identity while still being

able to see how they are positioned outside—the people I interviewed also held strongly to their national identity.

The interviewees differentiated what it is to be white in Cuba from what it is to adopt (or reclaim) whiteness in the United States. Given the irony of the fact Cuba continues to have many of its own problems around race, such distinctions, and the ways in which some respondents reclaimed and affirmed their Cuban identity, could be viewed by some as simplistic affirmations of racial democracy discourses or Castro's rhetoric. Yet I argue that making claim to such a space, wherein blackness has been officially celebrated, offers something different to people who embody blackness than it does for people who do not—it empowers them to draw on official discourses to contest white hegemony. I underscore that we should not interpret this to mean that blacks have it somehow better in Cuba than in the United States. Rather, the distinctions the respondents make offer a clearer view on how national contexts intervene in racialized experiences and intersect to determine the racialized experiences of Afro-Cuban immigrants in the United States. As they link the U.S.-based contentions between white and black Cubans to a white Cuban embrace of capitalist ideals and a U.S. brand of racism, the interviewees connect the source of division between black and white Cuban exiles to the embrace of U.S.-based ideals of worthy citizenship, making Cuban racism into something much bigger than simply "negative attitudes" on the part of white Cubans.

As we have seen, the Afro-Cuban interviewees affirmed, rather than rejected, their blackness in several ways in their negotiations of white Cuban racism: deliberately challenging Cuban exile anti-blackness in personal interactions; reminding us of Cuba's large black population; and critiquing the white Cuban impulse to separate from not only Cuban blackness but also from African Americans. As they draw on their abilities to navigate between the space of Cuba and the United States, they offer a challenge that could translate into better black–white Cuban and African American–Cuban relations because it promotes the questioning of all anti-blackness, regardless of the source.

On Being "Black" and Relations with African Americans

The Afro-Cuban critique of race in the United States challenges divisions between blacks and Latinos not only by indicting white Cubans but by also challenging African Americans who place limits on who qualifies as black (Greer 2013; Hintzen and Rahier 2003; Torres-Saillant 2010, 2002, 2003). Afro-Cubans present these critiques as they negotiate for themselves what it means to be black in the United States. One of the first people I spoke with for this project, Pedro, talks about the first time that he learned that his multiple identities would be a cause of confusion. He learned he would need to privilege his blackness as he distinguished among these identities. Because he was a Balsero who fled the scarcity of Cuba's "special period," the extreme abundance Pedro saw in the United States came as a shock and required a period of adjustment. When he first began searching for a job, he learned another aspect of U.S. culture he would need to adjust to besides the language—the question of "race" and what it would mean in his everyday life. The "race" question on his job application caused him much confusion. He explained, "I put on one application that I'm black when the guy, when I went to the interview, he looked at me and said, 'You ain't black, you're Cuban.' I said, 'Well'—now when I went across the room where he worked, I asked a lady, 'What color I am? And she said, 'You're black.' So after then, you see?"[22] It was not clear to Pedro how he should be defined—should he be defined by his place of birth, as the man who called him "Cuban" explained? Does "race" refer only to the color of his skin? Should the language he speaks define him? Because according to a politics of division he had to choose between identities on some forms, Pedro felt he could not represent his full self. He soon learned from others' reactions to him that being black stood out among his other identities.

Because of the ways their black identities stood out to others, the majority of the interviewees brought up the topic of race and blackness when answering questions about how others placed them within the U.S. racial structure. They pointed out that race is conceived of differently in Cuba, with intermediary terms such as *Jabao* and *mulato*.[23] Adapting to the U.S. context, the majority of interviewees reported that when filling out forms, they pick some combination of identities such as "Hispanic or Latino" or "black" or "other," depending on the choices offered. Those who said they pick "Hispanic" or "other" or "Cuban"—but generally did not choose "black" on forms—acknowledged that "black" was still a salient identity.

Ernesto, who arrived in the United States during Mariel and now lives in Los Angeles, indicated that he preferred to pick "black" alone. In response to a question about whether he believes black Cubans face more discrimination than white Cubans in the United States, he replied, "Oh, yeah, hey. When you're black they don't care if you're Cuban, they just look at your color. And I'm proud to be black. When I fill out an application, you know, I just put 'black'!" Because Ernesto realized he experienced more discrimination because he was black rather than because he was Latino, he sought to venerate and protect his black identity. He added that sometimes he chooses "black" and "Hispanic" to account for the fact he is a Spanish speaker, but being black was more of a salient identity than being Hispanic or Latino.

Being often mistaken for people from the greater African diaspora, Afro-Cubans learn to conceive of themselves as part of a wider African diaspora. In the U.S. context, as they search for community, relationships with other African-descended peoples such as African Americans become a prime option. In Chapter 3, I discussed the long history of Afro-Cuban and African American solidary building (Brock and Castañeda Fuertes 1998; Gómez-Garcia 1998; Greenbaum 2002; Guridy 2010; Hellwig 1998; Mirabal 2003, 1998). Although most of the people I interviewed lived in Cuban, Mexican, or mixed neighborhoods and did not always associate with African Americans on a daily basis, we could see that this tendency continues today. As discussed in Chapter 3, some respondents countered rejection by white Cuban exiles and other Latinos by bonding with African Americans. Carlos, who lives in an African American neighborhood in Miami, provides a further example. He expressed feeling more comfortable with or preferring to associate with African Americans than other Latinos. According to Carlos, when African Americans first notice he is not North American they seem to withdraw, but he said if he continues to reach out, they are usually accepting. He explained, "Personally, it is easier for me to deal with African Americans than Cubans, and I prefer them. They will accept me as an individual. We share similar values and many things. We have mutual respect and balanced relations, while with Cubans it is much more difficult." Previous research on black immigrants has suggested they face an identity choice in which their national identity and racial identity are in conflict—they may privilege a national rather than a racial identity in attempt to escape the stigma of a racialized black or African American identity (Bailey 2000, 2001; Bryce-Laporte 1972; Foner 2001; Landale and Oropesa 2002; Portes and Rumbaut 2001; Portes and Stepick 1994; Waters 1999). However, by the second generation, black immigrants may choose to associate and identify with African Americans because of their comparable social and financial capital, and experiences with discrimination and racism may promote them taking on an adversarial stance to white America (Bailey 2000, 2001; Cordero-Guzman, Smith, and Grosfoguel 2001; Greer 2013; Portes and Zhou 1993; Waters 1999). The respondents in this study, primarily first- or 1.5-generation immigrants, demonstrate how black immigrants' engagement with race can be even more complex.[24] As Carlos and others illustrate, rather than asserting national identities simply to distance themselves from blackness or from African Americans, they may assert their multiple identities (national, ethnic, racial) to account for the multiplicity of their experiences and identities, including their black identities. Moreover, in general, while negotiating what it means to be black in the United States, the Afro-Cuban interviewees in this study challenged anti-black impulses by demonstrating pride in their black identities.

Nevertheless, the issue of language can present a barrier between African Americans and Cubans. In the previous chapters, we saw how some African Americans in Miami lamented the fact that the Spanish language was gaining currency in Miami's labor sphere. In this chapter, Afro-Cubans discuss how being unable to speak each other's language makes it sometimes difficult for Afro-Cubans to make connections with African Americans, as Caridad spoke of at the beginning of the chapter. Similarly, when Juan first arrived in the United States in 1993, he noticed few African Americans could speak Spanish and communicate with him. Because he was perceived to be "black," sometimes African Americans disbelieved that he could not speak English well:

> [African Americans] see me black and I . . . with my broken English, sometimes, people thought that I was [crazy] or something, you know? It's funny, sometimes, you know. When I speak with the black dudes, they look at me like, "Come on, Bro." They think I am making an accent. You know, and they look at me like, "Come on. Cut it out, you know. Can you speak correctly, you know?" And they look at me like I am making fun or something.

For the African Americans Juan encountered, a black person who spoke with an accent or another language was so unusual that they believed he had to be faking it. This inability to communicate with African Americans, as well as being made fun of by some of them for his lack of English proficiency, created distance between Juan and the African Americans he desired to connect with. Like Juan, despite expressing either neutrality toward African

Americans or a preference for them over Latinos, some respondents realized that they were also not fully accepted by African Americans. Juan's experience attests to this in that his inability to speak English well seemed to be looked down upon. With the assertion that he needs to "speak correctly," they position him as less authentically black because even though he "looks" black, he does not speak English.

In cases when African Americans seem to position Afro-Cubans outside the ideal of a "true" black, some respondents spoke of avoiding confrontations by simply blending in and not revealing one's identity. Using such a strategy, they play on the limited knowledge of those around them to position themselves in a greater space of knowing (Gosin 2017). Luis illustrates this idea. He said, "For example, in African American circles, they think I am one of them and, eventually, say 'I thought you were African American.' [But] I stay quiet on purpose to see what they think and say." Charlie provides another example of this strategy. Because Charlie does not have a perceptible accent in English, he is able to blend in with African Americans until he speaks Spanish or hangs out with other Latinos. Then, African Americans at his job or elsewhere realize he is not "one of them":

[The African American person says,] "Yeah, man, you a Chico?"[25] I tell them, "Yeah, I'm a Chico, man." . . . Some of them, you know, if they know me for a long time, they're like, man, it ain't no thing, man. You're still down with me but others would be like, "You're a Chico, yeah." They're like, dang, you know, they like watch the way they be around me like, if, you know, so they got something against it. Whatever, you know, I say it's all good. It's all gravy, baby.

Rather than being put off by the fact that some of his African American co-workers feel "tricked" and become suspicious when his "true" identity is revealed, Charlie relishes letting others struggle with the discomfort of not knowing all of who he is. Charlie feels at home with both Latinos and blacks, speaks in African American slang, and has had experiences much like those experienced by urban black and Latino youths, including surveillance by the police. He views these challenges to his identity, wherein African Americans and others question him, as just part of the territory; they do not upset him. Using the strategy of pretense or simply blending in, Charlie, like other Afro-Cuban respondents, takes on what multiracial studies scholars call "protean identities," wherein people move between multiple identities simultaneously, feeling like insiders to each (Rockquemore and Brunsma 2002). In this way, they create spaces for themselves to belong in several communities while also firmly making claim to a black identity.

Respondents noted that while African Americans are a group particularly curious about their identities, often the questioning they receive from African Americans is less adversarial, seeming to emerge from the limited view among some African Americans about who is a "true black." However, other respondents felt angrier about being dismissed by African Americans. In these cases, some took it upon themselves to "educate" African Americans who "stripped" their black identities away from them. For instance, Digna, who lives in Miami, criticized the African American view that she was not a "real" black in a narrative about an encounter with a black security guard in a department store:

> I don't exactly recall what happened at a department store when I went to exchange a purchased item and the attending employee was a bit stressed. The store security guard said something like, "These black Latins are not *real* blacks." . . . I replied, "What are you saying?" Does that person think that I was born in an incubator, that [I] got this color from being in an "incubator"? . . . I told him, "My hen is from Africa, too." . . . So, the man was embarrassed and did not know how to respond.

Digna used the analogy of a hen (mother Africa) and her chicks (people of African descent) to argue that she too has a real black mother. In doing so, she reminds the African American person that Cubans can also make claim to the African diaspora and criticizes him for his belief that African Americans can make exclusive claims to blackness. Digna affirmed a strong black, or African, identity, and perhaps because of this, in her view, African Americans have learned racism from Anglo Americans. Making a critique similar to that argued in this book and by other anti-racist scholars, she contends that because there is so much racism in the United States, both Anglos and black Americans judge new immigrants as outsiders according to a native/foreigner frame (see also Hintzen and Rahier 2003). In confronting the U.S. racial structure and assumed notions of blackness, she and other black immigrants affirm the idea of a connected black diaspora while simultaneously challenging the idea that, on the ground, shared black skin is all that is needed to build solidarity.

Some respondents even argued that Cuban blacks have stronger connections to their African roots than many African Americans. For instance, Junior, a practitioner of Santería, argues, "black Americans, black people here don't feel any connection to their 'Africanness.' They're constantly espousing that they're 'African-*African*' and yet when you deal with them they don't deal in an African way." Although it is not entirely clear what he means by "an African way," in our discussion, Junior seemed to suggest that African Americans are generally unfamiliar with African languages, such as those used by practitioners of Santería, as well as other cultural manifestations of African culture that are prominent in Cuba. Moves to essentialize what it is to be African are problematic whether these moves are made by African Americans or Cubans. Nevertheless, several respondents demonstrated clear pride in their blackness or Africanness by embracing cultural traditions that, though widely practiced in Cuba, have African origins (and by taking pride in the fact that these practices and traditions have African origin). In this way, they further disrupt an African American hold on what it means to be black and illustrate the diversity of black cultures and experiences. They also affirm their own blackness by decisively making claim to a *Cuban* black identity.

Just as they negotiate their relationship to blackness, Afro-Cubans must also, in cities with so many Spanish speakers, negotiate their black identities in relation to the larger category "Latino." They are able to see that native-born, non-Latino Americans often call for the exclusion of Latino immigrants by asserting that Spanish speakers have an unfair advantage or that Latinos (viewed as immigrants) are taking American jobs. Both arguments have been prominent in African American–Latino conflict. Being both black and Cuban, how do Afro-Cubans fit within such debates? The interviewees provide many examples, as we have noted, of being discriminated against because of their language and their color, but in at least one instance, being a Spanish speaker was more of an advantage than being African American. Pedro recounted a story about applying for the same job as an African American, with whom he became friendly in the process. According to Pedro, although the African American was highly qualified, he was rejected because he could not speak Spanish, and Pedro got the job instead. As he told the story, it was clear that the incident still saddens him:

> So when it came down to—to the position—you know, they chose me because
> I was speaking Spanish. And they did not choose him. Boy, I wish you could

have seen that boy's face. . . . That was one of the things that I feel bad about that I was chosen over an American because I speak Spanish. It really hurt me. . . . And I said, "Brother, you know what, listen, my man, we can still hang together and you just have to speak Spanish, you have to learn how to speak Spanish."

Pedro's sadness about disenfranchising a "brother" reveals a consciousness that can be drawn upon by other Spanish speakers to try and bridge differences based on language. Pedro has very dark skin and his own blackness cannot be denied. He has adopted African American slang, so it is clear he does not seek to avoid being associated with African Americans. Pedro's positioning between black and Latino categories may thus enable increased awareness among African Americans that "Latinos" are not a faceless horde of people taking their jobs but include people who look like them who are also trying to navigate a system that pits brother against brother and sets one disenfranchised minority group against another.

Between Blackness and *Latinidad* in Los Angeles

> If you don't look like a Mexican, then you ain't no Hispanic.
> (Fermín, Los Angeles)

Afro-Cuban experiences negotiating race and place in Los Angeles offer a comparison piece to Miami, particularly when thinking about the promises and failures of the diversity of the United States in terms of breaking down ethnic barriers. They also offer a wider view into the question of how Afro-Cubans negotiate their subjectivity in relation to the panethnic configuration of Latinidad. People of Mexican descent are by far the largest Latino population in the United States and in Los Angeles. As Fermín observes, most people do not perceive Afro-Cubans as fitting the image of "Latino" because the predominant image of a "Latino" in Los Angeles is a person of Mexican descent. This idea that there is one way to look "Mexican" or "black" is related to the United States' racial/ethnic categorization paradigm and the historical desire to differentiate people of color from whites.

Los Angeles is highly diverse, but like Miami, it has its share of ethnic divisions, indicated by geographic separations. According to the 2010

Census, the population of Los Angeles County is 48 percent Latino, 28 percent white non-Latino, 14 percent Asian, and 9 percent black non-Latino.[26] Although people of Mexican descent in Los Angeles have not attained the power and influence that Cubans have in Miami, the Latino, and Mexican in particular, influence is quite dramatic. Though California has the fourth largest Cuban population in the United States, Los Angeles's Cuban population is quite small (Logan 2003). There is no one Cuban neighborhood, but an annual festival at Echo Park serves as a place to bring L.A. Cubans together. Echo Park, historically a Mexican enclave, hosts a Cuban festival on May 20 each year, in commemoration of Cuban Independence Day. The festival takes place at the lake, which includes a statue of Cuban patriot Jose Martí among its monuments. I met several of the people I interviewed for the first time at this festival, which many attend on a yearly basis. They indicated that the festival is a space where newly arrived Cubans can find other Cubans to help them get settled in the United States.

Los Angeles is known for its diversity and the idea that people generally get along and are not afraid to cross boundaries, but Juan's experiences contradict this view. When Juan came to the United States from Cuba, what he found most difficult about adjusting to life in Los Angeles was navigating the racial and ethnic social divisions of its geography:

> What really amazes me . . . is how people from the West LA . . . they don't go to the South Central . . . and, vice versa, no? People from the east, like my ex-wife, you know, she was Chicana, you know, 100 percent—"viva la Raza." Proud to be a Chicana. She and her friends, they never come to the west side. . . . Then, you have the white Americans . . . they don't go south—they don't pass from Pico and La Brea. So every time I talk to somebody, they're from a different, you know, group, I mean, *etnia*, or ethnicity, and I tell them that I went to this part of town and they look at me [and say], "You crazy! Don't go there!" And, people sometimes in that community when I go there . . . sometimes, they look at you like, "What are you doing here?"

Juan had come to the United States when he was thirty years old, during Cuba's "special period," to make a life with his wife at the time, an American citizen of Mexican descent. However, he would find that his daily life interactions meant learning how to cross various borders between communities, identities, and languages. With his multiple identities—a black person with a notable Spanish accent, from Cuba, a country many people he encountered did not know much about—it was not always clear to him where people thought he *did* belong. As a result, he says, "In general, I feel that I don't fit in any community. I mean, for me it was hard to understand why the Chinese live here and the blacks have to live here." He also found that despite having married a woman of Mexican descent, he would have trouble fitting in with other Mexicans, who rejected him because he is black.

Magaly similarly met rejections from people of Mexican descent and recounted what it was like to grow up in Los Angeles, to which she immigrated as a child. There were several incidences, she says, when people thought she did not know Spanish and, while speaking Spanish, said negative things are about her:

> You know especially when I was in high school and middle school, kids would think I would not understand what they saying, which I was like, I think I know more Spanish than them, you know, I know more, probably more about the culture than them, than they probably know themselves. . . . For example, I would . . . in school, girls would be behind my back, they'd say, "Oh look at her, she . . ." I don't know, maybe 'cause I'm chubby, I don't know, they would just bring something up, you know, just bothering people, and I would turn around and say "Oh my God, what are you saying," you know, in Spanish, in their language, and they'll just get stuck, like, "Oh, she knows it!"

Similar to the experiences of Cubans living in Miami, Magaly and most of the other respondents living in Los Angeles encountered other Latinos who assumed they were "black" and that they did not know Spanish. Often, respondents directly confronted these persons to challenge their assumptions.

Ernesto, like Fermín and other respondents, lamented the fact that he was not viewed as Latino because of his skin color and was angered by snubs from Mexicans. Ernesto critiqued his Mexican friends' disrespect of black history and culture:

> You know, I have a lot of Mexican friends, but they have issues with blacks, you know? They have issues with blacks. They're ignorant. Those that don't got an education, they're ignorant regarding blacks. That's what I hate, because those that live in a black neighborhood listen to the black music. . . . And they [Mexican men] love black sisters!

Ernesto also pointed to cultural appropriation among Mexicans (and whites), the tendency to like black culture but not black people.[27] However he defines the term "black," Ernesto finds value in blackness. Although his defense of that value also risks perpetuating stereotypes about Mexicans in such expressions of anger, Afro-Cubans, like Ernesto, belied a strong affective desire to assert their identities as Latinos and contest people who felt they could decide where they did and did not belong (Gosin 2017).

While some interviewees were quite angry about being underestimated by some of the people of Mexican origin that they encountered, given that Los Angeles generally does not have a large presence of Afro-Latinos, the confusion about racial identity could be seen as an honest mistake. Yet until recently, Mexico had officially downplayed the presence of Africans in Mexico, and such moves to dissociate from blackness could play a role in the rejections Afro-Cubans receive from recently arrived Mexican immigrants. Derogatory assessments of black identity are often actually directed at African Americans, since the Mexicans are mistaking Afro-Cubans for African Americans. Hence, anti-black attitudes among people of Mexican origin in Los Angeles speak to prejudices that also exist in their countries of origin, developed because of the legacy of colonization by whites, as well as the anti-black attitudes that are prevalent in the United States with which attitudes from the home country intersect (Roth and Kim 2013). Thus, paying attention to how Afro-Cubans challenged the assumptions of some of the people of Mexican origin they encountered reminds us of the need to combat the anti-black racism that some Latin American immigrants bring with them from their countries of origin, the anti-black racism of white Anglos, as well as the anti-black racism that results from a Latino buy-in to U.S.-based white dominant racial frames (Gosin 2017).

Though blackness remains under siege in Los Angeles, as can be seen in the economic disenfranchisement of African Americans and criminalization of black males, some black Cubans in Los Angeles found that not being immediately read as Latino could be an advantage. Such complexities illustrate the various forms the binary divides that compose worthy citizenship take and how they intersect. As Fermín observed:

> When supposedly the police or the immigration, when they attack people, they only attack a certain group. You know, if you look like this, you're Hispanic. And I could, like me, I'm Hispanic too, and I could be walking down

the street they won't mess with me, because I don't look like them. Which is what, a stereotype, right?

Fermín's comments remind us that because the Mexican stereotype leaves blacks out of the Latino category, Afro-Latinos can avoid the intense surveillance of, and stigma attached to, people identified as Mexican. Appearing African American may allow a certain privilege based on the perception that African American equals "American" and that Latino equals "foreign" or non-American according to a native/foreigner frame. There is a tremendous stigma attached to Mexican identity, not only in California but across the country, wherein they are viewed as "illegals." Mexican immigrants have been portrayed as a poor, law-breaking "problem" (Chavez 2001, 2013; Hayes-Bautista 2004; Santa Ana 2002). In California, public concerns over increased Mexican immigration inspired Proposition 187 (1994), which sought to refuse undocumented immigrants medical and educational services, and Proposition 227 (1998), which banned bilingual education. Such policy moves in California as well as similar moves in other parts of the country remind us of the strength of the native/foreigner frame that positions Latinos, along with (but quite differently from) blacks, into the role of "noncitizens."

Fermín's comments also remind us of the difference immigrant or refugee status makes for Cubans versus Mexicans (Dowling and Newby 2010; Newby and Dowling 2007). U.S. immigration policy has not welcomed Mexicans as it has Cubans, who were constructed as political rather than economic immigrants. In Florida, Anglos have viewed Cubans as threatening to take over, similar to the ways some Anglos in California view Mexicans. However, immigration policy has historically protected Cubans from the same types of instabilities experienced by people of Mexican descent who, regardless of citizenship status, are viewed as always already illegal. Thus, as Cubans, their experience of Latinidad has differed from that of many other Latinos because of the unique political concerns of Cuban refugees and the idea of Cuban exceptionalism. Thinking about all these complexities illuminates the fact that people of color are all demonized within a white elite–dominated system, albeit in different ways. Latinos and African Americans taking note of this reality can turn their angst away from one another and onto the problematic system that pits them against one another.

Such complexities and commonalities were not lost among the respondents. Along with negative interactions with people of Mexican origin, some respondents discovered the sense of community that can come from embracing their multiplicity—their identities as Spanish speakers and as immigrants. Though there are fewer Cubans in Los Angeles, as in Miami, Spanish television and radio thrive, and Spanish-language billboards pepper the city. One can speak Spanish daily. Thus, some interviewees spoke very specifically about having good relations with Mexicans and other Latinos based on a common language and the condition of being an immigrant. For example, Nancy stated,

> It does not matter if my friends are Mexican or from elsewhere, "unity" is the key. The truth is I don't care, nor do I ask, if they are Cuban or not. I just feel happy when I hear someone speaking Spanish. Instantly, people turn into friends and brothers—that's what happens. . . . The language unites us all. . . . And, necessity unites us, too. We can see that they came with the same intentions—in different ways—but to make a better life for themselves, to better educate their children, to take advantage of the opportunities afforded to us, and, so, they come for the same. So, aside from the differences, the same basic necessities unite us.

For Nancy, a common immigrant experience encouraged empathy with Mexicans and other immigrants in Southern California. If someone new to the country needs furniture, food, or other resources, Nancy feels compelled to help, as others helped her when she first arrived. Thus, as expressed by others, Nancy is able to feel at home with the other Latinos with whom she associates and enjoy Los Angeles's diversity and the blending of cultures.

Encouragingly, living among other Latinos in a city with no sizable Cuban community, Afro-Cubans in Los Angeles can draw on their multiple identities to find ways to connect with other Latinos and build on their commonalities. As Afro-Cubans negotiated the Latino identity in Los Angeles, several found ways to bond with other Latinos such as Mexicans in spite of also experiencing rejection from some of them. Scenarios wherein Mexicans spoke about them in a derogatory fashion, assuming they were African Americans, or challenged them for being among other Latinos, showed them that their blackness calls their identity as Latinos into question. Such experiences illustrate what is left out in the pan-ethnic category. Afro-Cubans took on various strategies to contest their exclusion, including direct confrontations, in order to challenge the shortsightedness of Latino anti-blackness as well as exclusive claims to a Latino identity. In doing so, they challenged anti-black impulses among some Latinos that may lead to conflict not only between black and nonblack Latinos but also between Latinos and African Americans. In these ways, they point to gaps and overlaps between blackness and Latinidad and also illustrate ways that other differences based on national origin, race, immigration status, and so on can be overcome.

Conclusion

The strength of the boundaries placed around blackness in particular is powerfully illustrated in the experiences of black Cuban immigrants recounted here, for whom it is necessary to think about blackness and racial identity not only when filling out forms but also when finding community. Though living in cities with rich racial/ethnic diversity such as Miami and Los Angeles, they report they are often questioned about their identities not only by people with innocuous curiosity but also from people who rejected them, deeming them too different to belong. In their stories, we see how they are viewed as not fully fitting in any group to which they would supposedly belong—Cuban, African American, Latino, immigrant, refugee, and so on. Yet their day-to-day lived experiences negotiating their multiple identities challenge such rigidity and illustrate the overlaps that exist between identities such as "Latino" and "black."

The testimonials of the Afro-Cuban respondents provide insight into the specific ways post-1980 Afro-Cuban immigrants experience and combat racism and micro-level rejections in the U.S. context, a subject that has been understudied. Embracing all their identities, they found ways to fit in as Cubans, blacks, and Latinos while also acknowledging their *mestizaje*—the fact that within the same immediate Cuban family one can find members of various colors. Moreover, in spite of the rejections Afro-Cubans sometimes face, they were able to emphasize commonalities, often drawing on perspectives on race and identity cultivated in Cuba. Discourses of racial democracy in Cuba are just as problematic as the idealism of color-blindness in the United States. Yet, respondents often "reclaimed" the ideals of Cuban racial fraternity to fight the racism they experienced in the United States. In their dealings with white Cubans, they took back their often-revoked Cuban identities, pointing back to Cuba, where being black and Cuban was normative. In doing so, they illuminate the role of ideology in creating separation between black and white Cuban identities in specific national contexts. Their strong attachment to being Cuban allowed them also to unite with some other white Cubans on the basis of shared culture and national identity. At the same time, they held a strong sense of the political and racial histories that determine the ways they as blacks are negatively positioned in Cuba and in U.S. society. When interacting with African Americans, they were able to create bridges and associations built on shared black or African pride. Similar experiences of discrimination on the basis of blackness also allowed them to connect with African Americans. With people of Mexican descent in Los Angeles, common immigrant and refugee experiences bonded some Afro-Cubans with recent immigrants, with the Spanish language connecting them to all Latinos. Afro-Cubans, like other Afro-Latinos, differ from English-speaking black immigrants because of their compounded identification with a stigmatized Latino identity. Thus, along with helping us challenge the persistence of anti-blackness in the hemisphere, their positionality evokes the conclusion that efforts intended to fight anti-black racism should be linked to the fight against anti-immigrant nativism. All in all, their multiplicity presents a challenge to bipolar and other rigid racial notions because, as their lived experiences illustrate, identities often viewed as discrete truly overlap in meaningful ways.

Their intervention goes deeper than simply breaking apart racial categories. As they directly challenged the rejections they faced, their experiences move beyond a suggestion that racial or cultural multiplicity is in and of itself the answer to racial binarisms. Indeed, an uncritical exaltation of racial hybridity or of racial diversity leaves little room for the critique of the injustices suffered by blacks, Latinos, and other racialized groups because such exaltations lend themselves to denials of racism (Gosin 2016; Jiménez Román 2005; Puri 2004). Afro-Cuban experiences and direct challenges to the rejections they face make clear the fallacy of racial democracy discourses and the idealism of color blindness, because the racism they are subjected to illuminates how deeply the legacies of white racism and imperialism are rooted in U.S. society and accepted to varying degrees by Americans of many different ethnic backgrounds. Moreover, they help remind us that in a racial system set up to maintain the place of whiteness atop a racial hierarchy, people of color are forced to preoccupy themselves with standard racial labels and identities as they undergo scrutiny from whites. They may dissociate from some identities to protect themselves from racial stigma or embrace identities for the purposes of political solidarity (Gosin 2017, 23; see also Bobo and Hutchings 1996; Dowling 2014, 115). Thus, what we see in Afro-Cuban interactions with white Cubans in Miami, Mexicans in Los Angeles, and African Americans in both places are the complicated ways people of color get caught up in the politics of race as they seek their place within the nation (Gosin 2017, 23).

Afro-Cuban experiences of race are similar to those of other Afro-Latinos when it comes to managing the stigma attached to blackness in the United States, but their case is also distinct. Cuban immigration waves have been racialized differently in part due to the politics of the historical political enmity between their homeland's government and that of the United States. Unlike other immigrant groups for whom previous migration cohorts are viewed as consistent in race or ethnicity, white and black Cuban Americans experience an artificial divide created by U.S.–Cuba relations and immigration cohort effects. Thus, Afro-Cubans must contend with the particular ways that Cuban exiles in the United States "reclaim" whiteness (López 2012) as they seek to affirm their status as worthy citizens. Among the "old guard" Cuban exiles in Miami are individuals who set themselves up as people that can determine who qualifies as "good immigrants" and who discriminate against newer arrivals—blacks in particular. In their critiques of such white Cuban racism, the Afro-Cuban respondents help remind us that Cuban exiles are rewarded for achieving parity to Anglo whites through their upward mobility. They are also rewarded for adopting ideologies of worthy citizenship, which function to create separations not only between Cubans based on race but also between other marginalized groups.

When thinking about the Latino category more broadly, Afro-Cubans enable a critical challenge to Latino whiteness because, by pointing out and directly challenging anti-blackness among Latinos, they underscore that although racial systems in the United States and Latin American countries differ, they are equally guilty of preserving the predominance of white over black (Aja 2016; López 2012; Oboler and Dzidzienyo, 2005; Rivera-Rideau et al. 2016). In the United States, the pan-Latino identification functions much like the hybrid identities that have been central to how national identity has been formulated in several countries in Latin America and the Caribbean (Gosin 2016). There is resistive potential in creating bonds among Latinos and in embracing the ambiguities inherent in the category "Latino."

Moreover, as Latinos are similarly stigmatized as "foreigners" or "illegals," it is crucial for us to continue to bring focus to the specificity of how the Latino stigma is deployed by the dominant order and negotiated by Latinos of various national origins. However, in an *uncritical* celebration of Latinidad, there is much that is obscured. As scholars of Afro-Latino studies have argued, it is essential for scholarship to engage with how racist notions from Latin America and the United States intersect and differentially affect the immigration incorporation of Afro-Latino immigrants into the specific national context of the United States (Flores-Gonzalez 1999; Gosin 2017; Jiménez Román and Flores 2010; Torres-Salliant 2002, 2003). Examining how Afro-Cuban immigrants negotiate the intersections of blackness and Latinidad and rejections they sometimes face from other Latinos allows an important critique of the ways white supremacist notions have been embraced or perpetuated by nonblack Latinos. Moreover, we also gain insights into how peoples' ideas about the politics of blackness shift or are clarified as they confront new domains of power in specific national contexts.

Rejection from white Cubans and other Latinos may push some Afro-Cubans to associate more with African Americans. Indeed, a sense of pride in blackness cultivated in Cuba may be a reason both to hold onto their Cuban identity and to align with other blacks. Still, in the United States, some Afro-Cuban respondents found that the borders around blackness were also policed by African Americans. As discussed in previous chapters, the idea of black unity was vital in African American civil rights struggles, and the desire among some African Americans to build solidarity with others of African descent according to a Pan-African ideal remains an important aim today toward the contestation of white supremacy. Perhaps as a result, in cases when black immigrants seem unwilling to join in ongoing struggles, or when they avoid affiliating themselves from African Americans, some African Americans see this as not only a rejection of an important political identification but as also a move by black immigrants to align themselves with whites and the dominant social order (Greer 2013; Torres-Salliant 2010). Yet, as some African Americans set themselves up as "ethnoracial border patrols" who can judge whether individuals have taken on the "proper" political alignment, they also set themselves up as "natives" who can decide who is and is not a "true black" (Torres-Salliant 2010, 2002, 2003). Like other black immigrants, Afro-Cuban immigrants illustrate in their negotiations of what it means to be black in the United States both the limits and the promises of Pan-African idealism. Furthermore, they challenge the idea that black identities should be defined by U.S. African Americans. By emphasizing their multiple positionality as blacks and Cubans and conceiving of race and identity as hybrid, Afro-Cubans like other Afro-Latinos teach African Americans that there are many different ways to be black and that this diversity does not preclude a consciousness that can be built upon by various (Afro) Latino groups to challenge anti-blackness.

The rejections Afro-Cubans experience in the United States happen within a specific racial context—one in which multiple identities are viewed as distinct and blackness is denigrated. During the Barack Obama presidency, the U.S. government seemed to signal a growing tolerance for ethnic, racial, and sexual difference in policies that were enacted. Moreover, that someone like Obama could be elected to the U.S. presidency was touted as evidence that the United States was moving toward a postracial promise (Da Silva 2014). Yet, that Obama himself, the son of a white American woman and a black African man, was almost always categorized in the media and by the public as "black" (rather than "white" or "mixed") is indicative of the persistence of the conception of "race" as fixed or essential and of the rigidity of the black/white binary. This point, as well as a racist anti-Obama backlash, made it clear that despite the emphasis on multiculturalism and color blindness that we saw during the period, very rigid ideas of what it means to be black remain popular among various groups.

As double minorities (Denton and Massey 1989), immigrants of African descent such as the Afro-Cubans in this chapter are profoundly affected by the U.S. historical and continued denigration of blackness. At the same time, they are affected by its reluctance to accept "unassimilable" immigrants. The implications of all this are that "although boundary crossing may be rising, and the color line fading, a shift has yet to occur toward a pattern of unconditional boundary crossing or a declining significance of race for all groups" (J. Lee and Bean 2004, 237). Thus, when thinking about race in multicultural America today, we must continue to understand the complexity that blackness brings to this question of the shifting color line, further examining how it intersects with anti-Latino and anti-immigrant sentiments. In doing so, we can continue to interrogate the role of anti-blackness in maintaining notions of worthy citizenship and assess how such notions affect relations between African Americans, Latinos, and other non-Anglo racial/ethnic groups.

Conclusion

In 2012 in Sanford, Florida, a "white" man, George Zimmerman, shot and killed Trayvon Martin based on the assumption that he did not belong in the neighborhood. The killing of Martin, an unarmed black teenager, would become another national wake-up call about the consequences of the white dominant view that black men are dangerous and would give rise to the modern Black Lives Matter movement. This movement gained steam as cases of police shootings of unarmed black men recurred during the decade. Yet, in the Martin/Zimmerman case, the framing of the shooting as another example of white-on-black antagonism was contested by Zimmerman and his family. Claiming that race played no part in his actions, his family revealed that Zimmerman was both white and Latino and drew on this Latino heritage as proof that he could not be racist. However, after Zimmerman was acquitted of guilt by a jury, outraged observers argued that presumptions about Zimmerman's whiteness and about Martin's blackness allowed jurors to see Zimmerman as "having his heart in the right place" when he took his job as a neighborhood watchman to a dangerous level.[1]

Though also identifying as a Latino, Zimmerman's whiteness gave him more credibility over Martin in determining who had the right to belong in his and Martin's shared space.

In the same year that Zimmerman was acquitted, the debate over which group—African Americans or Latinos—is most worthy of national belonging and which poses the greatest national threat also emerged at anti-immigrant rallies. Such rallies have become a stage for powerful white politicians to play African Americans against Latinos. At one rally opposing the 2013 proposed immigration reform bill, hundreds of protestors from across the country gathered at the U.S. Capitol to voice their discontent that the bill would grant amnesty to millions of undocumented immigrants. A key talking point of Republican representatives was the assertion that these immigrants would take jobs away from American citizens, particularly the most disenfranchised and especially African Americans. Professing concern that African Americans are being pushed out by immigrants made political sense in part because the late twentieth and early twenty-first centuries have seen the rise of "majority-minority" cities and states, with dwindling numbers of white residents and historically African American residential areas increasingly populated by Latino immigrants. The rally on Capitol Hill thus presented a striking example of how powerful actors can capitalize on possible conflicts between "native minorities" and immigrants to support their political agendas. Making the claim that African American citizens are being disenfranchised by Latinos, whose citizenship status (and thus worthiness) is always already in doubt, these leaders frame U.S. belonging as the prize in a zero-sum game that minority groups must battle over, during which whites make the final decisions about who has won.

While white voices are often at the forefront of pitting blacks and Latinos against each other, perceptions about the scarcity of resources and concerns about their own standing in the U.S. nation can also cause friction between these groups. At the 2013 rally, NPR interviewer Ailsa Chang spoke to Patty Pitchford, a black woman from Los Angeles, whose sentiments echo the conservative stance, which often conflates "Latino" and "immigrant" identities. Pitchford observed that in the county services office where she works, more and more Spanish speakers are being hired. She prefaced her dissenting comments by making the point that she was not a racist: "In my family, I have Vietnamese. In my family, I have Spanish. In my family, I have white. In my family, I have Trinidad. In my family, I have African." But, she argued, "If this amnesty pass, they will be taking our jobs. They're already taking over, period."[2] As an African American, Pitchford implied that the jobs in social services were "our" jobs, and her comments reaffirm the sentiments not only of some conservatives but also of members of the black public who have worried that the gains of the civil rights movement are being eroded. They maintain that immigrants will take the few jobs available to African Americans, particularly in the poorer classes. As such discussion about black disenfranchisement at anti-immigration rallies and the case of Zimmerman/Martin illustrate, people of color can be called on to perpetuate the racial status quo. Thinking about African American and Latino conflict in the present moment and in relation to the white power structure reminds us that, although whites are becoming the numerical minority, dominant white racial frames about worthiness continue to hold power. To continue forging effective alliances between various minority groups such as African Americans and Latinos, these frames must be fervently challenged.

In a historical sense, the nation has come far in regard to race, but the emergence of colorblind racism has come to exemplify one of the major obstacles to challenging dominant white racial frames (Bonilla-Silva 2018). For example, the election of Barack Obama to the presidency was touted by colorblind racists as proof that marginalized groups or individuals no longer had reason to complain about their treatment in the United States. There is certainly room to celebrate; for African Americans, who could not even vote in elections only fifty or so years before, the election of a man of African descent to the presidency was a major victory. However, the multiculturalist Obama moment lulled some into a very premature celebration of the end of racism. In reality, racism during the Obama era was characterized by a new insidiousness. As ethnic studies scholar Dylan Rodriguez notes, the Obama era "install[ed] a 'new' representative figure of the United States that, in turn, opens 'new' possibilities for history's slaves, savages, and colonized to more fully identify with the same nation-building project that requires the neutralization, domestication, and strategic elimination of declared aliens, enemies, and criminals."[3] In addition, a racist anti-Obama backlash, cases such as Martin/Zimmerman, as well as countless other occurrences of white officials' brutality toward blacks, illustrate that during the Obama presidency, more overt forms of racism had not abated.

Since the end of the Obama era and the election of Donald Trump, the nation has seen even more the virulent force with which white supremacist narratives and policies have come roaring back to undo any advances that had been made. Trump ran on a campaign overt in fomenting a U.S. politics of division—and despite this, he would win. Some voters, seduced by his promises to "Make America Great Again" through economic nationalism and the promise of jobs, were willing to ignore his early campaign trail comments equating Mexican immigrants with crime, drugs, and rapists.[4] Others voted for him because they were excited that Trump was willing to voice the racist and anti-immigrant sentiments they shared. Yet during the campaign, many predicted that someone like Trump could never win if everyone went out and voted—given demographic shifts, there simply were too many minorities and anti-racist whites that the numbers would be against him. Yet, as an NBC news story points out, "Republican elites infamously concluded after [Mitt] Romney's defeat [in 2012] that the party needed to grow more inclusive toward minorities. The GOP decided it needed to make inroads with Latinos or risk ceding all future presidential elections to Democrats. Trump . . . proved them all wrong."[5] Although Trump did lose the popular vote by a wide margin, his base came out in force. By winning the Electoral College, he was able to gain a historic win.

The show of resistance that would immediately follow in the form of a worldwide Women's March was also historic. During the march, hundreds of thousands of people allied with Black Lives Matter, gender equality, LGBTQ activism, and immigrant rights, among others, came together for a common good. The march, and subsequent resistance mounted against Trump administration policies, which target everyone from women, immigrants, Muslims, transgender people in the military, and African Americans, keep people hopeful that a politics of division, in the end, can be overcome.

Still, this historical moment gives us even more confirmation of the need to stay diligent and to not rest on a "presumed alliance" between marginalized groups.[6] We must be mindful of the fact that while Trump won just 28 percent of the Latino vote, the share of the Latino vote won by his challenger Hillary Clinton (66 percent) was less than the share Obama won in 2012 (71 percent).[7] And even though on the campaign trail Trump linked blacks to "inner cities" and crime, he also gained more support among African American voters than did his GOP predecessor Mitt Romney, during his 2012 run against President Obama.[8] The motivations of these voters continue to be analyzed. Some attribute the outcome to voters' excitement about Trump exhibiting the "strong-man," "get tough" qualities they attribute to a "real" leader; others say it was the failure of the Democratic candidate to appeal to minority voters. Either way, that Trump could get elected in the first place reminds us that ideologies that exemplify the white power base's exclusionary ideals of "the nation" have a strong appeal. Accordingly, we cannot simply rely on numbers—the numbers of anti-racist whites and the larger numbers of minorities—to ensure a change. Ethnic/racial multiplicity in and of itself is not the answer, because as long as just enough people support a racist agenda, either directly or indirectly, racist power dynamics securing the supremacy of whiteness will continue.

Thus, our scholarship must challenge us to answer the hard questions posed by Nicholas De Genova in his studies on the impact of Latino and Asian immigration on U.S. nationalism. While plenty of scholarship has, importantly, focused on the resistance efforts of people of color, De Genova asserts, "One of our critical tasks is to illuminate the ways that racially oppressed people do and do not make claims on Americanness. Do they disrupt, repudiate, subvert or endorse the hegemonic U.S. social formation? Are their efforts enlisted in the service of sustaining the resilience of their own or other's oppression? . . . We must have the political courage to soberly assess not only the heroism of our organized mobilizations but also the mundane struggles of our alienated everyday life" (2006, 17). With the prediction that by 2045 Anglos will become a U.S. numerical minority, we need to closely examine the ways racial conflict and racism endure and are reconfigured in a new demographic reality. Taking on this vital challenge, this book has examined antagonistic relations and discourses among non-Anglo groups in Miami to gain lessons from the past that can help clarify these contemporary questions of immigration, solidarity, and culture in the changing racial dynamics of the United States.

I take as a point of departure what W. E. B. DuBois wisely observed over a century ago; nonwhite groups have been seeking to more fully identify with the nation-building project all along. However, as DuBois highlights, this desire to be included in the nation is related to a deep longing to not be "a stranger in mine own house" (1982, 45–46). White elites have operated as the gatekeepers of the doors to the nation and have historically formulated membership in exclusionary terms to preserve power in the hands of the white few (Feagin 2010). "Others" have been required to prove they belong on the basis of "worthy citizenship," by conforming to proper "Anglo," middle-class, moral standards, such as being hard-working, self-reliant, law-abiding, and freedom-loving (Ong 2003; see also Gans 1999; Gray 1995; Urciuoli 1996). I have argued that as minority groups seek to position themselves more favorably in society, they sometimes draw on the language and ideals of worthy citizenship because, as Nicholas De Genova maintains, "nativism appears to be necessary for the production of national identity" (2005, 7). By extension, adopting a nativist stance, to some degree, is necessary for national inclusion. A nativist stance relies on, indeed requires, asserting one's own more deserving positionality in reference to "unworthy others" (Cacho 2012; De Genova 2005; Ong 2003). Part of my work, then, has been to critique the embrace of the ideals of worthiness by racialized groups. Yet just as or perhaps more importantly, I am also emphatic that we cannot read these dynamics as racialized groups simply "doing to each other what white people have done to them."[9] Emphasizing the power of ideology in perpetuating white dominance as well as the prevailing white power dynamics involved, I underscore that when the fundamental philosophies of nation building that enabled its creation are adopted and enacted by minority groups, it is because the nation offers what *looks like* inclusion but is in reality an elusive racial bribe (Guinier and Torres 2002).

In this book, I have highlighted three overarching discursive, or racializing, frames, which I contend compose worthy citizenship. One is the black/white frame, a primary frame through which whites historically positioned black as opposite to American (Ellison 1952; Feagin 2010; Morrison 1992, 1994). New immigrants learn that they must define themselves not only in relation to U.S. whites but also in relation to U.S. notions of blackness (Noguera 2003; see also Horsman 1981; Ong 2003). The second, the good/bad immigrant frame, draws on the model-minority idea, which requires immigrants to demonstrate that they compare favorably against African Americans in terms of social mobility, crime statistics, health, and so on. They become "model minorities" when they prove they are contributors rather than a burden to society (R. G. Lee 1999). With the good immigrant frame, immigrants also self-impose these requirements to affirm their own acceptance in U.S. society and to maintain a sense of power (Saito 2001; see also Aranda et al. 2009). The third frame is the native/foreigner dichotomy, in which groups claim to be more entitled to citizenship on the grounds that their group has a longer history of time or investment in the United States. This claim can also include arguments that because of a longer history of oppression and suffering, one's group has already proven they are more worthy of inclusion than the Other. Though these frames are sometimes distinct, they usually overlap to help to maintain the dominant order, which ultimately continues to position whiteness at the top of the racial hierarchy.

I have argued that because race in the United States operates through a politics of division, interminority conflict is rooted in these racialized ideologies of "worthy citizenship" as they come to be internalized by minority groups themselves. Previous scholars have noted that minority groups can perpetuate white racial frames but do not illustrate *how* (Feagin 2010; Kim 2000; Picca and Feagin 2007). Using examples from the late twentieth century and focusing on the complexity of relations among African Americans and Cuban Americans, generations of Cuban immigrants, and white and black Cubans, I looked closely at official media discourses to reveal how efforts to secure status as true Americans can become a reinscription of white racializing frames and demonstrate how these racializing frames come to be accepted as the commonsense approach to becoming a part of the nation.

These central claims reveal a host of implications for the future study of race making in multicultural America. What will be at stake for groups of color still seeking to establish their place in U.S. culture when or if other racialized groups, rather than whites, are viewed as their main competition? How will "native minority" groups continue to receive new immigrants? How will we as researchers and activists work to challenge white supremacy as it is manifested in different forms, even perpetuated by people of color? How might people on the margins continue to challenge dominant racialization paradigms? In cases of black–Latino conflict in particular, what possible solutions could people embodying both black and Latino identities, such as Afro-Cubans, provide for easing interethnic conflict? In the sections that follow, I reflect on such questions as I explore how the Miami case provides a way forward for both scholars and activists in this new era of race relations in the United States.

Interethnic Conflict and Dominant Discourses about Belonging

Focusing on African Americans and a Spanish-speaking population in Miami, this book is in conversation with the growing field of research on African American and Latino relations. This scholarship emphasizes that conflict is not the primary mode in which African Americans and Latinos interact and argues that the media's depiction of relations between these groups has been problematic. Indeed, news magazine reports have emphasized individual and group-level animosities and contentious battles over space, providing virtually no historical context for such battles (Cacho 2012; Shah and Thornton 2004). Blacks have been depicted as victims of the growing immigration. Yet, at the same time, rather than the empathy often linked with depictions of victimhood, African Americans are portrayed as "complainers," simply finding someone else to blame for their failures to properly assimilate and "get a job." The concerns of members of both Latino and African American communities are reduced in these reports to contemptible squabbling (Shah and Thornton 2004). More recently, as Lisa Marie Cacho explains, "the official narrative of black-Latina/o conflict and competition works to pathologize both groups, regardless of which side we take," pitting them against each other and demonizing both: Latinos steal jobs; blacks steal because they have no jobs (2012, 18). Whether it is Latinos or African Americans who are painted as the victim in the individual stories, each narrative positions the groups as complicit in protecting the borders and boundaries of the United States, resulting in an official narrative that vacillates in its characterization of both groups, exchanging their oppositional roles as protectors and destroyers of the nation. This vacillation is indicative of the ways white elites strategically employ dominant gatekeeping narratives of worthiness to maintain their positioning atop a racial hierarchy, pitting groups of color against one another.

There is great reason to be optimistic about relations between African Americans and Latinos and the prospects of coalition, particularly in the political arena (Hero and Preuhs 2013; Márquez 2014; Sawyer 2006; Telles et al. 2011). My optimism is substantiated not only by research but also by personal life experience. Indeed, I come to this topic as someone who has experienced more cooperation than conflict between African Americans and Latinos in my personal life. As a young child, I was a military brat who lived in Spain for some years. When I moved back to the States and to Southern California, I lived in areas where there were few African Americans. Often the only one in my grade school classes, I found a welcoming social group among many friends of Mexican or Latin American origin. Perhaps my familiarity with the Spanish language and other aspects of Latin cultures allowed me to feel at home among these friends and their families. What started as a childhood social connections developed in college into a lifelong commitment to anti-racism—motivated not only by my own experience navigating U.S. society as an African American, with parents from the Deep South who lived through the end of the Jim Crow era, but also by my real-time observations of what was happening around me as my Latino friends fought against stereotypes and faced an expressly anti-Latino political climate. In my personal life, the overlaps between African American and Latino political concerns have been abundantly clear. My early experiences benefitting from the camaraderie that can exist between groups of color has heightened my commitment to challenging existing divisions and highlighting the links between African Americans, nonblack Latinos, and Afro-Latinos, and among other groups. I have also been witness to many other encouraging shows of solidarity today, such as those on my own campus as politically motivated student representatives of Black Lives Matter prominently supported rallies against the Trump administration's immigration policies, specifically the ending of the Deferred Action for Childhood Arrivals (DACA) program, an Obama-era program intended to defer punitive action for young adults and children who were brought to the United States as children and thus do not have citizenship status.

Still, I have also been privy to conversations among African Americans outside my scholarly circles lamenting the Latino "takeover," and I have heard Latino friends, to my surprise, making derogatory statements or assumptions about black people in my presence. I realized that although conflict is not the primary mode of interaction between African Americans and Latinos, there is still pressing need to challenge the divisions that exist. Indeed, research has pointed to the current reality of contentious relations, such as those I discuss in this book, among African Americans and Latinos, especially in new Latino immigrant destination sites. For lower-class blacks and Latinos, the real inequalities and scarcity over jobs and battles over turf may be more impactful (Gay 2006; Marrow 2011). Moreover, studies on racial attitudes demonstrate that Latinos may have more negative views of African Americans when it comes to stereotypes (Gay 2006; Kaufmann 2003; McClain et al. 2007; Mindiola, Niemann, and Rodriguez, 2002; Oliver and Wong 2003; Vaca 2004). Although African Americans generally have less negative attitudes toward Latinos than the reverse, they still may harbor negative attitudes toward Latinos, viewing them as economic competition (Betancur 2005a; McClain et al. 2007; McClain and Karnig 1990). In times of perceived crisis (such as the Mariel exodus and the Balsero crisis the tragedy of

September 11, 2001, or, more recently, economic recessions), politicians often play on fears about the perception of scarce jobs and resources and the need for "national security." The realities of poverty and unemployment, as well as fear narratives perpetuated on a national stage, can promote increased competition among some minority groups when they are convinced the other is their main threat.

Because context matters in analyses of interethnic conflict, I have paid close attention to the complexities of the local context and local concerns in Miami, which are distinct from other areas of the country. For instance, it is essential to keep in mind the larger context of the nation's imperialist project in the U.S.–Cuba conflict, as well as the complexities of how whiteness and blackness are regarded in Cuba, to fully understand the views expressed by members of the affected communities in *El Nuevo Herald* and the *Miami Times*. This context heightened African American and Cuban American concerns about the impact of these particular immigration waves. The more powerful and higher-class position of some members of the Cuban community adds an element in the Miami case of African American–Cuban relations that is different than black–Latino relations in other cities where Latinos are not as prominent in the economic and political arena. Moreover, Cubans differ significantly from other Latino groups in that they were invited to the United States as exiles rather than being viewed as needy and impoverished immigrants. Cubans gained tremendously from being favored in U.S. immigration policy. Today, the contradictions between the United States' Cold War–era policies that rewarded Cubans for risking all to gain freedom and current immigration policy moves that penalize migrants from Mexico and Central America for seeking the same goal are abundant. Thus, Cubans often do not fit well within U.S. Latino political imaginaries.

Still, the cases this book explores offer the opportunity to develop a wider understanding of the dynamics at play for minority groups in competition with each other writ large. This is because on a day-to-day basis, Cubans are often lumped together with other Latinos when it comes to fights over who belongs in the nation. Regardless of ethnicity, Latinos have historically been reduced by native-born non–Latino Americans to "foreigners" or "unwanted immigrants." Cubans too have suffered from the "Latino threat narrative" (Chavez 2013)—racialized discursively as immigrants threatening to "take over" (Grenier and Pérez 2003). Moreover, although there are key differences in how conflict between African Americans and Cubans manifests in Miami as compared with black–Latino conflict elsewhere, the simultaneous and contradictory idea that Cubans are threatening to take over but are also more favored by whites also plays a major role in negative relations between African Americans and Latinos in other areas of the country. Studies have shown that in spite of restrictive immigration policies toward various Latino groups, in places such as North Carolina, California, and Texas, whites' preference for Latinos over blacks (in hiring, for instance) plays into black resentment against Latinos (Betancur 2005a; Fabienke 2007; Gay 2006; Marrow 2011; McClain et al. 2007; McClain and Karnig 1990; Mindiola et al. 2002). These conflicting notions wherein Latinos, including Cubans, are perceived to be too numerous, threatening to take over, but simultaneously favored over African Americans, reveal what Cubans have in common with other Latino groups and frame the dynamics of black–Latino conflict not only in Miami but across the nation. Furthermore, as I have discussed, many Latinos bring anti-black notions from their home countries or adopt anti-black perspectives as they learn to disparage African Americans. Thus, as research focusing on El Nuevo South and other areas of the country attests, strained relations between African Americans and Latinos today is a matter of great concern (Gay 2006; Marrow 2011; McClain et al. 2007).

In this context, Miami serves as a cautionary tale. By 1980, the racial dynamics that are now occurring across the country as whites become the numerical minority had already occurred in this highly diverse city. The intense interethnic conflict between the two largest minority groups, African Americans and Cuban Americans, which occurred in Miami, can be viewed as an example of the worst-case scenario that could occur across the country (Grenier and Stepick 2001). The divisions set up between African Americans and Cubans and between black and white Cubans in the Miami scenario illustrate how the same black versus white dynamics of the city's past manifested themselves during a time when Miami was transitioning into one of the most diverse cities in the nation. In today's multiethnic society, it is necessary to examine how the poles of "black" and white" continue to be entrenched in our society. Sticking to black/white and white/other racism functions as a type of nostalgia for some people who long for the "simpler" times when "others" knew their place and did not pose as much of a threat. These binary racial poles create divisions even between different minority groups.

Toward addressing these tensions, I have challenged existing scholarship, which primarily attributes interminority conflict to causes such as limited resources or demographic shifts, by focusing on discourse and ideology as primary factors in its emergence. Clearly, the material realities of structural inequities in relation to jobs and other economic concerns play a starring role. Yet the abundant examples of coalition building among people of color in order to attack mutually experienced economic and social problems remind us that conflict is not the only response to scarcity. To take on an oppositional stance toward the "Other" is a choice that is made. In regards to this choice, I accede that minority or racialized groups are agents in disparaging blackness when they do so (as did some of the white Cubans in this book) and in promoting anti-immigrant sentiments and policies (as did some African Americans in Miami). However, I seek to remind us that the decisions made by minority groups or individuals to compete with other minority groups are often shaped by dominant ideologies that dictate how groups can achieve social membership in the nation. For instance, white Cuban exiles indeed brought anti-black and pro-white attitudes with them to the United States, these attitudes also intersect with their particular configurations in the context of the United States, heightened by the role of state intervention as it historically designated Cuban exiles preferred or "good immigrants" in its foreign policy. Moreover, the precariousness of Cuban American whiteness due to their differentiation from white Anglos and their being lumped in with other immigrants as a "foreign threat" create compounding dynamics in which they might be compelled to "reclaim" whiteness (López 2012). In short, even when it is clear that members of these groups hold strongly to anti-black or anti-immigrant sentiments, we must still remember that the decisions made by minority groups to engage in conflict cannot be decontextualized from the already existing power dynamics of the country, as if these choices are not constrained in any way by the exclusionary framework of worthy citizenship perpetuated from above (Ong 2003).

Indeed, it is mainstream society that needs to change its exclusionary practices, as minority groups are reacting to existing parameters of racial oppression. As Kim (2000) suggests, our scholarship on interethnic conflict must avoid decontextualization, depoliticization, and the delegitimation of the concerns of minority groups (4). We must take seriously minority concerns about finding jobs, maintaining families, and obtaining a modicum of dignity. We must understand that by voicing their concerns, the communities discussed in this book seek to challenge the idea that they are not true Americans. Such concerns should be taken seriously, even when they are manifested in ways we as scholars and activists would not promote. Again, I want to be careful in my critique of the operationalization of notions of worthy citizenship by some people of color. We have seen, since the grand resurgence of white supremacy today, pundits blaming this resurgence on "identity politics." They argue that by calling attention to racial or sexual difference (and the problems associated with the othering of those differences), activists, scholars, and other individuals have undermined American unity and have in fact caused the backlash against "political correctness."[10] These same folks might be quick to assert that people of color can be equally guilty of racism. My scholarship adamantly rejects such notions. I contend that we must remember that interminority conflict occurs within a context in which things are not and have never been equal. Minorities have been historically excluded from the nation and even when seemingly included or even preferred (in the case of Cuban exiles), their current standing is always placed into flux (their status as true Americans can at any time be revoked or called into question). Keeping prevailing power dynamics in mind, we must differentiate the uses of dominant racializing frames by people of color from the ways these frames are used by privileged whites. Taking all this into account is necessary in future research to avoid a simplistic blaming of the groups themselves in cases of interethnic conflict when they arise.

Immigration, Race, and the Reframing of the Nation

Future research needs to continue exposing white supremacy in the "new America" not only by challenging actions made by white actors but by also delving into how it is adapted by nonwhite or non-Anglo groups. But on a more fundamental level, research needs to continue to challenge the widely accepted notion of the United States as a white nation, which is at the root of the tendency to ignore concerns of minority groups. As Picca and Feagin (2007) point out, another manifestation of white racial framing is taking for granted the idea that various social institutions are normally white controlled, without questioning white dominance and privilege. The normative framing of the nation is everywhere: in the talk of police officials declaring whites the appropriate arbiters of morality onto "deviant" black populations and in the speeches of politicians who frame who "we" are as a nation by excluding

Latino immigrants. As Entman and Rojecki have observed about another arena where this normative framing is quite evident, the news, "At the most general level the color pattern of the news conveys a sense that America is essentially a society of White people with minorities . . . as adjunct members who mainly cause trouble or need help" (2000, 63). We must reframe the nation, underscoring that the nation is not just a neutral geographical space that immigrant groups enter, or a white land with "adjunct members," but a nation in which minority groups are integral. In doing this work, we must also take seriously the idea that even relatively recent immigrants sometimes see themselves as (and are) unequivocal Americans.

The taken-for-granted construction of the U.S. nation as "white" is reinscribed in immigration research. Though immigration researchers have explicitly questioned white privilege by noting how assimilation processes for immigrants of color have been hampered by racism, the insistence on continuing to define immigrant adaptation by the extent to which they approximate whites socially, economically, and residentially is problematic. Although such comparisons capture the realities of U.S. power dynamics, they do not often capture the types of adaptation immigrants of color must make because they enter into a U.S. racial and linguistic caste system. Paying closer attention to this aspect of how immigrants adapt to life in the United States, as I do in this book, allows us to further bridge the separation between studies on race (emphasizing the black/white or white/nonwhite divide) and scholarship on immigration (which focuses primarily on the assimilation processes of immigrants of color). As recent scholarship has pointed out, theoretical approaches to the study of migration continue to largely ignore the role race plays in immigrants' lives (Sáenz and Manges Douglas 2015; Valdez 2017; Valdez and Golash-Boza 2017). Paying close attention to the role of race in immigrants' lives, along with examining the traditional measures of assimilation—economic mobility, home ownership, acquisition of the English language, and so forth—we can further examine adaptation processes that are about staking a claim to an American identity. As new (and even old) immigrants meet racist and nativist challenges to their right to belong, there are multiple ways they work to challenge these assertions. Capturing this complexity helps clarify often unexplored tensions involved in how immigrants assimilate into the context of the United States.

For instance, in this book I examined the role race plays in (white) Cuban exile adaption processes by revealing some of the ways they made claims to an American identity as captured in the Spanish-language press in the specific context of a Cuban immigrant backlash. At the same time that I levied a critique against such claims when they reinforced the idea of white supremacy and black inferiority, I also treated Cubans of all colors as a minority group. I sought to unpack the complexity of Cuban American whiteness, the whitening of the exiles in the United States due to U.S. designation of them as anti-communist heroes, as well as the precariousness of this whiteness (Aja 2016; López 2012). The precariousness of Cuban whiteness is related, in part, to the fact that Cubans are subjected to anti-immigrant sentiments held by members of the public and to the fact that in the United States, Cuban mestizaje and blackness (or blackening) make them "not quite white" in the context of the United States.

Because Cuban exiles must negotiate intersecting and transnational racial ideologies, I engaged with how race is framed in Cuba and with how white Cuban deployment of anti-blackness is related, in part, to those frames. However, I do not take a transnational approach. Transnational immigration studies scholars emphasize the idea that immigrants are not bounded by the nation-state (Aparicio 2006; Schiller, Basch, and Blanc-Szanton 1992). Such a perspective is important because it focuses on how immigrants can reconfigure their position of marginalization in the United States by creating a new sense of community through their involvement in the home country (Levitt 2001). However, "scholars focusing on transmigrant activity do not sufficiently analyze the extent to which immigrants organize in ways that are not transnational" (Aparicio 2006, 7). Seeking to better capture the struggles of immigrant groups that are related to their worries about access to local resources, I followed Nancy Raquel Mirabal's (2003) call for more studies (focused on Cuban exiles) that place emphasis on what it means to "ser de aqui"—to be from "here," putting roots in the United States and building identities around an American identity.

Another way in which this book has worked to integrate the study of race and immigration is in its focus on how immigrant incorporation is related not only to how immigrants are accepted by whites but also to how they are accepted by other traditional minority groups. I address this by exposing varying and sometimes contradictory degrees of willingness among African Americans and Cuban exiles in Miami, and also people of Mexican descent in Los Angeles, to accept other groups. Given demographic shifts, some immigrants are more likely to interact with other minorities rather than whites on a daily basis. Incorporating critical race perspectives into the future of im-migration research allows us to better examine the multilayered dynamics of interminority relations in such areas.[11] Examining these relations, even those that are antagonistic, allows us to more effectively examine the complex ways race relations manifest in a demographically transformed U.S. society. We capture not only how immigrants must adapt to and contest their exclusion from the nation but also the ways they can also operate as local state-level actors and producers seeking to gain and assert a modicum of privilege in a white hegemonic sphere (Aja 2016, 7–8). In the case of Cuban exiles, this not only means celebrating how they resist traditional assimilation models by gaining success and upward mobility by holding fast to their own culture and traditions (as we see in the scholarship of proponents of the segmented assimilation model) but means also challenging instances when they deem newer immigrants "bad immigrants" and instances when they disparage Afro-Cuban and African American blackness. In taking on this challenge to understand how immigrants of color can turn around and stigmatize or malign other minority groups or more recent immigrants, our scholarship must continue examining how the racial understandings immigrants held before coming to the United States intersect with the ideals about race they may acquire in the new and different racial climate of the United States (Roth and Kim 2013). In the case of studies on immigrants coming from Latin America, doing so allows us to contribute to Latino and Afro-Latino stud-ies, accounting for the multiple ways transnational histories of white settler and colonial domination overlap and intervene in intra-Latino relations in the geographical context of the United States. Taken together, integrating scholarship on race and immigration can allow us to examine the multiple layers involved in how immigrants experience race in the United States as they work to be included or, at least, survive in the "host" county.

Extending African American Unity

Just as it is important to take notice of the struggles of immigrant groups to be included and survive in the host county, in an era of Black Lives Matter we must continue to recognize the legitimacy of African American concerns about their social, economic, and political losses. The strength of racism and the continued disenfranchisement of African Americans justify black leaders' continued attempt to organize around black identities and create a united front. The social devaluation of blackness has been and remains foundational to how race is made in the nation and is related to the historical positioning of African Americans "others" against white "citizens." The unequal conditions and life chances endured by African Americans are in part a result of continued racial discrimination and white privilege. As Stuart Hall argues, African Americans become conscious of their subordination through race, and thus they understandably use that modality to resist subordination (1978, 347). Therefore, they may look to bond with other blacks for a common cause. In their efforts to combat this inequality, African Americans have also traditionally sought to frame race relations within a structural framework; hence, they have often organized their struggle in a manner inclusive of other immigrant groups who, because they share the experience of living in a white supremacist society bent on preserving the status quo, also share a similar history of racism and discrimination. However, the complaint of some African Americans, as expressed in the *Miami Times* for instance, was that this stance of advocating for everyone else's rights places African Americans at a disadvantage because no one else is looking out for African Americans.

How can African Americans continue to work toward social justice for themselves while also building alliances with other minorities? How will they incorporate non–African American blacks and other immigrants without an African heritage? As this book discusses in Chapters 3 and 4, the *Miami Times* demonstrated that Pan-African ideals were important to the community the newspaper served, especially during the time of Mariel, but there was some evidence that the ideals were less important during the Balsero crisis, perhaps because of growing anti-immigrant sentiment in the country as a whole. For instance, Haitians, who were placed under the African American umbrella, were somewhat less accepted. In the *Miami Times*, Afro-Cubans could be integrated with African Americans because of their blackness, but because the newspaper often painted Cuban Americans and other Latinos as Spanish speakers taking their jobs, in reality a dichotomy was set up that would also exclude Afro-Cubans because they speak Spanish and are Latinos. This exclusion was further corroborated by the interviews with Afro-Cubans, who reported that they were at times viewed as outsiders by African Americans, a fact that further attests to the limits of the Pan-African ideal. In Miami today, the numbers of African Americans are decreasing, with much of the growth of the black population attributed to the increasing numbers of

Afro-Caribbeans. More widely, research by scholars on African American acceptance of other black immigrants, such as Jamaicans, Haitians, and so on, indicates that a shared black identity is not always enough to form alliances, especially when black immigrants are viewed as taking African American jobs and when they do not automatically support causes championed by African Americans (Greer 2013; Kasinitz 1992; Waters 1999). Thus, demographic shifts and the question of how black Cubans and other black immigrants fit within or outside a Pan-African or black identity present new dilemmas for African Americans, disrupting their long-standing reliance on black racial identity for political mobilization.

Asians, Latinos, and other immigrants of color have challenged the logics behind native/foreigner divides, and black immigrants such as the Afro-Cubans in this study challenge the meaning of "black" or, more specifically, of black *American*. The experiences of Afro-Cubans and that of other non–African American blacks challenge African Americans to reassess the models they use for organizing and challenge the impulse among some African Americans to measure true blackness by an American identity and the use of the English language.[12] As African Americans not only in Miami but across the nation as a whole are confronted with these challenges, they continue to grapple with how to truly fold immigrants into their fight for African American civil rights. Material realities, such as the fact that at 13 percent in 2013 unemployment among African Americans was twice the national average, often inspire the fears expressed by blacks taking on a nativist stance (like Pitchford at the 2013 rally, described at the beginning of this chapter). Still, the African American dedication to the ideals of the civil rights movement also remain strong, as revealed in the *Miami Times* coverage that did provide some examples of how some African Americans saw coalition with immigrants as a possible solution to African American social problems. Black leaders also cautioned the African American public not to fall into a trap set by dominant whites of divide and conquer. Such perspectives point to the resistance efforts African Americans have and can continue to put forth against the black/white binary and the native/foreigner frame.

Though African Americans and Latino immigrants often share residential space, the experiences of African American communities are often lacking in immigration scholarship. Moreover, African American scholarship tends not to capture how the lives and struggles of immigrants overlap with the struggles of African Americans. In our research on the dynamics of race in multicultural America, we can contribute to African American studies by further examining African American concerns about the impact of immigration on their communities and by examining the dynamics of relations between African Americans and other minority groups. Given their continued systematic disempowerment, we must be careful not to forget the specificity of African American experiences and the particularities of their situation when it comes to race. In the spirit of a commitment to examining the specificity of African American experiences, I chose to give their perspectives focused attention in this book. Because they are the descendants of enslaved Africans who endured the "peculiar institution," de jure segregation, and other efforts by white elites to disenfranchise and disparage them, their experiences differ from those of recent immigrants regardless of race or origin. But given the realities of demographic change, African Americans must also continue to look to what they share with other marginalized groups. As they gain greater understanding of how racism affects Afro-Cubans and other Afro-Latinos in particular, African Americans across the country can draw on similarities to solve problems facing not only African Americans but all blacks in the United States. At the same time, they can continue to draw parallels between their experiences and those of immigrant groups who are currently being disparaged and criminalized by dominant elites in order to achieve mutually beneficial social justice goals.

Rethinking Racial Paradigms

Earlier in this chapter, I discussed how Afro-Cubans and other Afro-Latinos mount a challenge against limited notions among some African Americans about what it means to be black. My focus on Afro-Cubans in this book also allowed for a challenge to the stigma attached to blackness as accepted not only by white Americans but also by Latino groups such as Cubans and Mexicans. By weaving the voices of black Cubans throughout the text, this book also provided a lens into how antagonistic racial discourses affect individual lives. As such, the research contributes to a "critical Latino whiteness studies" (López 2010, 190; see also Aja 2016). Furthermore, the Afro-Cubans interviewed for this book allow us to broaden our thinking about black and Latino identities and the boundaries between them. Their lived experiences illustrate the porousness of the boundaries that were being placed around identities such as white, black, native, foreigner, Cuban, and African American. As blacks and Latinos, the Afro-Cubans in this study helped illustrate how people on the margins can challenge dominant racialization paradigms because their multiple positionality allows them to act as mediators, translators, and interpreters at crucial sites of encounter (Anzaldúa 1999; Jiménez Román and Flores 2010). There is a long history of U.S. familiarity with Afro-Cubans through enjoyment of Afro-Cuban music, from the popularity of Mario Bauzá in the 1930s to the "boom Cubano" of the late 1990s and the popularity of the late Celia Cruz (Gosin 2016; Hernández 2002; Knaur 2001). There is much to be celebrated about Afro-Cuban contributions to music and culture, but when Afro-Cubanidad is relegated to the realm of "the cultural," this reaffirms dominant stereotypes about difference, particularly blackness, and signifies an inclusion predicated on the idea of exclusion (Dávila 2001; De la Fuente 2001). This book complicates research on Cubans, other Latinos, and African Americans in the United States by listening to Afro-Cuban immigrant voices and paying attention to their experiences as political subjects, particularly their views on how race is lived in the United States.

Focusing on post-1980 Afro-Cuban immigrants and race, I contribute to Cuban studies by adding my voice to the growing scholarship analyzing anti-blackness among Cuban Americans. The words of Dora Amador, the Afro-Cuban award-winning journalist from *El Nuevo Herald*, captures why this is such a touchy topic as she comments on responses to articles she wrote on black Cuban experiences with white Cuban discrimination in the United States:

> On two more occasions, I have taken on the issue of racism in my writings; on both I have met with the same despicable objections to bringing up this topic: that it fosters division in the exile community, that it hurts the Cuban cause, that Fidel Castro uses it for his own ends, that this is not the time to talk about this—interestingly enough, it is never the right time—that first we have to free the motherland, and later there will be time to talk about such things, etc.[13]

Amador goes on to take a very strong stance against the excuses made by critics, arguing that now is the time to broach the issue of racism among Cubans to help unite the Cuban community. *El Nuevo Herald*'s general depiction of a singular Cuban voice is disrupted by her and other articles that illustrated how black Cubans experience the exile identity differently. These perspectives underscore the experiences recounted by Afro-Cubans I interviewed, who found that Miami Cubans sometimes disparaged them and were surprised when they did seem educated or upwardly mobile. The newspaper coverage and the voices of black Cubans interviewed for this book undermine the "happy" picture of the Cuban American family unified in their exaltation of the American ideals of freedom and democracy and anticommunism. Furthermore, Afro-Cubans disrupt the boundaries between "white" and "black" Cubans by drawing on ideals of Cuban racial fraternity in ways different from their white counterparts (who often used them to stifle black claims of racism) to challenge anti-black frames of reference as they are manifested in the context of the United States.

When thinking about the Latino category more broadly, we are able to see the ways Afro-Cubans challenge the tendency within Latino studies to emphasize the idea of Latinos as *mestizo* and transnational subjects in ways that obscure the problem of anti-blackness among Latinos (Rivera-Rideau et al. 2016). With the rise of the U.S. Latino population, the Pan-Latino identification has grown in significance in the United States; however, many scholars have disputed the use of the ethnic umbrella terms "Hispanic" as well as "Latino," because the labels obscure the localized differential experiences of peoples of Latin American and Caribbean heritage based on national origin, gender or sexuality, and race (Beltrán 2010; Flores-Gonzalez 1999; Frank et al. 2010). Yet in specific settings, Spanish-speaking peoples from disparate groups have found families of resemblance, adopted one another's cultural practices, and broadened their sense of identity to include a collective one. William Flores and Rina Benmayor (1997) have argued that in the context of the United States, this construction resists imposed binaries of race, gender, or national origin and emphasizes the ability of marginalized groups to reconfigure race. But the experiences of black Latinos (and other immigrants of African descent) in the United States also demonstrate that according to the one-drop rule, they are expected to identify according to their race of black identity over and above their other identities (Bailey 2000, 2001; Landale and Oropesa 2002; Torres-Salliant 2010; Waters 1999, 2001). Thus, investigations of the "Latino" experience must also examine, as does the current research, what has been made invisible in the discussion of pan-ethnic identities.

The rejection of Afro-Cubans by some white Cubans can in part be attributed to attitudes about black inferiority held among whites in Cuba; in the U.S. Afro-Cubans are also directly affected by the negative evaluations by some white Cubans of African Americans. For instance, the blackening of Mariel Cubans in *El Nuevo Herald* on the basis of qualities used in the United States to disparage African Americans could be seen in the stories focusing on criminality and using the word "ghetto" to discuss a set of behaviors among the Marielitos not sanctioned in U.S. society. Furthermore, Afro-Cubans in Miami and Los Angeles explicitly attest to the fact they are affected by the stigma attached to an African American identity when they are mistaken for African Americans by white Cubans and Mexicans. Seeing the particular ways Afro-Cubans drew on their Cuban heritage to contest anti-blackness as experienced in the United States and deployed not only by whites but also other Latinos, we gain insight into how ideas about blackness shift as Afro-Latino immigrants move across space and time. As we see the ways they affirmed their blackness, we also add to Afro-Latino scholarship by "further mov[ing] us away from the assumption that . . . Afro-Latinos are somehow prone to pathologically deny[ing] their blackness" (Rivera-Rideau et al. 2016, 13).

Future research on Afro-Cubans and other Afro-Latinos would do well to investigate their political orientations. The interviewees in this research were not directly asked about their political stance, in regards to either U.S. or Cuban politics, so we do not know if they are more inclined to support Latino or African American leaders and causes. What will be their response if Latino groups vie for their support as Latinos, and African Americans seek to include them as blacks? A larger study might reveal reliable patterns and a more conclusive answer to the question of how their racial identities intersect with their political choices.

The responses from the Afro-Cubans interviewed for this study capture just a segment of Afro-Cuban immigrant experiences, but they challenge us to think about what we can do in our daily interactions to undermine racism and inequality. We see clear problems in their everyday experiences—in the African American rejection of Afro-Cuban foreignness, sometimes rooted in language issues, as African Americans tend to associate English with a true African American identity. Latinos, in contrast, may associate Afro-Cubans with an African American identity, which is also stigmatized among some Latinos. But some of the Afro-Cubans interviewed demonstrated a willingness to cross boundaries viewed as rigid by others, in an effort to connect with others on the basis of shared race, culture, immigration status, and language. By drawing attention to gaps and overlaps, the Afro-Cubans interviewed for this project challenge us to answer the hard questions about race and nationalism, belonging, and the boundaries drawn as we create political communities. This book's investigation of the Afro-Cuban experiences indicates that their complex racial identities contribute to their manipulation of otherness, revealing overlaps between African American and Latino communities. Together, these racialized minorities can provide and take advantage of spaces for resisting dominant racializing frames, thus enhancing the possibilities for greater interethnic understanding and alliances. Such alliances do not simply reinscribe the use of race as the principal basis of identity. Rather, these sorts of alliances are about going beyond the limits of racial/ethnic identities to find common ground that can then be galvanized for the fight against already existing racial and racist institutions and orders.[14]

Miami Today

Decades removed from the crises discussed in this research, the Miami of today has continued to transform. While Cubans continue to hold power and influence and represent more than half the Latino population in Miami, the Latino population has greatly diversified.[15] In Little Havana, one can find the growing presence of other Latin American immigrants, who run businesses and restaurants there. As mentioned earlier, the African American population has also declined overall, with the growth of the black population today being attributed to immigration from the Caribbean. While in previous decades incidents would flare up because of the tensions between African Americans and Cuban Americans, today these populations generally do not often interact with one another. Tensions between African Americans and Cubans may thus seem to be a thing of the past, but the fact that these populations, who could gain so much from coalition, generally avoid one another *is* a problem. What we do see today in Miami is that the traditional mode of race making, which positions blacks at the bottom of the social order, is still in effect. The interviews in the current study, corroborated by Alan Aja's work (2016), demonstrate that white Cuban racism against black Cubans and other blacks is not a thing of the past. Furthermore, as Aja (2016) found, in general, black populations in Miami, whether native born or immigrant, are struggling economically disproportionately compared with other local groups in Miami-Dade County. As Aja contends, Cubans, along with Latinos from South American countries who on the U.S. Census are most likely to report themselves as "white," tend to fare considerably better than blacks in the area. All these factors illustrate that, in a diversifying Miami, race continues to be a strong mediating factor in the social and economic situation of Miamians.[16]

Cubans have a well-deserved reputation of being an insular and staunchly conservative community; thus, scholars have been pessimistic that they will play an active role in working to create more equal conditions in Miami. Concerning African American and Cuban relations in particular, scholars have been even more pessimistic about the prospects for political cooperation because they traditionally support opposing political parties, Democratic and Republican, respectively. However, the actual diversity in thought and opinion that has always existed but was submerged in the insistence on a united anti-Castro posture became more apparent during President Obama's first run for president. For the first time in history, a Democratic candidate won the majority of the Miami's Latino vote. The Latino victory was largely due to the strong non-Cuban Latino presence that had grown in Miami during the first decade of the twenty-first century. But 55 percent of Cubans aged twenty-nine and younger voted for Obama. This contrasted sharply with the proportion of Cubans sixty-five and older, 84 percent of whom continued to vote Republican. Hence, we saw a growing division within the Miami Cuban community, as the older Cubans remained loyal to the Republican ticket while younger Cuban Americans voted more in line with Latinos across the country.[17] The increasingly moderate and liberal views of the second and third generations provide room to be hopeful that political alignment among younger Cubans, Afro-Cubans, African Americans, and the increasing population of black Caribbeans can allow greater understanding and coalition to work toward solving problems affecting all these groups in Miami.[18]

Still, dramatic political transformations spurred a backlash and tightening of the exile identity among some members of the exile community. During the Obama administration, dramatic moves were made to reestablish diplomatic relations with Cuba, such as the softening of travel restrictions for U.S. citizens seeking to visit Cuba, slackening import restrictions, and expanding the ability for U.S. imports to Cuba. Cuba was also taken off the terrorism list, and a U.S. embassy in Havana was reestablished. The Cuban old guard was strongly opposed to these moves, and Trump's promises to undo the warming on U.S.–Cuba relations enhanced the support he gained among Miami's Cubans, half of whom voted for him. Thus, it appears at least for the near future, the unique conflict between the U.S. and Cuba will continue to play a strong role in Cuban exile politics and may also determine the nature of relations between Cubans and other groups in Miami that remain marginalized.

There is a new political economy Cubans seeking refuge in the United States are forced to navigate, however. With the death of Fidel Castro and the transfer of power from his brother Raúl to Miguel Díaz-Canel, it is not clear how the political climate in Cuba will develop and how (or if) the United States' relationship with the nation will shift in response. Moreover, the United States recently made the historic move of closing the open door to Cuban immigration. At the end of his presidential term in January 2017, Obama ended the "Wet Foot, Dry Foot" policy that had specially benefited Cuban refugees. Although the policy was originally meant to be restrictive, it still allowed Cubans to be given access to immediate asylum if they entered the United States by land. Obama's move was meant to make the immigration and asylum process more equitable for migrants regardless of national origin. Advocates for immigrants from other countries other than Cuba see this as a very positive development, but for Cubans, it does signal the end of an era when the United States deemed them "favored" migrants. Despite the many Trump administration moves to undo Obama-era policies, "Wet Foot, Dry Foot" has not been reinstated. Thus, the plight of Cuban migrants is currently more similar to that of others seeking U.S. entry. Future scholarship on Cuban Miami will likely need to examine how Cuban Americans contend with the new contradictions they may face as politicians seek to simultaneously castigate the Cuban government and maintain its intensified focus on immigration restrictions, particularly if this comes to involve increased surveillance and the ramping up of deportations of Cuban nationals. This research could also examine whether such changes in the political economy might heighten the prospects of greater community building between groups in Miami that have traditionally found themselves on opposite sides of the political spectrum.

In the face of rigidly drawn borders, such as those drawn in cases of interethnic conflict in Miami and across the nation, we must take stock of the greater complexity of a political climate in which anti-immigrant, anti-refugee policies and continued efforts to reverse civil rights movement gains are enacted simultaneously and in concert. Today, an official voice from the White House has argued that the Statue of Liberty is not actually a beacon for all the world's tired and poor to come to America. Denying the ability of migrants to seek asylum and working to limit even legal forms of immigration, the administration is moving even further away from the pretense that the nation cares about suffering and human rights. The nation is currently experiencing a strong (white) nativist backlash that, according to scholars such as Juan Gonzalez (2011), has been long in the making, beginning in 1980, the year that marked the beginning of a period known as "the Browning of America." This backlash goes right along with a "get tough on crime" narrative and policy moves that position the establishment against "errant blacks." In this book, examining the case of African Americans, Cuban Americans, and Afro-Cubans reminded us of these greater social and political issues that overlap in the lives of people, some of whom are both blacks and Latinos, who are in reality all affected by the strength of the native/foreigner frame that dangerously positions Latinos, along with (but differently from) blacks, in the role of "noncitizens." They are also all affected by the entrenched anti-blackness that has continued to spur the need for activists to remind the nation that "black lives matter." This is because in a white elite-dominated system, people of color are all often demonized but in different ways. Latinos and African Americans taking this into account can resist dominant efforts to pit them against one another.

We have reason to be hopeful that those opposed to anti-immigrant, anti-Latino, and anti-black policy moves will bond together to oppose them, given that African Americans and Latinos have historically worked together in the past to redress their shared disenfranchisement (Behnken 2016; Johnson 2013; Kun and Pulido 2013; Márquez 2014). However, the changes in the economy since the 1970s, U.S. labor needs, housing discrimination, increased urbanization, and political competition have affected immigrant and African American populations in different ways, jeopardizing such alliances (Betancur 2005b; Vaca 2004). In this book, I have emphasized the role and importance of such structural forces by contextualizing Miami's interminority conflict within histories of structural racism and illustrating how these structures set the stage for interminority conflict. Such observations make clear that along with attending to the issue of discourse and ideology also discussed in this book, the larger structural issues affecting competition need to be addressed to forge effective alliances. Indeed, my main focus on ideologies driving interethnic conflict does not preclude the importance of the objective structural factors that intervene.

Still, this book advocates that we continue to expose the inextricable links between material realities and ideologies. We must continue to expose the important role of ideology in how people of color might be recruited to carry out ideals of worthy citizenship or might be convinced, themselves, of the legitimacy of a nativism that cloaks itself in the mantle of "national security" or of the need to get tough on (black) crime. The white power base has long promoted exclusionary ideals of "the nation" as a tool for asserting power, unity, and identity. More recently, the Trump administration has placed a premium on immigrants and native-born Americans demonstrating their worthiness to belong on the basis of their "patriotism" or the approved "American" ideologies to which they adhere. According to the terms of worthy citizenship, such ideals, and the qualities that supposedly make people ideal citizen-subjects, come to be taken for granted as having moral value. Thus, as people seek to place themselves on a moral high ground, some may be convinced that not only should they police themselves in these ways but that they should also police others. As such policing reinforces the status quo and existing power dynamics, we as scholars and activists are tasked with resisting and challenging the pull to embrace white dominant exclusionary ideologies, in all their forms, as we continue working toward new ways of defining American belonging.

NOTES

Introduction

1. Mirta Ojito, "Best of Friends, Worlds Apart," *New York Times,* June 5, 2000, http://www.nytimes.com/learning/general/featured_articles/000606tuesday.html. This summary appears as the subheading to the article.

2. Racial categorization works differently in Cuba as intermediary categories between black and white are officially recognized. In addition, prevailing discourses privilege national identity over racial identity. Such "racial democracy" discourses are related to Cuban Patriots' efforts to unify the country during the struggle for independence from Spain between 1868 and 1898 by repudiating racial separatism. However, such discourses have also served to silence anti-racist efforts.

3. The distinction being made here between a "black" and "white" Cuban is specific to the U.S. context. Ojito's article implies that these men were not "black" and "white" in the same way before emigrating but are cast as black and white by Anglos, African Americans, and other Cubans in a way that "matters." Though divisions between white and black Cubans indeed exist in Cuba, the men's experiences point to the idea that there is a particular way the divide between white and black Cubans in the United States is "artificial" and created in this national context.

4. Ojito, "Best of Friends."

5. Membership in these groups is, of course, not mutually exclusive. However, in Miami, African Americans were often distinguished from "Cubans" without accounting for the racial diversity among Cubans; generations of Cuban immigrants shared a culture and country of origin but had differing political perspectives and U.S. experiences based on immigration cohort effects; and divisions were manifest between black and white Cubans regardless of cultural and other similarities.

6. Rather than referring to the idea of citizenship as defined through legal processes, I use the term "citizenship" broadly to refer to a sense of being accepted or included within the nation. My use is similar to Cainkar and Maira's notion of "cultural citizenship," which they define as "the everyday experience of belonging to the nation-state in relation to experiences of inclusion and exclusion" (2005, 3).

7. As I am primarily concerned with discussing the dynamics of race as it operates in the context of the United States, in this book I use the terms "white," white supremacy," and "whiteness" to capture the overarching power dynamic, put in place by white Anglo settlers and the United States' slave societies, which frames racial relations in the United States.

8. Here I am referencing Flores and Jiménez Román's (2009) "triple consciousness," which argues that Afro-Latinos in the United States have a compounded experience of discrimination on the basis of their race and their ethnicity, while also being viewed as not "true blacks" by some African Americans. Because of such experiences, Afro-Latinos see the world through several lenses.

9. In the book, the term "Miami" refers to both the city of Miami and the larger Miami-Dade metro area.

10. Black immigrants are current U.S. residents born outside the United States who indicate that their race is black or is mixed-race black, regardless of whether they also claim to be of Hispanic origin (U.S. Census 2010).

11. For instance, according to the 2010 Census, the Miami metro area ranks among the top ten of the U.S. metro areas with both the largest black populations and highest black-white segregation. It also has significant Latino-white segregation (see Logan and Stults 2011).

12. According to Maria Cristina García's sources, anywhere from 10 to 40 percent of the Marielitos were black (García 1996, 60). An *El Miami Herald* article put the percentage of blacks in Mariel at 19.6 percent (Voboril 1980, 4), while Bach, Bach, and Triplett (1981–1982) cite the percentage of blacks as 40 percent. During the fourth wave, or Balsero crisis, the percentage of blacks and *mulatos* was also significant, 8.3 percent as compared with the 3 percent that arrived before 1980 (Ackerman and Clark 1995).

13. It should be noted that because of resettlement efforts and discriminatory practices, black Cubans do not always end up settling in Miami once they migrate to the United States. According to figures from the Metro-Dade County Planning Department (cited in Dunn 1997, 336), there were about 2,629 blacks from Cuba in the county in 1980 (accounting for about 8 percent of all blacks) and 6,382 blacks from Cuba in the county in 1990 (accounting for about 6.5 percent of all blacks).

14. There is quantitative evidence that backs up the problems with the "worthiness" narrative positioned here. Such studies demonstrate that although blacks are out-educating and out-saving whites, they do not receive the same material returns. See, for

example, Hamilton, Darity, Price, and Sridharan 2015; Nam, Hamilton, Darity, and Price 2015.

15. John J. Betancur (2014, 363) also emphasizes such strategies of divide and conquer in his work on black-Latino relations, arguing that relations between these groups are manipulated by dominant actors within a racial matrix of structural and institutional power.

16. Here I am mainly discussing white Cuban Americans, but we should also take into consideration Cuban diversity when thinking about this. It could be argued also that many nonwhite (mixed-race) and black Cubans have more in common with other Latinos in terms of racialized experiences, especially if they live outside Miami.

17. See also Neil Foley's (2010) riveting analysis of the failures of black-brown solidarity efforts in Texas during and after World War II.

18. For example, Márquez (2014), Marrow (2011), and Ribas (2015).

19. Exceptions include Woltman and Newbold (2009) and Skop (2001), which are studies focusing specifically on race. For studies that mention the role of blackness in the Mariel stigma see Aguirre (1984); Bach et al. (1981–1982); Hufker and Cavender (1990, 33); Portes and Stepick (1994); Soruco (1996, 10); and Boswell and Curtis (1984).

20. "Mariel" and "Marielito" refer to the port, Mariel, from which the third wave of refugees departed. The diminutive term *Marielito*, though widely used in scholarly writing, began as a derogatory term.

21. The founder of the *Miami Times,* Henry Ethelbert Sigismund Reeves, was Bahamian-born (Rose 2015, 24).

22. An analysis of these *periodiquitos* is not included in the current discussion. However, in a study of a sample of *periodiquitos* published in 1980, I found Cuban American perspectives in these sources to be consistent in their general tone with my findings in *El Miami Herald.*

23. While African American and Spanish-language newspapers provided an archive of perspectives emanating from these communities, no comparable post-1980 "Afro-Cuban immigrant archive" exists.

1. Race Making

1. The controversial people Mandela thanked for their financial and military support of the African National Congress included Yasir Arafat, Muammar Gaddafi, and Fidel Castro (Sawyer 2006).

2. This is not to deny the agency of both groups—agency that was surely expressed in the adroitness with which they appealed to these gatekeepers.

3. See http://www.miamiandbeaches.com/. Accessed July 15, 2016.

4. See Dunn (2013; 2016) and Connoly (2014) for more on the history of black exploitation in the area and details of the horrendous violence blacks experienced.

5. See Dunn (1997) and Rose (2015) for more information on Afro-Caribbean/West Indian migration to Miami and the important role Bahamians played in Miami's history.

6. The post–Fidel Castro revolution Cuban community came to the United States in four distinctive waves. The third and fourth waves will be discussed in more detail in coming chapters. Though not the topic of this book, it should be noted that Cubans had a long history of migration to the United States (in smaller numbers) well before the Castro revolution (see Greenbaum 2002; López 2010; Shell-Weiss 2009).

7. The 1973 ordinance had officially declared Miami a bilingual city. The Metro Commission (an elected board tasked with representing the citizens of the county's districts) and Mayor Jack Orr had decided to make this declaration as the city sought to further integrate Cuban refugees and to adapt to the fact that government officials and first responders needed to be able to communicate with Miami-Dade County's rapidly growing Spanish-speaking population.

8. See Darity (2011) for an excellent take-down of "underclass" theory and the victim-blaming discourse in relation to this topic.

9. See De Genova (2005, 298) for a discussion of other early African American intellectuals who have critiqued the erasure of African Americans from the idea of who can be "American."

10. Aja and Marchevsky (2017) examine similar good/bad immigrant undercurrents related to "Dreamers," undocumented immigrants, and recent deportation policy.

11. This idea of what makes one a "good immigrant" is also similar to Espiritu's (2006, 2014) notion of the "good refugee" who is a grateful contributor the U.S. nation and its national interests.

12. I use the term "native" instead of Kim's term "insider" to link the idea of nativism. See also De Genova (2006) for an integral discussion of nativism and constructions of immigrant foreignness.

13. See Guinier and Torres's use of the term "nativism" to describe black attitudes toward Mexicans in Los Angeles (2002, 241).

14. John J. Betancur (2014, 353) refers to this game (that blacks and Latinos in his analysis are compelled to take part in) as "the game of racial domination."

2. Marielitos, the Criminalization of Blackness, and Constructions of Worthy Citizenship

1. Right before the Mariel exodus began, the U.S. government had passed the Refugee Act of March 1980. According to this act, the Marielitos could not be accepted automatically as refugees; their status would be determined by review on a case-by-case basis. The act limited Cuban immigration by establishing a yearly quota of 19,500 Cuban refugees and required individual case reviews to determine eligibility for refugee status. If approved, refugees could become permanent residents after two years (Masud-Piloto 1996).

2. This characterization did lasting damage: studies on the adaptation of Marielitos, years after they first arrived, show signs that Mariel immigrants continued to suffer social consequences, such as higher rates of imprisonment than other Cubans, likely due to the greater surveillance they received (Aguirre 1984; G. A. Fernández 2002; Lisandro Pérez 2001).

3. As Gonzalez (2011) argues, this nativist backlash, beginning in 1980, was the third major eruption since the nation's founding.

4. Likely due to the differences in the way racial categories are understood in the United States and in Cuba (affecting self-reports), there is variation in official statistics about the racial makeup of the Mariel wave. For instance, an *El Miami Herald* article (Voboril 1980, 4) put the percentage of blacks in Mariel at 19.6 percent, while Bach, Bach, and Triplett (1981–1982) cite the percentage of blacks as 40 percent.

5. The "one-drop rule" refers to the idea in the United States that the children of black and white unions are black (rather than white or "biracial"). Even people whose forebears are mostly white but can trace back to at least one black grandparent or forebear would be counted as black (F. J. Davis 2001).

6. Although marriage between blacks and whites was officially prohibited in 1805, this law was not enforced until 1864 (Martinez-Alier 1989).

7. Cheryl Brownstein, "Llegan familiares de cubano que sobrevivió al paredón," [news story] *El Miami Herald*, April 15, 1980, 2. Throughout this book, English translations of the original Spanish from both *El Miami Herald* and *El Nuevo Herald* are used. The original Spanish was translated by a professional translator of Cuban descent who lives in Miami.

8. "Mujeres y niños duermen en barracas en Cayo Hueso" [news story], *El Miami Herald*, April 26, 1980, 5.

9. Guillermo Martínez, "Alternativas de nuevos exilados son reducidas" [news story], *El Miami Herald*, April 9, 1980, 4.

10. Johnson, L. B. (1966). *Public Papers of the Presidents of the United States: Lyndon B. Johnson, 1965*. Vol. 2. Washington, DC: Government Printing Office.

11. Roberto Fabricio, "Que vengan los asilados!" [editorial], *El Miami Herald*, April 12, 1980, 4.

12. Roberto Fabricio, "Un problema de imagen" [op-ed], *El Miami Herald*, July 3, 1980, 8.

13. Dan Williams, "'Escoria' es lastre y sambenito del nuevo exilio" [top news story], *El Miami Herald*, September 1, 1980, 1, 3.

14. Luis R. Caceres Jr., "Apuntes de lo del Mariel" [op-ed], *El Miami Herald*, September 23, 1980, 4.

15. Juan J. Alborna Salado, "Los jóvenes del Mariel" [op-ed], *El Miami Herald*, September 8, 1980, 6.

16. "Antonio" is the only interviewee quoted here who would not be considered "black" by others or based on self-identification, but he was interviewed because of his connections to other Afro-Cubans who arrived during Mariel.

17. Melquíades B. Fuentes, "El exilio nuevo si tiene iniciativa" [letter to the editor], *El Miami Herald*, September 6, 1980, 4.

18. Romilio Espinosa Pereda, "Condena ataques a los recién llegados" [letter to the editor], *El Miami Herald*, September 8, 1980, 6.

19. Braulio Sáenz, "Los refugiados no son escoria" [letter to the editor], *El Miami Herald*, September 30, 1980, 4.

20. Williams, "'Escoria' es lastre y sambenito del nuevo exilio."

21. Dan Williams, "Nuevo exilio es 'clase obrera sólida,' dice estudio" [news story], *El Miami Herald*, September 1, 1980, 3.

22. The Mariel exodus led to the creation of an organization that was expressly tasked with counteracting all the anti-Cuban articles and stereotypes that were circulating. The organization, FACE (Facts about Cuban Exiles), also worked to promote a positive image of Cubans through articles and films. Although the organization began in Miami, it grew to have chapters across the country (Portes and Stepick 1994, 35).

23. George Stein and Guillermo Martinez, "Cifras policiales comprometen a refugiados" [news story], *El Miami Herald*, September 18, 1980, 1, 3.

24. Zita Arorcha, "Abarrotada la cárcel de Dade por refugiados" [news story], *El Miami Herald*, September 11, 1980, 1; Eric Rieder, "Refugiados matan a hombre en bar" [news story], *El Miami Herald*, September 22, 1980, 2.

25. Dan Williams and Joan Fleischman, "Achacan a refugiados alza del crimen en Miami Beach" [news story], *El Miami Herald*, July 25, 1980, 2.

26. Ibid.

27. Portes and Stepick's 1994 study corroborates my findings that Cubans had consolidated negative views of the Marielitos. They provide evidence from their survey research, which also demonstrated that Mariel Cubans perceived that older Cubans discriminated against them (see pages 31–33 for some examples of the comments they gleaned from their survey).

28. Cesar E. Montejo, "Benefició a Castro éxodo del Mariel" [letter to the editor], *El Miami Herald,* September 1, 1980, 4.

29. George Stein and Guillermo Martinez, "Cifras policiales comprometen a refugiados" [news story], *El Miami Herald*, September 18, 1980, 1, 3.

30. Williard P. Rose and Stephen Doig, "Furiosos, achacan a Cubanos" [news story], *El Miami Herald*, May 29, 1980, 1.

31. More details on the McDuffie case and uprising will be provided in Chapter 3.

32. "Falta un plan para asimilar al nuevo exiliado Cubano" [editorial], *El Miami Herald*, May 31, 1980, 6.

33. Guillermo Martinez, "Ciudad de carpas: 'Ghetto' Cubano en Miami" [news story], *El Miami Herald*, August 24, 1980, 1, 5.

34. Dan Williams, "Esperanza y desesperación en el campamiento de carpas," [news story] *El Miami Herald*, August 31, 1980, 10. Other stories that reported on the larger number of blacks among the newcomers include an April news story, "The Situation in the Peruvian Embassy Is Tense," which reported on "the extraordinary diversity of the previous ones, between the blacks, whites, and mulattos that are there" (Guillermo Martínez and Dan Williams, "Tensa la situación en embajada peruana," *El Miami Herald*, April 10, 1980), 1. In May, two news stories provided estimates of the percentage of blacks among the Marielitos. One states that almost 20 percent of the new arrivals were black but notes that the majority (a little over 80 percent) were white (Mary Voboril, "Sumase al éxodo lo más valioso de la población de Cuba," *El Miami Herald*, May 5, 1980, 4). The other, "The Recently Arrived: Younger and Poorer," cites research by sociologist Juan Clark from Miami-Dade Community College, along with statistics taken from the Opa-locka Center for Refugees and the Elgin Air Force Base, which also states that blacks constituted 20 percent of the Marielitos. The article describes the new

arrivals: "The overwhelming majority are men, which represents a notable change from the previous Cuban immigrants; there are also many more blacks than ever before" (Guy Gugliotta, "Recién llegados: Mas jóvenes y pobres," *El Miami Herald*, May 11, 1980,1).

35. "Urge unidad a los Cubanos exiliados" [unsigned letter to the editor], *El Miami Herald*, July 7, 1980, 4.

36. Helio Nardo, "Comportamiento en Estados Unidos" [letter to the editor], *El Miami Herald*, July 12, 1980, 6.

37. Jose Cobo, "Refugiados: Están en nación de leyes" [letter to the editor], *El Miami Herald*, June 2, 1980, 6.

38. "Carter cavila mientras los refugiados se enfurecen" [editorial], *El Miami Herald*, June 3, 1980, 4.

39. Because I was also interested in whether the paper noted the larger presence of Afro-Cubans, every story that mentioned the word "black" or "Afro-Cuban," as well as those that contained pictures of Cubans who appeared to be black, was also collected to determine the context in which the words were mentioned and black Cubans were depicted.

40. Juan Casanova, "Diez mil buscaban refugio y hallaron el infierno" [feature article], *El Miami Herald*, June 1, 1980, 1.

41. Ileana Orozo, "Exiliados del Mariel tienen vida nueva" [feature article], *El Miami Herald*, June 21, 1980, 8.

42. Ileana Orozo, "Familia no se desalienta, a pesar de problemas: Los Casanova se adaptan, poco a poco" [feature article], *El Miami Herald*, July 26, 1980, 10.

43. Ileana Orozo, "Los Casanova van adaptándose al exilio" [feature article], *El Miami Herald*, September 6, 1980, 7.

44. Ibid.

45. Ibid.

46. Just one of the articles describes an incident when Juan faced discrimination, from a pair of women who refused to give him a ride after he answered "yes" to their question of whether he was Cuban. It is not clear from the story what the ethnic and racial backgrounds of the women were (whether they were African American or Anglos).

47. Orozo, "Familia no se desalienta," *El Miami Herald*, 10.

48. See Espíritu (2006, 2014) for a discussion of how such redemption stories of "good refugees" were also expected of Vietnamese refugees who came to the United States in the 1970s and 1980s.

49. Orozo, "Familia no se desalienta," 10.

50. Juan Casanova, "Diez mil buscaban refugio y hallaron el infierno" [feature story], *El Miami Herald*, June 1, 1980, 1.

51. Martínez and Williams, "Tensa la situación en embajada peruana," 1; Voboril, "Sumase al éxodo lo más valioso," 4; Gugliotta, "Recién llegados," 1.

52. As noted earlier, since many of the news stories were written first in English and then translated, it is also possible that the inattention to race, at least in news stories, was related to the perspectives of writers or editors from the English-language paper. These writers or decision makers may have ignored the issue of race in reporting on Cubans.

3. And Justice for All?

1. See Antonio López (2012, 157) for more discussion on the Cuban cop involved in this brutality case.

2. See Connolly (2014) for more details on how whites utilized real estate practices to continue to disenfranchise blacks.

3. The first Haitian boat people, most threatened by the Duvalier regime, began arriving in Miami in September 1963. By 1964, members of the middle classes also began leaving, and during the 1960s and 1970s, some members of the lower classes began to leave (primarily for New York) (Stepick 1992).

4. This amount of coverage is still significant given that the publication is a weekly rather than daily newspaper. However, it is a smaller number in comparison to the newspaper's coverage of other timely topics.

5. "America's Partiality to Cubans" [editorial], *Miami Times*, May 1, 1980, 4.

6. "Government Should Accommodate Those Cubans Wanting to Go Back" [editorial], *Miami Times*, August 21, 1980, 5.

7. "'No Habla Español' Costs Black Maids Their Jobs" [news story], *Miami Times*, August 7, 1980, 1. This proposal, also referenced in earlier chapters, would prohibit the use of Metro funds for programs that used any language other than English (García 1996).

8. "Bilingualism an Excuse for Discrimination" [letter to the editor], *Miami Times*, October 9, 1980, 35.

9. "Cubans Should Not Be "One up" on Blacks" [letter to the editor], *Miami Times*, May 15, 1980, 35.

10. "Bilingualism an Excuse for Discrimination," 35.

11. See also "Immigrants Insist on Bilingualism" [letter to the editor], *Miami Times*, September 6, 1980, 39.

12. "South Florida's Goal: Keep out Haitians" [letter to the editor], *Miami Times*, September 30, 1980, 13A.

13. Bayard Rustin, "Tragedy in Miami: Oppressed vs. Oppressed" [op-ed], *Miami Times*, June 5, 1980, 5.

14. See Stepick (1992) for a more complete discussion of the changes in immigration policy toward Cubans and Haitians in the 1980s.

15. Ricky Thomas, "Immigration Policies Should Be Colorblind" [op-ed], *Miami Times*, April 17, 1980, 6.

16. Ibid.

17. Ricky Thomas, "Cuban Sealift Illegal" [op-ed], *Miami Times*, April 1980, 5.

18. The United States had recently passed the 1980 Refugee Act. This act was more restrictive toward Cuban immigration in that it made Cuban acceptance into the United States less automatic, but the act was viewed as an important move to make immigration and asylum policy more equitable for people arriving from other countries (such as Haiti).

19. "Haitian Refugees Finally Noticed" [editorial], *Miami Times*, May 6, 1980, 1.

20. Vernon Jordan, "A Fair Break for Haitian Refugees" [op-ed], *Miami Times*, June 5, 1980, 5.

21. Rustin, "Tragedy in Miami," 5.

22. "NAACP Decries Anti-Bilingual Petition" [news story], *Miami Times*, August 18, 1980, 25.

23. "Cuban Refugees and Haitian Refugees" [editorial], *Miami Times*, May 15, 1980, 4.

24. Haiba Jabali, "Reflection" [op-ed], *Miami Times*, April 24, 1980, 24.

25. Haiba Jabali, "Afro-Cuban Refugee Point of View" [op-ed], *Miami Times*, May 15, 1980, 11.

26. "Cuban Refugees and Haitian refugees," 4.

27. "South Florida's Goal," 13A.

28. This is not to deny that there are also some Afro-Cubans who align with white Cubans and attempt to dissociate from African Americans. See Michelle Hay's (2009) study for her take on the important role their exposure to African American political culture and philosophies played in the lives and self-identifications of the Florida and New York-based Afro-Cuban immigrants she interviewed.

29. The adoption of AAVE was less noticeable among women. For the five men who adopted this manner of speaking, four lived in Los Angeles, where they became proficient in African American English because jobs and neighborhoods put them in contact with black Americans. In Miami, interviewees on the whole were less proficient in English in general and in AAVE in particular.

4. Framing the Balsero Crisis

1. It should be noted that suffering also has later associations with other important African American social movements, such as Black Lives Matter.

2. See Louis A. Pérez (1995) for a more complete discussion of the impact of the "special period" on the Cuban economy.

3. See Soderlund (2003) and Girard (2004) for more detailed discussion of the reasoning behind political opposition to Clinton's stance on Haiti.

4. During the George H. W. Bush administration, a coup in Haiti took out the U.S.-backed Jean Bertrand Aristide in 1991, and in 1994 Clinton made moves to intervene and restore the ousted leader with a military invasion of Haiti (Girard 2004).

5. See Chapter 3 for a brief discussion of the complicated political relationship the United States has had with Haiti. This relationship, which alternated in U.S. support and condemnation of the Haitian leadership, likely contributed to the contradictions in the U.S. government and general public's stance on Haiti during the 1990s.

6. On September 19, 1994, U.S. troops went to Haiti, but the conflict was ultimately resolved without war, and Aristide was successfully reinstated to power through a deal negotiated by Jimmy Carter, Colin Powell, and others (Girard 2004).

7. In an effort to appease the Cuban American community, on August 20 Clinton requested a meeting with Miami leaders, including the influential Jorge Mas Canosa, the leader of the Cuban American National Foundation. In the meeting, Clinton promised to further strengthen the embargo against Cuba in exchange for support of his new policy (Henken 2005). The president was able to appease some Cubans with these

agreements, but others lamented the fact that repatriation was now an option and that refugees found at sea would not be immediately brought to the United States.

8. To investigate the discursive framing of the Balseros and the crisis in *El Nuevo Herald*, I analyzed 319 articles, the results from a search for the key word "Balsero" in the online database of *El Nuevo Herald* between the dates of July 1, 1994, and December 31, 1994. The online database allows searches for articles from 1982 to the present. The term "Balsero" was the common word used within the media to describe the refugees who arrived on rafts, and thus a search for this word was most likely to yield stories about the refugees fleeing Cuba at the time. Of those articles, I counted only those stories dealing with the Balseros in the United States, Cuba, and Guantánamo, leaving out stories reporting on their condition in other resettlement countries such as Panama, the Cayman Islands, and Spain. Stories that made only passing reference to the Balseros were also excluded. The overall tone of the articles and the most prevalent themes regarding the reception of the Balseros by the established Cuban community were identified. Only six stories about the Balseros have a negative tone.

9. Ramón Cotta, "El costo es moral" [editorial], *El Nuevo Herald*, October 5, 1994, A10.

10. Christopher Marquis, "Se desvanece el trato especial para los cubanos" [news story], *El Nuevo Herald*, November 20, 1994, A1.

11. María A. Morales, Jannice Reyes, Ivan Román, and Maydel Santana, "Freno a éxodo provoca furia y lágrimas" [news story], *El Nuevo Herald*, August 20, 1994, A1.

12. Roberto Suarez, "Cuba: Peligro en la orilla" [editorial], *El Nuevo Herald*, September 4, 1994, A22.

13. Cynthia Corzo, "Llega de cuba madre de balsero ahogado" [news story], *El Nuevo Herald*, November 5, 1994, B1.

14. Liz Balmaseda, "Cuba se desangra en cada balsa" [news story], *El Nuevo Herald*, August 17, 1994, B1.

15. Ana Santiago, Ivan Román, and Francisco García Azuero, "Fugitivos de cuba afirman hubo tiroteo al dejar Mariel" [news story], *El Nuevo Herald*, August 11, 1994, A1.

16. Ironically, the U.S. blockade is likely one of the reasons there was no milk.

17. Francisco Garcia Azuero and Jannice Reyes, "No regresa a la base de Guantánamo niño refugiado" [news story], *El Nuevo Herald*, September 29, 1994, B1.

18. The plight of immigrating children has been a subject of the national debate more recently. The United States made the controversial move (April 2018) to ramp up punishment of migrants attempting to cross the U.S.–Mexico border. Rather than rewarding migrants for giving their children a chance at "a better life," the United States began separating children from their parents (even those seeking asylum) as a deterrent for illegal entry into the United States. However, the moral outcry among members of the U.S. public was dramatic, and in response, on June 20 of that year, President Trump signed an executive order to end the practice, which his attorney general, Jeff Sessions, had initiated.

19. Agencia Reuter, "Profesionales crean 'incipiente democracia' en Guantánamo" [news story], *El Nuevo Herald*, November 5, 1994, A12.

20. Gustavo Peña, "Diez de octubre en la vorágine" [editorial], *El Nuevo Herald*, October 10, 1994, A10.

21. Joanne Cavanaugh, "Balseros se ayudan mutuamente tras el paso de Gordon" [news story], *El Nuevo Herald*, November 16, 1994, A8.

22. Francisco García Azuero and Ivan Roman, "Agencias tramitan casos de cientos de refugiados," [news story] *El Nuevo Herald*, August 19, 1994, B1.

23. Elaine De Valle, "Misivas de niños escolares infunden esperanza a los refugiados" [news story], *El Nuevo Herald*, September 4, 1994, B3.

24. Aminda Marques Gonzalez, "*Herald* galardona a 6 activistas de la comunidad" [news story], *El Nuevo Herald*, September 30, 1994, B1. That year (1994), *El Nuevo Herald* proved its own endorsement of such activities by honoring community activists for their support of the newcomers.

25. Ivan Roman, "'Red' ayuda a balserosa conseguir trabajo" [news story], *El Nuevo Herald*, September 1, 1994, B1.

26. Maydel Santana, "Grupo femenino presiona por ayuda a balseros" [news story], *El Nuevo Herald*, September 15, 1994, B1. William Allen happens to be Afro-Cuban. Special thanks to Holly Ackerman and her extensive knowledge of the Miami community during the Balsero crisis for pointing this out.

27. Daniel Mórcate, "El año de la reconcentración" [editorial], *El Nuevo Herald*, November 3, 1994, A16.

28. Clemence Fiagome, "Attorneys Demand Release of Names of Haitian Refugees Held at Guantánamo: Double Standard Policy Protected," *Miami Times*, September 8, 1994, 1.

29. William D. C. Clark, "We Are a Community Controlled by Others and Failed by Our Leaders," *Miami Times*, November 24, 1994, 5A.

30. In an op-ed, Jackson weighs in on Clinton's policy toward Cuba with a stance that expresses sympathy for members of the Cuban American community and with a position aligned with liberal anti-imperial politics. See Jesse Jackson, "Clinton Is Digging a Deeper Hole with Hard-Line Cuban Policy [column: "New Ideas for America"], *Miami Times*, September 1, 1994, 5A.

31. A search for articles in the *Miami Times* in bound newspaper archives and on microfilm covering the Balsero crisis and its aftermath between the dates of July 1, 1994, and December 31, 1994, yielded twenty-two articles. Articles with a focus on Afro-Cubans numbered eight, including op-eds by Rosa Reed, a Miami Afro-Cuban businesswoman.

32. "The Haitian Impasse" [editorial], *Miami Times*, July 14, 1994, 5A.

33. Seleatha Virgille, "President Clinton's New Cuba Policy Is Welcome" [letter to the editor], *Miami Times*, September 1, 1994, 4A.

34. "What about Haiti?" [editorial], *Miami Times*, August 25, 1994, 4A.

35. "Street Talk: What Should the U.S. Do about Mariel II?" [feature article], *Miami Times*, August 11, 1994, 5A.

36. "Street Talk: What Effect Will the Cuban Crisis Have on the Black Community? [feature article], *Miami Times*, September 1, 1994, 5A.

37. Christopher Marquis, "Se desvanece el trato especial para los cubanos" [news story], *El Nuevo Herald*, November 20, 1994, 1A.

38. Fabiola Santiago, "Listas 40,000 libras de donaciones para Guantánamo" [news story], *El Nuevo Herald*, September 8, 1994, 12A.

39. Lizette Álvarez, "Miami se prepara para recibir miles de balseros" [news story], *El Nuevo Herald*, November 17, 1994, 1A.

40. Blacks and mulattos were 8.3 percent of this population. They were 3.1 percent of the pre-1980 population (Ackerman and Clark 1995).

41. To determine how and if Afro-Cubans came into conversations about the Balsero crisis, I conducted a search for the key words "negro/a," "mulato/a," and "afrocubana/o" within the Balsero articles. After eliminating articles with a nonracial use of these terms, the search yielded only five articles; three made reference to Afro-Cuban gods to whom Balseros prayed for safe journey, and the other two discussed discrimination experienced by Afro-Cubans. The database does not include pictures; therefore, it could not be determined whether the paper included black Cubans in photos.

42. Here Amador is referring to Clinton's efforts to reinstate Haiti's ousted leader Jean Bertrand Aristide.

43. Dora Amador, "A puerta cerrada" [op-ed], *El Nuevo Herald*, September 22, 1994, A16.

44. Mohamed Hamaludin, "Immigrants as Scapegoats" [op-ed], *Miami Times*, October 6, 1994, 5A.

45. Manning Marable, "Blacks and Latinos Must Identify Common Interest and Seek to Unite" [op-ed], *Miami Times*, December 29, 1994, 5A.

46. "Afro-Cuban Dissident Takes Refuge in Miami," *Miami Times*, July 14, 1994, 2A.

47. The Malecón riot that broke out on August 5, 1994, when outraged Cubans gathered and broke store windows, is an example of the extent of unrest that Cubans were experiencing during the "special period."

48. Ricardo E. Gonzalez, "Race at Heart of Cuba Crisis" [op-ed], *Miami Times*, September 1, 1994, 4A.

49. "Thousands Flee from Castro's Failed Revolution" [photo essay], *Miami Times*, September 1, 1994, 3A.

50. "Rafter Stocking up for Sea Trip" [photo essay], *Miami Times*, September 8, 1994, 2A.

51. However, the "Afro-Cuban" was dropped from her byline in September.

52. Rosa Reed, "Support the President on His Tough Stand against Castro" [op-ed], *Miami Times*, August 25, 1994, 2A.

53. Ibid.

54. Rosa Reed, "Is Castro Winning the Immigration Stalemate?" [op-ed], *Miami Times*, September 1, 1994, 4A. Aja (2016) picks up on this idea of Afro-Cuban invisibility in his book's title and content.

55. Teele was a high-profile politician who ran for mayor of Miami in 1996 but lost to Alex Penelas. He had a successful but troubled political career, and as he was awaiting trial in 2005 for fraud charges, he walked into the *Miami Herald* building and shot himself to death. His supporters claim that his "trial and conviction by the media" can be blamed for his death.

56. Rosa Reed, "Cuban Power in Miami" [op-ed], *Miami Times*, December 22, 1994, 4A.

57. Rosa Reed, "Elect Candidates Who Are Caring" [op-ed], *Miami Times*, November 3, 1994, 5A.

5. Afro-Cuban Encounters at the Intersections of Blackness and Latinidad

1. Parts of this chapter previously appeared in "'Other' than Black: Afro-Cubans Negotiating Identity in the United States," in *Una Ventana a Cuba y los Estudios Cubanos: A Window into Cuba and Cuban Studies*, ed. Amalia Cabezas, Ivette N. Hernandez-Torres, Sara Johnson, and Rodrigo Lazo. A joint publication of the University of California—Cuba Academic Initiative, and Ediciones Callejon, Puerto Rico.

2. The findings of my investigation of Afro-Cuban experiences with people of Mexican descent in Los Angeles corroborate those of scholars who have examined Afro-Cuban experiences in other geographic contexts with large Mexican populations such as Albuquerque, New Mexico, and Austin, Texas (e.g., Dowling and Newby 2010; Newby and Dowling 2007), but builds on them, identifying points of division between Afro-Cubans and Mexicans in Los Angeles and spotlighting particular nuances that can provide a basis for a shared Latino identity.

3. Elsewhere I have defined "micro-level rejections" as "irritating personal affronts that uphold rigid or racist ideals and exclude [people] from what they perceive as their rightful membership in certain groups." Micro-level rejections are distinguished from "microaggressions" because they are perpetrated not by whites but by members of minority groups (Gosin 2017, 21).

4. All names are pseudonyms. Interviews conducted in Spanish have been translated.

5. In Alan Aja's book (2016) on Afro-Cubans in Miami, along with examples of Afro-Cubans who readily defended their blackness, he also encountered several examples of Afro-Cubans being less affirming of blackness and seeking like their white compatriots to "identify up" or dissociate from blackness (17). That my respondents were less likely to do so may be attributed to several factors such as their self-selection to be a part of a study focused on race, the fact that many of my respondents were active in preserving African elements of Cuban culture in their work and leisure, and the fact that I the interviewer am not only black but African American. Accordingly, I can only purport to have captured a sample of Afro-Cuban immigrant experiences. Nevertheless, the findings provide important insights into the differential ways particular segments of the Afro-Cuban immigrant population encounter and deal with race in the U.S. context.

6. While the extent to which Martí truly cared about the condition of blacks themselves is suspect for some scholars, he did seek to convince his white compatriots of the value of black inclusion in the nation, thereby emphasizing a need to relinquish anti-black impulses for a "greater good."

7. Miscegenation laws were overturned in 1967 in the landmark case of *Loving v. the State of Virginia*.

8. The U.S. Census does allow people to claim multiracial identities in the fact that they can choose more than one race. However, they cannot choose a term than signifies a "new" category based on mixture, such as "multiracial" or "mestizo." Some multiracial activists in the United States have advocated for such a term because they believe it would better capture who they perceive themselves to be.

9. Race and ethnicity technically differ from each other. However, they are often conflated in the wider racial hierarchy of U.S. society, and they are also not mutually exclusive (Cornell and Hartman 1998).

10. It should be noted that the idealization of racial democracy varies and is configured differently in specific Latin American national contexts.

11. Some hybrid identity terms include creole, jíbaro, mestizo, and mulato. Depending on specific national contexts, these terms are used to indicate racial mixture and/or cultural mixture (see Wade 1997).

12. See Martínez-Echazábal (1998) for a critical overview on the discourse of African/European mestizaje and its use in defining Latin American national identities.

13. It must be noted that a situational use of labels could also come from a more "positive" place as individuals use such labels to signify their connections to various communities. Many thanks to Tere Ceseña Bontempo for this reminder.

14. The respondents were less likely to interact with Anglo whites on a daily basis, but some did provide stories about negative interactions with whites. I center my focus on their experiences with other minorities, however, as I am interested in placing focused attention on the race-related interactions between groups of color in the geographical contexts of Miami and Los Angeles.

15. This translates as "Cuban croquettes" and a "fried beef dish."

16. Mark Hugo Lopez and Daniel Dockterman, "U.S. Hispanic Country of Origin Counts for Nation, Top 30 Metropolitan Areas," Pew Hispanic Center, May 26, 2011, http://www.pewhispanic.org/2011/05/26/ii-metropolitan-area-diversity/.

17. See also Aja's (2016) discussion of how despite the idealization of Cuban national identity as a delicious "ajiaco" or soup wherein people of various colors come together to compose it (Fernando Ortiz 1940), Afro-Cubans have been "evicted" from the white Cuban American exile community.

18. The Castro government took on the project of celebrating Cuba's African heritage, particularly its contributions to music and dance. These efforts have been criticized as merely superficial by many in and out of Cuba. Still, efforts by Castro to honor the African contribution to Cuban national identity and to equalize the society after his revolution did allow some gains for black Cubans (De la Fuente 2001; Gómez-Garcia 1998; Sawyer 2006).

19. In this book, I am primarily concerned with the operations of race in the U.S. context and therefore am taking a neutral analytical stance regarding Cuba.

20. See Clealand (2017) for her crucial contribution to the conversation of how race operates in Cuba today, wherein she provides important context and findings that illuminate the variations of political racial consciousness among black Cubans still on the island.

21. This process of relying on racial ideologies from the home country to contest U.S. experiences of race is similar to what Joe Feagin (2010) calls "home culture frames,"

wherein immigrants make use of racial frames of reference from the home culture in order to maintain their distinctive values and resist assimilation into the U.S. dominant majority (see also Dowling 2014; Gosin 2017).

22. One of Aja's (2016) respondents had a remarkably similar exchange about his racial/ethnic identity.

23. In Cuba, these terms refer to specific phenotypes. A "mulato" can range in skin tone from light to medium brown, while a person described as "jabao" often has light skin with a reddish tone, with "kinky," sometimes reddish hair and "African" features. The term "jabao" is similar to the African American term "redbone."

24. A 1.5-generation immigrant refers to a person who emigrated as a child and so has mostly grown up in the receiving country.

25. "Chico" is a slang term used by some African Americans to refer to people of Latino descent.

26. U.S. Census Bureau, "State and County QuickFacts," http://quickfacts.census .gov/qfd/states/06/06037.html.

27. The term "Mexican" was often used by interviewees to refer to anyone of Mexican descent with no distinction made for immigration status or generation. The Mexican population is composed of very different cohorts, including newly arriving immigrants, old immigrants and their children, and a small representation of the descendants of Mexicans native to California.

Conclusion

1. This comment refers to a statement made by Juror B37 while being interviewed by CNN journalist Anderson Cooper (2013). See Cooper, "Juror B37: Zimmerman's Heart Was in the Right Place," Anderson Cooper 360, July 16, 2013, http://ac360.blogs .cnn.com/2013/07/16/juror-b37-zimmermans-heart-was-in-the-right-place/?iref =allsearch.

2. Ailsa Chang, "Critics: Immigration Reform Takes Jobs away from Black Workers," NPR, July 15, 2013, http://www.npr.org/templates/story/story.php?storyId=202 401675.

3. Dylan Rodriguez, "Inaugurating Multiculturalist White Supremacy," Colorlines, November 10, 2008, http://www.colorlines.com/articles/dreadful-genius-obama-moment.

4. See Michelle Ye Hee Lee, "Donald Trump's False Comments Connecting Mexican Immigrants and Crime," *Washington Post,* July 8, 2015, https://www.washingtonpost .com/news/fact-checker/wp/2015/07/08/donald-trumps-false-comments-connecting -mexican-immigrants-and-crime/?utm_term=.e767aef50c83.

5. See Amanda Sakuma, "Trump Did Better with Blacks, Hispanics, Than Romney in '12: Exit Polls," NBC News, November 9, 2016, https://www.nbcnews.com /storyline/2016-election-day/trump-did-better-blacks-hispanics-romney-12-exit-polls -n681386.

6. One of the earliest writers on the subject of black and Latino conflict, Nicolas Vaca (2004), warned us against thinking that an alliance can always be presumed, or taken for granted, as historical conditions and specific contexts change.

7. See Jens Manuel Krogstad and Mark Hugo Lopez, "Hillary Clinton Won Latino Vote but Fell Below 2012 Support for Obama," Pew Research Center, November 29, 2016, http://www.pewresearch.org/fact-tank/2016/11/29/hillary-clinton-wins-latino-vote-but-falls-below-2012-support-for-obama/.

8. See Sakuma, "Trump Did Better with Blacks."

9. See also arguments made by Betancur (2005b).

10. See Molly Roberts, "Stop Blaming White Supremacy on 'Identity Politics,'" *Washington Post*, August 14, 2017, https://www.washingtonpost.com/blogs/post-partisan/wp/2017/08/14/stop-blaming-charlottesville-on-identity-politics/?utm_term=.c976af0780a8.

11. See Robinson and Chang (2017) for good examples of the directions of such scholarship.

12. Although a discussion of black African immigrant experiences is outside the scope of this book, there is a growing body of scholarship on African immigrants that adds further insight into these themes.

13. Dora Amador, "A puerta cerrada," *El Nuevo Herald*, September 22, 1994, A16.

14. For more on these ideas see Beltrán (2010) and Dean (1996) on notions of "reflective solidarity" and on how "we" political identities are generated and performed.

15. See Planning Research, Department Of Planning And Zoning, "Hispanics by Country of Origin in Miami-Dade" Issue 16 (2011) for a percentage breakdown of the Latino population in Miami based on data from the 2010 census, https://www.miamidade.gov/planning/library/reports/data-flash/2011-hispanics-by-origin.pdf.

16. Aranda et al. 2009; 2014 provide an illuminating discussion of how the good immigrant ideal is deployed by various other immigrant groups in Miami that are not included in the current analysis.

17. Casey Woods, "Obama First Democrat to Win Florida's Hispanic Vote," *Miami Herald*, November 5, 2008, https://www.mcclatchydc.com/news/politics-government/article24508822.html. I would like to note that this discussion about political parties does not mean to imply that simply being a Democrat makes one more "progressive," nor does simply being a Republican make one more prone to racism.

18. Pop culture attests to this; popular second-generation (white) Cuban American rapper Pit Bull commonly collaborates with African American and Haitian artists, and his record label, Bad Boy Latino, is a brainchild of African American producer P. Diddy and Latin Music producer and Miami cultural icon Emilio Estefan. By naming two of his albums to reappropriate the image of the Marielitos, for example, *El Mariel* (2006) and *The Boatlift* (2007), Pit Bull employs a practice that recalls the celebration by hip hop artists of the main character in the movie *Scarface*. The movie, depicting a Marielito who is a gangster and criminal anti-hero, has been criticized for its stereotypical depiction of Cubans who arrived during the Mariel exodus. As Antonio López (2012) notes, the lead actor, Al Pacino, was literally in brownface in the role. Still, Pit Bull invokes the character in the tradition of hip hop's glorification of movie gangster anti-heroes in order to tell stories from the perspective of "the underdog."

References

Ackerman, Holly. 1996. "The Balsero Phenomenon, 1991–1994." *Cuban Studies* 26: 169.

Ackerman, Holly, and Juan Clark. 1995. *The Cuban Balseros: Voyage of Uncertainty*. Miami: Policy Center of the Cuban American National Council.

Aguirre, Benigno E. 1984. "Cuban Mass Migration and the Social Construction of Deviants." *Bulletin of Latin American Research* 13(2): 155–183.

Aguirre, Benigno E., Rogelio Sáenz, and Brian Sinclair James. 1997. "Marielitos Ten Years Later: The Scarface Legacy." *Social Science Quarterly* 78(2): 487–507.

Aja, Alan A. 2016. *Miami's Forgotten Cubans: Race, Racialization, and the Miami Afro-Cuban Experience*. New York: Palgrave Macmillan.

Aja, Alan A., and Alejandra Marchevsky. 2017, March 17. "How Immigrants Became Criminals." *Boston Review*. http://bostonreview.net/politics/alan-aja-alejandra-marchevsky-how-immigrants-became-criminals.

Alba, Richard D., and Victor G. Nee. 2005. *Remaking the American Mainstream: Assimilation and Contemporary Immigration*. Cambridge, MA: Harvard University Press.

Anzaldúa, Gloria. 1999. *Borderlands: La Frontera*. San Francisco: Aunt Lute Books.

Aparicio, Ana. 2006. *Dominican-Americans and the Politics of Empowerment*. Gainesvillle: University Press of Florida.

Aranda, Elizabeth, Rosa Chang, and Elena Sabogal. 2009. "Racializing Miami: Immigrant Latinos and Colorblind Racism in the Global City." Pp. 149–165 in José A. Cobas,

Jorge Duany, and Joe Feagin (Co-Eds.) *How the United States Racializes Latinos: White Hegemony and its Consequences.* Boulder CO: Paradigm Publishers.

Aranda, Elizabeth M., Sallie Hughes, and Elena Sabogal. 2014. *Making a Life in Multi-ethnic Miami: Immigration and the Rise of a Global City.* Boulder, CO: Rienner.

Asante, Molefi Kete. 2003. *Afrocentricity: The Theory of Social Change.* Chicago: African American Images.

Bach, Robert L., Jennifer B. Bach, and Timothy Triplett. 1981–1982. "The Flotilla 'Entrants': Latest and Most Controversial." *Cuban Studies* 11/12: 29–48.

Bailey, Benjamin. 2000. "Language and Negotiation of Ethnic/Racial Identity among Dominican Americans." *Language in Society* 29(4): 555–82.

——. 2001. "Dominican-American Ethnic/Racial Identities and United States Social Categories." *International Migration Review* 3(135): 677–708.

——. 2007. "Shifting Negotiations of Identity in a Dominican American Community." *Latino Studies* 5(2): 157–181.

Bean, Frank D., Cynthia Feliciano, Jennifer Lee, and Jennifer Van Hook. 2009. "The New U.S. Immigrants: How Do They Affect Our Understanding of the African American Experience?" *ANNALS of the American Academy of Political and Social Science* 621(1): 202–220.

Behnken, Brian. 2011. *Fighting Their Own Battles: Mexican Americans, African Americans, and the Struggle for Civil Rights in Texas.* Chapel Hill: University of North Carolina Press.

Behnken, Brian D., editor. 2016. *Civil Rights and Beyond: African American and Latino/a Activism in the Twentieth-Century United States.* Athens: University of Georgia Press.

Beltrán, Cristina. 2010. *The Trouble with Unity: Latino Politics and the Creation of Identity.* Oxford: Oxford University Press.

Benson, Devyn Spence. 2012. "Owning the Revolution: Race, Revolution, and Politics from Havana to Miami, 1959–1963." *Journal of International American Studies* 4(2): 1–30.

——. 2013. "Cuba Calls: African American Tourism, Race, and the Cuban Revolution, 1959–1961." *Hispanic American Historical Review* 93(2): 239–271.

——. 2016. Antiracism in Cuba: The Unfinished Revolution. Chapel Hill: University of North Carolina Press.

Betancur, John J. 2005a. "Black-Latino Relations." In The Oxford Encyclopedia of Latinos and Latinas in the United States. Edited by Suzanne Oboler and Deena J. González. Oxford: Oxford University Press.

Betancur, John J. 2005b. "Framing the Discussion of African American-Latino Relations: A Review and Analysis." In *Neither Enemies nor Friends: Latinos, Blacks, Afro-Latinos,* edited by A. Dzidzienyo and S. Oboler, 159–172. New York: Palgrave Macmillan.

Betancur, John J. 2014. "How Much Control Do Latinos and African Americans Have of their Mutual Relations?" *Latino Studies* 12(3): 353–373.

Bobo, Lawrence, and Vincent L. Hutchings. 1996. "Perceptions of Racial Groups Competition: Extending Blumer's Theory of Group Position to a Multiracial Social Context." *American Sociological Review* 61(6): 951–972.

Bonilla-Silva, Eduardo. 2004. "From Bi-Racial to Tri-Racial: Towards a New System of Racial Stratification in the USA." *Ethnic and Racial Studies* 27(6): 931–950.

———. 2010. *Racism without Racists: Color-Blind Racism and the Persistence of Racial Inequality in the United States*. Third Edition. Lanham, MD: Rowman & Littlefield.

———. 2018. *Racism without Racists: Color-Blind Racism and the Persistence of Racial Inequality in the United States*. Fifth Edition. Lanham, MD: Rowman & Littlefield.

Bosniak, Linda S. 1997. "'Nativism' the Concept: Some Reflections." In *Immigrants Out! The New Nativism and the Anti-Immigrant Impulse in the United States*, edited by J. F. Perea, 279–299. New York: New York University Press.

Boswell, Thomas D., and James R. Curtis. 1984. *The Cuban-American Experience: Culture, Images, and Perspectives*. Totowa, NJ: Rowman and Allanheld.

Brock, Lisa, and Digna Castañeda Fuertes, eds. 1998. *Between Race and Empire: African-Americans and Cubans before the Cuban Revolution*. Philadelphia: Temple University Press.

Brunsma, David L. 2006. "Public Categories, Private Identities: Exploring Regional Differences in the Biracial Experience." *Social Science Research* 35(3): 555–576.

Bryce-Laporte, Roy S. 1972. "Black Immigrants: The Experience of Invisibility and Inequality." *Journal of Black Studies* 4(1): 29–56.

Cacho, Lisa Marie. 2012. *Social Death: Racialized Rightlessness and the Criminalization of the Unprotected*. New York: New York University Press.

Cainkar, Louise, and Sunaina Maira. 2005. "Targeting Arab/Muslim/South Asian Americans: Criminalization and Cultural Citizenship." *Amerasia Journal* 31: 1–27.

Camayd-Freixas, Yohel. 1988. *Crisis in Miami: Community Context and Institutional Response in the Adaptation of 1980 Mariel Boatlift Cubans and Undocumented Haitian Entrants in South Florida*. Boston: Boston Urban Research and Development Group.

Castro, Max. 1992. "On the Curious Question of Language in Miami." In *Language Loyalties: A Source Book on the Official English Controversy*. James Crawford, editor, 178–186 London: University of Chicago Press.

Chavez, Leo R. 2001. *Covering Immigration: Popular Images and the Politics of the Nation*. Berkeley: University of California Press.

———. 2013. *The Latino Threat: Constructing Immigrants, Citizens, and the Nation*. Stanford, CA: Stanford University Press.

Clealand, Danielle P. 2013. "When Ideology Clashes with Reality: Racial Discrimination and Black Identity in Contemporary Cuba." *Ethnic and Racial Studies* 36(10): 1619–1636.

———. 2017. *The Power of Race in Cuba: Racial Ideology and Black Consciousness During the Revolution*. New York, NY: Oxford University Press.

Connolly, N. D. B. 2014. *A World More Concrete: Real Estate and the Remaking of Jim Crow South Florida*. Chicago: University of Chicago Press.

Cordero-Guzmán, Héctor R., Robert C. Smith, and Ramón Grosfoguel. 2001. *Migration, Transnationalization, and Race in a Changing New York*. Philadelphia: Temple University Press.

Cornell, Stephen E., and Douglas Hartmann. 1998. *Ethnicity and Race: Making Identities in a Changing World*. Thousand Oaks, CA: Pine Forge Press.

Darity, William A. 2011. "A New (Incorrect) Harvard/Washington Consensus: Review of William Julius' Wilson's *More Than Just Race.*" *Du Bois Review* 8(2): 467–476.

Da Silva, Denise Ferreira. 2014. "Extraordinary Times: A Preface." *Cultural Dynamics* 26(1): 3–8.

Dávila, Arlene. 2001. *Latinos Inc.* Berkeley: University of California Press.

Davis, F. James. 2001. *Who Is Black? One Nation's Definition.* University Park: Pennsylvania State University Press.

Dean, Jodi. 1996. *Solidarity of Strangers: Feminism after Identity Politics.* Berkeley: University of California Press.

De Genova, Nicholas. 2005. *Working the Boundaries: Race, Space, and "Illegality" in Mexican Chicago.* Durham, NC: Duke University Press.

———, ed. 2006. *Racial Transformations: Latinos and Asians Remaking the United States.* Durham, NC: Duke University Press.

De la Fuente, Alejandro. 2001. *A Nation for All: Race, Inequality, and Politics in Twentieth-Century Cuba.* Chapel Hill: University of North Carolina Press.

Denton, Nancy A., and Douglas S. Massey. 1989. "Racial Identity among Caribbean Hispanics: The Effect of Double Minority Status on Residential Segregation." *American Sociological Review* 54(5): 790–808.

Deters, Kathleen A. 1997. "Belonging Nowhere and Everywhere: Multiracial Identity Development." *Bulletin of the Menninger Clinic* 61(3): 368–384.

Diamond, Jeff. 1998. "African-American Attitudes towards United States Immigration Policy." *International Migration Review* 32(2): 451–470.

Didion, Joan. 1987. *Miami.* New York: Simon and Schuster.

Dominguez, Virginia. 1997. *White by Definition.* New Brunswick, NJ: Rutgers University Press.

Dowling, Julie A. 2014. *Mexican Americans and the Question of Race.* Austin: University of Texas Press.

Dowling, Julie A., and C. Alison Newby. 2010. "So Far from Miami: Afro-Cuban Encounters with Mexicans in the U.S. Southwest." *Latino Studies* 8(2): 176–194.

Duany, Jorge. 2005. "Neither White nor Black: The Representations of Racial Identity among Puerto Ricans on the Island and in the U.S. Mainland." In *Neither Enemies nor Friends: Latinos, Blacks, Afro-Latinos*, edited by Anani Dzidzienyo and Suzanne Oboler, 173- 188, New York: Palgrave Macmillan.

DuBois, W. E. B. 1982. *The Souls of Black Folk.* New York: New American Library.

Dunn, Marvin. 1997. *Black Miami in the Twentieth Century.* Gainesville: University Press of Florida.

———. 2013. *The Beast in Florida: A History of Anti-Black Violence.* Gainesville: University Press of Florida.

———. 2016. *A History of Florida: Through Black Eyes.* North Charleston, SC: CreateSpace Independent Publishing Platform.

Dunn, Marvin, and Alex Stepick III. 1992. "Blacks in Miami." In *Miami Now! Immigration, Ethnicity, and Social Change*, edited by G. J. Grenier and A. Stepick, 41–56. Gainesville: University Press of Florida.

Ellison, Ralph. 1952. *Invisible Man.* Signet Books.

Entman, Robert M., and Andrew Rojecki. 2000. *The Black Image in the White Mind: Media and Race in America*. Chicago: University of Chicago Press.

Espíritu, Yến Lê. 2006. "Towards a Critical Refugee Study: The Vietnamese Refugee Subject in U.S. Scholarship." *Journal of Vietnamese Studies* 1(1–2): 410–432.

———. 2014. *Body Counts: The Vietnam War and Militarized Refuge(es)*. Berkeley: University of California Press.

Fabienke, D. 2007. "Beyond the Racial Divide: Perceptions of Minority Residents on Coalition Building in South Los Angeles." The Tomás Rivera Policy Institute.

Feagin, Joe R. 2010. *The White Racial Frame: Centuries of Racial Framing and Counter-Framing*. New York: Routledge.

Ferguson, James. 1987. *Papa Doc, Baby Doc: Haiti and the Duvaliers*. Oxford: Basil Blackwell.

Fernández, Alfredo A. 2000. *Adrift: The Cuban Raft People*. Houston: Arte Público.

Fernández, Gastón A. 2002. *The Mariel Exodus Twenty Years Later: A Study on the Politics of Stigma and a Research Bibliography*. Miami: Universal.

Fernandez, Ronald. 2008. *America Beyond Black and White: How Immigrants and Fusions Are Helping Us Overcome the Racial Divide (Contemporary Political And Social Issues)*. Ann Arbor: University of Michigan Press.

Ferrer, Ada. 1998. "The Silence of Patriots: Race and Nationalism in Marti's Cuba." In *José Martí's "Our America": From National to Hemispheric Cultural Studies*, edited by J. Belnap and R. Fernández, 228–249. Durham, NC: Duke University Press.

———. 1999. *Insurgent Cuba: Race, Nation, and Revolution, 1868–1898*. Chapel Hill: University of North Carolina Press.

Fiske, John. 2000. "White Watch." In *Notes on Ethnic Minorities and the Media: Changing Cultural Boundaries*, edited by S. C. Buckingham, 50–66. Philadelphia: Open University Press.

Flores, Juan, and Miriam Jiménez Román. 2009. "Triple-Consciousness? Approaches to Afro-Latino Culture in the United States." *Latin American and Caribbean Ethnic Studies* 4(3): 319–328.

Flores, William V., and Rina Benmayor, eds. 1997. *Latino Cultural Citizenship: Claiming Identity, Space and Politics*. Boston: Beacon.

Flores-Gonzalez, Nilda. 1999. "The Racialization of Latinos: The Meaning of Latino Identity for the Second Generation." *Latino Studies Journal* 10(3): 3–31.

Foley, Neil. 2010. *Quest for Equality: The Failed Promise of Black-brown Solidarity*. Cambridge, MA: Harvard University Press.

Foner, Nancy. 2001. *Islands in the City: West Indian Migration to New York*. Berkeley: University of California Press.

Frank, Reanne, Ilana Redstone Akresh, and Bo Lu. 2010. "Latino Immigrants and the U.S. Racial Order." *American Sociological Review* 75(3): 378–401.

Freedman, Lawrence. 2000. *Kennedy's Wars: Berlin, Cuba, Laos, and Vietnam*. New York: Oxford University Press.

Fuchs, Lawrence H. 1990. "The Reactions of Black Americans to Immigration." In *Immigration Reconsidered: History, Sociology, and Politics*, edited by V. Yans-McLaughlin, 293–314. New York: Oxford University Press.

Gans, Herbert J. 1999. "The Possibility of a New Racial Hierarchy in the Twenty-First-Century United States." In *The Cultural Territories of Race: Black and White Boundaries*, edited by M. Lamont, 371–390. Chicago: University of Chicago Press.

García, María Cristina. 1996. *Havana U.S.A.: Cuban Exiles and Cuban-Americans in South Florida, 1959–1994*. Berkeley: University of California Press.

Gay, Claudine. 2006. "Seeing Difference: The Effect of Economic Disparity on Black Attitudes toward Latinos." *American Journal of Political Science* 50(4): 982–997.

Girard, Philippe. 2004. *Clinton in Haiti: The 1994 U.S. Invasion of Haiti*. Gordonsville, VA: Palgrave Macmillan.

Gómez-García, Carmen. 1998. "Cuban Social Poetry and the Struggle against Two Racisms." In *Between Race and Empire: African-Americans and Cubans before the Cuban Revolution*, edited by L. Brock and D. Castañeda Fuertes, 205–248. Philadelphia: Temple University Press.

Gonzalez, Juan. 2011. *Harvest of Empire*. New York: Penguin Books.

Gordon, Milton M. 1964. *Assimilation in American Life: The Role of Race, Religion, and National Origins*. New York: Oxford University Press.

Gosin, Monika. 2010. "'Other' than Black: Afro-Cubans Negotiating Identity in the United States." In *Una Ventana a Cuba y los Estudios Cubanos*, edited by A. Cabezas, I. N. Hernandez-Torres, S. Johnson, and R. Lazo, 155–178. Puerto Rico: Ediciones Callejon.

———. 2016. "The Death of 'La Reina de la Salsa': Celia Cruz and the Mythification of the Black Woman." In *Afro-Latin@s in Movement: Critical Approaches to Blackness and Transnationalism in the Americas*, edited by P. R. Rivera-Rideau, J. A. Jones, and T. S. Paschel, 85–107. New York: Palgrave Macmillan.

———. 2017. "'A Bitter Diversion': Afro-Cuban Immigrants, Race, and Everyday-Life Resistance." *Latino Studies* 15(1): 4–28.

Gray, Herman. 1995. *Watching Race: Television and the Struggle for "Blackness."* Minneapolis: University of Minnesota Press.

Greenbaum, Susan. 2002. *More than Black: Afro-Cubans in Tampa*. Gainesville: University Press of Florida.

Greenhill, Kelly M. 2002. "Engineered Migration and the Use of Refugees as Political Weapons: A Case Study of the 1994 Cuban Balsero Crisis." *International Migration* 40(4): 39–72.

———. 2010. *Weapons of Mass Migration: Forced Displacement, Coercion, and Foreign Policy*. Ithaca, NY: Cornell University Press.

Greer, Christina M. 2013. *Black Ethnics: Race, Immigration, and the Pursuit of the American Dream*. New York: Oxford University Press.

Grenier, Guillermo J., and Max J. Castro. 1999. "Triadic Politics: Ethnicity, Race and Politics in Miami, 1959–1998." *Pacific Historical Review* 68(2): 273–292.

Grenier, Guillermo J., and Lisandro Pérez. 2003. *The Legacy of Exile: Cubans in the United States*. Boston: Allyn and Bacon.

Grenier, Guillermo J., and Alex Stepick III, eds. 1992. *Miami Now! Immigration, Ethnicity, and Social Change*. Gainesville: University Press of Florida.

———. 2001. "Blacks and Cubans in Miami." In *Governing American Cities: Interethnic Coalitions, Competitions, and Conflict*, edited by M. Jones-Correa, 137–157. New York: Russell Sage Foundation.

Grosfoguel, Ramón. 2003. *Colonial Subjects: Puerto Ricans in a Global Perspective.* Berkeley: University of California Press.

Guinier, Lani and Gerald Torres. 2002. *The Miner's Canary: Enlisting Race, Resisting Power, Transforming Democracy.* Cambridge, MA: Harvard University Press.

Guridy, Frank Andre. 2010. *Forging Diaspora: Afro-Cubans and African Americans in a World of Empire and Jim Crow.* Chapel Hill: University of North Carolina Press.

Hall, Stuart. 1978. *Policing the Crisis: Mugging, the State, and Law and Order.* London: Macmillan.

———. 1997. "What Is This 'Black' in Black Popular Culture?" In *Representing Blackness: Issues in Film and Video*, edited by V. Smith, 123–133. New Brunswick, NJ: Rutgers University Press.

Hallin, Daniel C. 1986. *The Uncensored War: The Media and Vietnam.* New York: Oxford University Press.

Hamilton, Darrick, William A. Darity Jr., Anne E. Price, Vishnu Sridharan, and Rebecca Tippett. 2015, April. "Umbrellas Don't Make It Rain: Why Studying and Working Hard Isn't Enough for Black Americans." http://www.insightcced.org/wp -content/uploads/2015/08/Umbrellas_Dont_Make_It_Rain_Final.pdf.

Hamm, Mark S. 1995. *The Abandoned Ones: The Imprisonment and Uprising of the Mariel Boat People.* Boston: Northeastern University Press.

Harris, Cheryl. 1993. "Whiteness as Property." *Harvard Law Review* 106(8): 1707.

Harris, David R., and Jeremiah Joseph Sims. 2002. "Who Is Multiracial? Assessing the Complexity of Lived Race." *American Sociological Review* 67(4): 614–627.

Hay, Michelle. 2009. *I've Been Black in Two Countries: Black Cuban Views on Race in the U.S.* El Paso, Texas: LFB Scholarly Publishing.

Hayes-Bautista, David E. 2004. *La Nueva California: Latinos in the Golden State.* Berkeley: University of California Press.

Helg, Aline. 1995. *Our Rightful Share: The Afro-Cuban Struggle for Equality, 1886–1912.* Chapel Hill: University of North Carolina Press.

Hellwig, David J. 1981. "Black Leaders and United States Immigration Policy, 1917–1929." *Journal of Negro History* 66(2): 110–127.

———. 1987. "The Afro-American Press and Woodrow Wilson's Mexican Policy, 1913–1917." *Phylon* 48(4): 261–270.

———. 1998. "The African-American Press and the United States Involvement in Cuba, 1902–1917." In *Between Race and Empire: African-Americans and Cubans before the Cuban Revolution*, edited by L. Brock and D. Castañeda Fuertes, 70–84. Philadelphia: Temple University Press.

Henken, Ted. 2005. "*Balseros, Boteros*, and *el Bombo*: Post-1994 Cuban Immigration to the United States and the Persistence of Special Treatment." *Latino Studies* 3: 393–416.

Hernández, Tanya K. 2002. "The Buena Vista Social Club: The Racial Politics of Nostalgia." In *Latina/o Popular Culture*, edited by M. Habell-Pallan and M. Romero, 61–72. New York: New York University Press.

Hero, Rodney E., and Robert R. Preuhs. 2012. *Black–Latino Relations in U.S. National Politics: Beyond Conflict or Cooperation.* Cambridge: Cambridge University Press.

Hintzen, Percy Claude, and Jean Muteba Rahier. 2003. *Problematizing Blackness: Self-Ethnographies by Black Immigrants to the United States.* New York: Routledge.

Hoeffel, Paul Heath. 1980, December 21. "Fort Chaffee's Unwanted Cubans," *New York Times Magazine*, 47.

Hollinger, David A. 1995. *Postethnic America: Beyond Multiculturalism*. New York: Basic Books.

Horsman, Reginald. 1981. *Race and Manifest Destiny: The Origins of American Racial Anglo-Saxonism*. Cambridge, MA: Harvard University Press.

Hufker, Brian, and Gary Cavender. 1990. "From Freedom Flotilla to America's Burden: The Social Redefinition of the Mariel Immigrants." *Sociological Quarterly* 31(2): 321–335.

Ignatiev, Noel. 1995. *How the Irish Became White*. New York: Routledge.

Jacobs, Ronald N. 2000. *Race, Media, and the Crisis of Civil Society: From Watts to Rodney King*. Cambridge: Cambridge University Press.

Jaynes, Gerald D. 2000. "Introduction: Immigration and the American Dream." In *Immigration and Race: New Challenges for American Democracy*, edited by G. D. Jaynes. P. 1–43. New Haven, CT: Yale University Press.

Jiménez Román, Miriam. 2005. "Looking at That Middle Ground: Racial Mixing as Panacea?" *Wadabagei: A Journal of the Caribbean & Its Diasporas* 8(1): 65–79.

Jiménez Román, Miriam, and Juan Flores, eds. 2010. *The Afro-Latin@ Reader: History and Culture in the United States*. Durham, NC: Duke University Press.

Johnson, Gaye Theresa. 2013. *Spaces of Conflict, Sounds of Solidarity: Music, Race, and Spatial Entitlement in Los Angeles*. Berkeley: University of California Press.

Jones, Jennifer A. 2011. "Who Are We? Producing Group Identity through Everyday Practices of Conflict and Discourse." *Sociological Perspectives* 54(2): 139–162.

Jones, Nicholas A., and Jungmiwha Bullock. 2012. *The Two or More Races Population: 2010*. United States Census Bureau. https://www.census.gov/library/publications/2012/dec/c2010br-13.html.

Jordan, Winthrop. 1977. *White over Black: American Attitudes toward the Negro, 1550–1812*. New York: Norton.

Joseph, Ralina L. 2013. *Transcending Blackness: From the New Millennium Mulatta to the Exceptional Multiracial*. Durham, NC: Duke University Press.

Kasinitz, Philip. 1992. *Caribbean New York: Black Immigrants and the Politics of Race*. Ithaca, NY: Cornell University Press.

Kasinitz, Philip, John Mollenkopf, and Mary C. Waters. 2002. "Becoming American/Becoming New Yorkers: Immigrant Incorporation in a Majority Minority City." *International Migration Review* 36(4): 1020–1036.

Katz, Michael B. 2013. *The Undeserving Poor: America's Enduring Confrontation with Poverty*. Oxford: Oxford University Press.

Kaufmann, Karen M. 2003. "Cracks in the Rainbow: Group Commonality as a Basis for Latino and African-American Political Coalitions." *Political Research Quarterly* 56(2): 199–210.

Khanna, Nikki, and Cathryn Johnson. 2010. "Passing as Black: Racial Identity Work among Biracial Americans." *Social Psychology Quarterly* 73(4): 380–397.

Kim, Claire Jean. 2000. *Bitter Fruit: The Politics of Black–Korean Conflict in New York City*. New Haven, CT: Yale University Press.

Knaur, Lisa Maya. 2001. "Eating in Cuban." In *Mambo Montage*, edited by A. Lao-Montes and A. Dávila, 425–447. New York: Columbia University Press.

Kun, Josh, and Laura Pulido. 2013. *Black and Brown in Los Angeles: Beyond Conflict and Coalition.* Berkeley: University of California Press.

Landale, Nancy S., and Ralph. S. Oropesa. 2002. "White, Black, or Puerto Rican? Racial Self-Identification among Mainland and Island Puerto Ricans." *Social Forces* 81(1): 231–254.

Lee, Jennifer, and Frank D. Bean. 2004. "America's Changing Color Lines: Immigration, Race/Ethnicity, and Multiracial Identification." *Annual Review of Sociology* 30: 221–242.

Lee, Robert G. 1999. *Orientals: Asian Americans in Popular Culture.* Philadelphia: Temple University Press.

Levitt, Peggy. 2001. *The Transnational Villagers.* Berkeley: University of California Press.

Lewis, Amanda E. 2004. "'What Group?' Studying Whites and Whiteness in the Era of 'Colorblindness.'" *Sociological Theory* 22(4): 623–646.

Lipsitz, George. 2006. *The Possessive Investment in Whiteness: How White People Profit from Identity Politics.* Philadelphia: Temple University Press.

Loescher, Gil. 1986. *Calculated Kindness: Refugees and America's Half-Open Door, 1945 to the Present.* New York: Free Press.

Logan, John R. 2003. *Pew Hispanic Fact Sheet.* Albany, NY: Lewis Mumford Center for Comparative Urban and Regional Research, SUNY. http://mumford.albany.edu /census/BlackLatinoReport/BlackLatino01.htm.

John R. Logan and Brian Stults. 2011. "The Persistence of Segregation in the Metropolis: New Findings from the 2010 Census," Census Brief prepared for Project US2010 (http://www.city-data.com/forum/city-vs-city/1404162-persistence-segregation -metropolis-new-findings-2010-a.html#ixzz5Tf5yrvsD).

López, Antonio. 2010. "Cosa de Blancos: Cuban-American Whiteness and the Afro-Cuban-Occupied House," *Latino Studies* 8(2): 220–243.

———. 2012. *Unbecoming Blackness: The Diaspora Cultures of Afro-Cuban America.* New York: New York University.

Márquez, John D. 2014. *Black–Brown Solidarity: Racial Politics in the New Gulf South.* Austin: University of Texas Press.

Marrow, Helen B. 2011. *New Destination Dreaming: Immigration, Race, and Legal Status in the Rural American South.* Stanford, CA: Stanford University Press.

Martinez-Alier 1989. Marriage, class and colour in nineteenth-century Cuba: a study of racial attitudes and sexual values in a slave society. University of Michigan.

Martinez, Ramiro, Jr. 1997. "Homicide among Miami's Ethnic Groups: Anglos, Blacks, and Latinos in the 1990s." *Homicide Studies* 1(1): 17–34.

Martínez-Echazábal, Lourdes. 1998. "Mestizaje and the Discourse of National/Cultural Identity in Latin America, 1845–1959." *Latin American Perspectives* 25(3): 21–42.

Masud-Piloto, Felix Roberto. 1996. *From Welcomed Exiles to Illegal Immigrants: Cuban Migration to the U.S., 1959–1995.* Lanham, MD: Rowman & Littlefield.

McClain, Paula D., and Albert K. Karnig. 1990. "Black and Hispanic Socioeconomic and Political Competition." *American Political Science Review* 84(2): 535–545.

McClain, Paula, Monique L. Lyle, Niambi M. Carter, Victoria M. DeFrancesco Soto, Gerald F. Lackey, Kendra Davenport Cotton, Shayla C. Nunnally, Thomas J. Scotto,

Jeffrey D. Grynaviski, and J. Alan Kendrick. 2007. "Black Americans and Latino Immigrants in a Southern City: Friendly Neighbors or Economic Competitors?" *DuBois Review: Social Science Research on Race* 4(1): 97–117.

McNulty, Thomas L., and Paul E. Bellair. 2003. "Explaining Racial and Ethnic Differences in Serious Adolescent Violent Behavior." *Criminology* 41(3): 709–747.

Miami-Dade County Facts. 2009. Miami-Dade County Department of Planning and Zoning, Research Section. Miami, Florida. http://www.miamidade.gov/planning /library/reports/2009-miami-dade-county-facts.pdf.

Mindiola, Tatcho, Jr., Yolanda Flores Niemann, and Nestor Rodriguez. 2002. *Black–Brown Relations and Stereotypes*. Austin: University of Texas Press.

Mirabal, Nancy Raquel. 1998. "Telling Silences and Making Community: Afro-Cubans and African-Americans in Ybor City and Tampa, 1899–1915." In *Between Race and Empire: African-Americans and Cubans before the Cuban Revolution*, edited by L. Brock and D. Castañeda Fuertes, 49–69. Philadelphia: Temple University Press.

———. 2003. "'*Ser de aquí*': Beyond the Cuban Exile Model." *Latino Studies* 1: 366–382.

———. 2005. "Scripting Race, Finding Place: African Americans, Afro-Cubans, and the Diasporic Imaginary in the United States." In *Neither Enemies nor Friends: Latinos, Blacks, Afro-Latinos*, edited by A. Dzidzienyo and S. Oboler, 189–207. New York: Palgrave Macmillan.

Mohl, Raymond A. 1990. "On the Edge: Blacks and Hispanics in Metropolitan Miami since 1959." *Florida Historical Quarterly* 69(1): 37–56.

Molina-Guzman, Isabel. 2008. "Rescuing Elián: Gender and Race in Stories of Children's Migration." In *Immigrant Rights in the Shadows of Citizenship*, edited by R. I. Buff, 179–189. New York: New York University Press.

Mora, G. Cristina. 2014. *Making Hispanics: How Activists, Bureaucrats, and Media Constructed a New American*. Chicago: University of Chicago Press.

Morrison, Toni. 1992. *Playing in the Dark: Whiteness and the Literary Imagination*. Cambridge, MA: Harvard University Press.

———. 1994. "On the Backs of Blacks." In *Arguing immigration: The debate over the changing face of America*, ed. Nicolaus Milla, 97–100. New York: Simon and Schuster.

Nackerud, Larry, Alyson Springer, Christopher Larrison, and Alicia Issac. 1999. "The End of the Cuban Contradiction in U.S. Refugees Policy." *International Migration Review* 33(1): 176–192.

Nam, Yunju, Darrick Hamilton, Wiliam A. Darity, and Anne E. Price. 2015, September. "Bootstraps Are for Black Kids: Race, Wealth, and the Impact of Intergenerational Transfer on Adult Outcomes. Research Brief. http://www.insightcced.org /wp-content/uploads/2015/07/Bootstraps-are-for-Black-Kids-Sept.pdf.

Newby, C. Alison, and Julie Dowling. 2007. "Black and Hispanic: The Racial Identification of Afro-Cuban Immigrants in the Southwest." *Sociological Perspectives* 50(3): 343–366.

Noguera, Pedro A. 2003. "Anything but Black: Bringing Politics back to the Study of Race." In *Problematizing Blackness: Self-Ethnographies by Black Immigrants to the United States*, edited by P. C. Hintzen and J. Muteba Rahier, 193–200. New York: Routledge.

Oboler, Suzanne, and Anani Dzidzienyo. 2005. "Flows and Counterflows: Latinas/os, Blackness, and Racialization in Hemispheric Perspective." In *Neither Enemies nor Friends: Latinos, Blacks, Afro-Latinos*, edited by A. Dzidzienyo and S. Oboler, 3–35. New York: Palgrave Macmillan.

Okihiro, Gary Y. 1994. *Margins and Mainstreams: Asians in American History and Culture*. Seattle: University of Washington Press.

Oliver, J. Eric. 2010. *The Paradoxes of Integration: Race, Neighborhood, and Civic Life in Multiethnic America*. Chicago: University of Chicago Press.

Oliver, J. Eric, and Janelle Wong. 2003. "Intergroup Prejudice in Multiethnic Settings." *American Journal of Political Science* 47(4): 567–582.

Omi, Michael. 2001. "The Changing Meaning of Race." In *America Becoming: Racial Trends and Their Consequences*, edited by N. Smelser, W. J. Wilson, and F. Mitchell, 243–263. Washington, DC: National Academy Press.

Omi, Michael, and Howard Winant. 1994. *Racial Formation in the 1960s to the 1990s*. New York: Routledge.

Ong, Aihwa. 2003. *Buddha Is Hiding: Refugees, Citizenship, the New America*. Berkeley: University of California Press.

Oxford, Connie G. 2008. "Acts of Resistance in Asylum Seekers' Persecution Narratives." In *Immigrant Rights in the Shadows of Citizenship,* edited by R. I. Buff, 40–54. New York: New York University Press.

Pamphile, Leon D. 2001. *Haitians and African Americans: A Heritage of Tragedy and Hope*. Gainesville: University Press of Florida.

Park, Robert Ezra. 1950. *Race and Culture*. Glencoe, IL: Free Press.

Pastor, Manuel, Jr., and Enrico A. Marcelli. 2004. "Somewhere over the Rainbow? African Americans, Unauthorized Mexican Immigration, and Coalition Building." In *The Impact of Immigration on African Americans*, edited by S. Schulman, 107–136. Edison, NJ: Transaction.

Pedraza, Silvia. 1996. "Cuba's Refugees: Manifold Migrations." In *Origins and Destinies: Immigration, Race, and Ethnicity in America*, edited by S. Pedraza and R. G. Rumbaut, 1–42. Belmont, CA: Wadsworth.

Pedraza-Bailey, Silvia. 1985. "Cuba's Exiles: Portrait of a Refugee Migration." *International Migration Review* 19(1): 4–34.

Pérez, Lisandro. 2001. "Growing up Cuban in Miami: Immigration, the Enclave, and New Generations." In *Ethnicities: Children of Immigrants in America*, edited by R. Rumbaut and A. Portes, 91–125. Berkeley: University of California Press.

Pérez, Louis A. 1995. *Cuba: Between Reform and Revolution*. New York: Oxford University Press.

———. 2003. *Cuba and the United States: Ties of Singular Intimacy*. Athens: University of Georgia Press.

Pew Research Center. 2013. Mapping the Latino Population, by State, County, and City. http://www.pewhispanic.org/2013/08/29/iii-ranking-latino-populations-in-the-nations-counties/.

Picca, Leslie Houts, and Joe R. Feagin. 2007. *Two-Faced Racism: Whites in the Backstage and Frontstage*. New York: Routledge.

Porter, Bruce, and Marvin Dunn. 1984. *The Miami Riot of 1980: Crossing the Bounds.* Lexington, MA: Lexington Books.

Portes, Alejandro, and Ruben G. Rumbaut. 2001. *Legacies: The Story of the Immigrant Second Generation.* Berkeley: University of California Press.

Portes, Alejandro, and Alex Stepick. 1994. *City on the Edge: The Transformation of Miami.* Berkeley: University of California Press.

Portes, Alejandro, and Min Zhou. 1993. "The New Second Generation: Segmented Assimilation and Its Variants." *Annals of the American Academy of Political and Social Science* 530(1): 74–96.

Puri, Shalini. 2004. *The Caribbean Postcolonial: Social Equality, Post-Nationalism, and Cultural Hybridity.* New York: Palgrave Macmillan.

Rama, Angel. 1996. *The Lettered City.* Edited and translated by John Charles Chasteen. Durham, NC: Duke University Press.

Rhodes, Jane. 1995. "The Visibility of Race and Media History." In *Gender, Race, and Class in Media: A Text-Reader,* edited by G. Dines and J. M. Humez, 33–39. Thousand Oaks, CA: Sage.

Ribas, Vanesa. 2015. *On the Line: Slaughterhouse Lives and the Making of the New South.* Berkeley: University of California Press.

Rieff, David. 1987. *Going to Miami: Exiles, Tourists, and Refugees in the New America.* Boston: Little, Brown.

Rivera-Rideau, Petra R., Jennifer A. Jones, and Tianna S. Paschel, eds. 2016. *Afro-Latin@s in Movement: Critical Approaches to Blackness and Transnationalism in the Americas.* New York: Palgrave Macmillan.

Robert, Joseph F. (publisher), Janice B. Lewis (editorial director), and Norma J. McAlister (Research Director). 1980. *The Working Press of the Nation: Newspaper and Allied Services Directory.* Vol. 1. Chicago: National Research Bureau.

Robinson, Greg, and Robert S. Chang, eds. 2017. *Minority Relations: Intergroup Conflict and Cooperation.* Jackson: University of Mississippi Press.

Robinson, Piers. 2002. *The CNN Effect: The Myth of News Foreign Policy and Intervention.* New York: Routledge.

Rockquemore, Kerry Ann, and David L. Brunsma. 2002. "Socially Embedded Identities: Theories, Typologies, and Processes of Racial Identity among Black/White Biracials." *Sociological Quarterly* 43(3): 335–356.

Rodriguez, América. 1999. *Making Latino News: Race, Language, Class.* Thousand Oaks, CA: Sage.

Rodríguez, Clara E. 2000. *Changing Race: Latinos, the Census, and the History of Ethnicity in the United States.* New York: New York University Press.

Rodríguez, Dylan. 2014. "Goldwater's Left Hand: Post-Raciality and the Roots of the Post-Racial Racist State." *Cultural Dynamics* 26(1): 29–51.

Roediger, David R. 1991. *The Wages of Whiteness: Race and the Making of the American Working Class.* London: Verso.

———. 2002. *Colored White: Transcending the Racial Past.* Berkeley: University of California Press.

Rojecki, Andrew. 1999. *Silencing the Opposition: Antinuclear Movements and the Media in the Cold War.* Urbana: University of Illinois Press.

Romero, Mary. 2008. "Crossing the immigration and race border: A critical theory approach to immigration studies." *Contemporary Justice Review* 11 (1): 23–37.

Rose, Chanelle N. 2016. *The Struggle for Black Freedom in Miami: Civil Rights and America's Tourist Paradise, 1896–1968*. Baton Rouge: Louisiana State University Press.

Roth, Wendy D., and Nadia Y. Kim. 2013. "Relocating Prejudice: A Transnational Approach to Understanding Immigrants' Racial Attitudes." *International Migration Review* 47(2): 330–373.

Sáenz, Rogelio, and Karen Manges Douglas. 2015. "A Call for the Racialization of Immigration Studies: On the Transition of Ethnic Immigrants to Racialized Immigrants." *Sociology of Race and Ethnicity* 1(1): 166–180.

Saito, Leland T. 2001. "The Politics of Adaptation and the 'Good Immigrant': Japanese Americans and the New Chinese Immigrants." In *Asian and Latino Immigrants in a Restructuring Economy: The Metamorphosis of Southern California*, edited by M. C. Lopez-Garza, 332–349. Palo Alto, CA: Stanford University Press.

Santa Ana, Otto. 2002. *Brown Tide Rising: Metaphors of Latinos in Contemporary American Public Discourse*. Austin: University of Texas Press.

Sawyer, Mark Q. 2006. *Racial Politics in Post-Revolutionary Cuba*. New York: Cambridge University Press.

Sawyer, Mark, and Tianna S. Paschal. 2009. "Contesting Politics as Usual: Black Social Movements, Globalization, and Race Policy in Latin America." In *New Social Movements in the African Diaspora*, edited by Leith Mullings. 13–32, New York: Palgrave Macmillan.

Schiller, Nina G., Linda Basch, and Cristina Blanc-Szanton. 1992. "Towards a Definition of Transnationalism." *Annals of the New York Academy of Sciences* 645(1): ix–xiv.

Schulman, Steven, ed. 2004. *The Impact of Immigration on African Americans*. New Brunswick, NJ: Transaction.

Shah, Hemant, and Michael. C. Thornton. 2004. *Newspaper Coverage of Interethnic Conflict: Competing Visions of America*. Thousand Oaks, CA: Sage.

Shell-Weiss, Melanie. 2009. *Coming to Miami: A Social History*. Gainesville: University Press of Florida.

Skop, Emily H. 2001. "Race and Place in the Adaptation of Mariel Exiles." *International Migration Review* 35(2): 449–471.

Smith, Robert C. 2006. *Mexican New York: Transnational Lives of New Immigrants*. Berkeley: University of California Press.

Soderlund, Walter C. 2003. "The Cuban Balsero Crisis." In *Mass Media and Foreign Policy: Post-Cold War Crises in the Caribbean*, edited by W. C. Soderlund, 113–138. Westport, CT: Praeger.

Soruco, Gonzalo R. 1996. *Cubans and the Mass Media in South Florida*. Gainesville: University Press of Florida.

Stedman, Stephen John, and Fred Tanner. 2003. *Refugee Manipulation: War, Politics, and the Abuse of Human Suffering*. Washington, DC: Brookings Institution Press.

Steinberg, Stephen. 1995. *Turning Back: The Retreat from Racial Justice*. Boston, MA: Beacon Press.

Stepick, Alex, III. 1992. "The Refugees Nobody Wants: Haitians in Miami." In *Miami Now! Immigration, Ethnicity, and Social Change*, edited by G. J. Grenier and A. Stepick, 57–82. Gainesville: University Press of Florida.

Stepick, Alex, Guillermo Grenier, Max Castro, and Marvin Dunn. 2003. *This Land Is Our Land: Immigrants and Power in Miami*. Berkeley: University of California Press.

Telles, Edward. 2006. *Race in Another America: The Significance of Skin Color in Brazil*. Princeton, NJ: Princeton University Press.

Telles, Edward, Mark Sawyer, and Gaspar Rivera-Salgado, eds. 2011. *Just Neighbors? Research on African American and Latino Relations in the United States*. New York: Russell Sage Foundation.

Thornton, Michael C., and Yuko Mizuno. 1999. "Economic Well-Being and Black Adult Feelings toward Immigrants and Whites, 1984." *Journal of Black Studies* 30(1): 15–44.

Ticktin, Miriam. 2011. *Casualties of Care: Immigration and the Politics of Humanitarianism in France*. Berkeley: University of California Press.

Torres-Saillant, Silvio. 2002. "Problematic Paradigms: Racial Diversity and Corporate Identity in the Latino Community." In *Latinos: Remaking America*, edited by Marcelo Suárez-Orozco, 435–455. Berkeley: University of California Press.

———. 2003. "Inventing the Race: Latinos and the Ethnoracial Pentagon." *Latino Studies* 1: 123–151.

———. 2010. "Divisible Blackness: Reflections on Heterogeneity and Racial Identity." In *The Afro-Latin@ Reader: History and Culture in the United States*, edited by M. Jiménez Román and J. Flores, 453–465. Durham, NC: Duke University Press.

Urciuoli, Bonnie. 1996. *Exposing Prejudice: Puerto Rican Experiences of Language, Race, and Class*. Boulder, CO: Westview Press.

———. 2003. "Boundaries, Language, and the Self: Issues Faced by Puerto Ricans and Other Latina/o College Students." *Journal of Latin American Anthropology* 8(2): 152–173.

Vaca, Nicolás C. 2004. *The Presumed Alliance: The Unspoken Conflict between Latinos and Blacks and What It Means for America*. New York: Rayo.

Valdez, Zulema. 2017. *Beyond Black and White: A Reader on Contemporary Race Relations*. Thousand Oaks, CA: Sage.

Valdez, Zulema, and Tanya Golash-Boza. 2017. "U.S. racial and ethnic relations in the twenty-first century," *Ethnic and Racial Studies* 40(13): 2181–2209.

Vanderbush, Walt, and Patrick J. Haney. 1999. "Policy toward Cuba in the Clinton Administration." *Political Science Quarterly* 114(3): 387.

Van Dijk, Teun. 1987. *Communicating Racism: Ethnic Prejudice in Thought and Talk*. Newbury Park, CA: Sage.

———. 1993. "Principles of Critical Discourse Analysis." *Discourse and Society* 4(2): 249–283.

Voboril, Mary. "Sumase al éxodo lo más valioso de la poblacion de Cuba," *El Miami Herald*, May 5, 1980, 4.

Wade, Peter. 1997. *Race and Ethnicity in Latin America*. London: Pluto.

Waters, Mary C. 1990. *Ethnic Options: Choosing Identities in America*. Berkeley: University of California Press.

———. 1996. "Optional Ethnicities: For Whites Only?" In *Origins and Destinies: Immigration, Race, and Ethnicity in America*, edited by S. Pedraza and R. Rumbaut, 444–454. Belmont, CA: Wadsworth Press.

———. 1999. *Black Identities: West Indian Immigrant Dreams and American Realities*. New York: Russell Sage Foundation.

———. 2001. "Ethnic and Racial Identities of Second-Generation Black Immigrants in New York City." *International Migration Review* 28(4): 795–820.

West-Durán, Alan. 2004. "Rap's Diasporic Dialogues: Cuba's Redefinition of Blackness." *Journal of Popular Music Studies* 16(1): 4–39.

Wetherell, Margaret and Jonathan Potter. 1992. *Mapping the Language of Racism: Discourse and the Legitimation of Exploitation*. New York: Columbia University Press.

Wilsbank, William. 1984. *Murder in Miami*. New York: University Press of America.

Woltman, Kelly, and K. Bruce Newbold. 2009. "Of Flights and Flotillas: Assimilation and Race in the Cuban Diaspora. *Professional Geographer* 61(1): 70–86.

Yancey, George. 2003. *Who Is White? Latinos, Asians, and the New Black/Nonblack Divide*. Boulder, CO: Rienner.

Zhou, Min, and Carl L. Bankston. 1998. *Growing Up American: How Vietnamese Children Adapt to Life in the United States*. New York: Russell Sage Foundation.

INDEX